AAT

Qualifications and Credit Framework (QCF)

AQ2013

LEVEL 4 DIPLOMA IN ACCOUNTING

(QCF)

QUESTION BANK

Financial Statements

2015 Edition

For assessments from September 2015

Third edition June 2015
ISBN 9781 4727 2205 8

Previous edition
ISBN 9781 4727 0939 4

British Library Cataloguing-in-Publication Data
A catalogue record for this book is available from the British Library

Published by
BPP Learning Media Ltd
BPP House
Aldine Place
London W12 8AA

www.bpp.com/learningmedia

Printed in the United Kingdom by Martins of Berwick
Sea View Works
Spittal
Berwick-Upon-Tweed
TD15 1RS

BPP
LEARNING MEDIA

CONTENTS

Introduction   v

Question and answer bank

A NOTE ABOUT COPYRIGHT

BPP
LEARNING MEDIA

INTRODUCTION

This is BPP Learning Media's AAT Question Bank for Financial Statements. It is part of a suite of ground-breaking resources produced by BPP Learning Media for the AAT's assessments under the Qualification and Credit Framework.

The Financial Statements assessment will be **computer assessed**. As well as being available in the traditional paper format, this **Question Bank is available in an online environment** containing tasks similar to those you will encounter in the AAT's testing environment. BPP Learning Media believe that the best way to practise for an online assessment is in an online environment. However, if you are unable to practise in the online environment you will find that all tasks in the paper Question Bank have been written in a style that is as close as possible to the style that you will be presented with in your online assessment.

This Question Bank has been written in conjunction with the BPP Text, and has been carefully designed to enable students to practise all of the learning outcomes and assessment criteria for the units that make up Financial Statements. It is fully up to date as at June 2015 and reflects both the AAT's unit guide and the sample assessments provided by the AAT.

This Question Bank contains these key features:

- Tasks corresponding to each broad topic area. Some tasks are designed for learning purposes, but most of them are of assessment standard

- AAT's sample assessments and answers for Financial Statements and further BPP practice assessments

The emphasis in all tasks and assessments is on the practical application of the skills acquired.

Approaching the assessment

When you sit the assessment it is very important that you follow the on screen instructions. This means you need to carefully read the instructions, both on the introduction screens and during specific tasks.

When you access the assessment you should be presented with an introductory screen with information similar to that shown below (taken from the introductory screen from the AAT's AQ2013 Sample Assessment for Financial Statements).

We have provided the following assessment to help you familiarise yourself with AAT's e-assessment environment. It is designed to demonstrate as many as possible of the question types you may find in a live assessment. It is not designed to be used on its own to determine whether you are ready for a live assessment.

This assessment contains 8 tasks and you should therefore attempt and aim to complete EVERY task.
Each task is independent. You will not need to refer to your answers to previous tasks.
Read every task carefully to make sure you understand what is required.

Please note that in this sample assessment only your responses to tasks 1, 2, 5, 6 and 7 will be marked.
The equivalents of tasks 3, 4 and 8 will be human marked in the live assessment.

In tasks 1, 2 and 6 you will see there are tables that can be used as workings for your proformas.
You don't have to use the workings to achieve full marks on the task, but data entered into the workings tables will be taken into consideration if you make errors in the proforma.

Where the date is relevant, it is given in the task data.

Both minus signs and brackets can be used to indicate negative numbers UNLESS task instructions say otherwise.

You must use a full stop to indicate a decimal point.
For example, write 100.57 NOT 100,57 or 100 57

You may use a comma to indicate a number in the thousands, but you don't have to.
For example, 10000 and 10,000 are both OK.

Other indicators are not compatible with the computer-marked system.

The actual instructions will vary depending on the subject you are studying for. It is very important you read the instructions on the introductory screen and apply them in the assessment. You don't want to lose marks when you know the correct answer just because you have not entered it in the right format.

In general, the rules set out in the AAT Sample Assessments for the subject you are studying for will apply in the real assessment, but you should again read the information on this screen in the real assessment carefully just to make sure.

A full stop is needed to indicate a decimal point. We would recommend using minus signs to indicate negative numbers and leaving out the comma signs to indicate thousands, as this results in a lower number of key strokes and less margin for error when working under time pressure. Having said that, you can use whatever is easiest for you as long as you operate within the rules set out for your particular assessment.

You have to show competence throughout the assessment and you should therefore complete all of the tasks. Don't leave questions unanswered.

In the Financial Statements assessment the written tasks are human marked. In this case you are given a blank space or table to enter your answer into. You are told in the assessments which tasks these are.

If these tasks involve calculations, it is a good idea to decide in advance how you are going to lay out your answers to such tasks by practising answering them on a word document, and certainly you should try all such tasks in this question bank and in the AAT's environment using the sample/practice assessments.

When asked to fill in tables, or gaps, never leave any blank even if you are unsure of the answer. Fill in your best estimate.

Note that for some assessments where there is a lot of scenario information or tables of data provided, you may need to access these via 'pop-ups'. Instructions will be provided on how you can bring up the necessary data during the assessment. For example, the following is taken from the introductory screen the AAT AQ2013 sample assessment for Financial Statements.

Note:
Data is provided in tasks 1, 6 and 7 in the form of pop-ups. You can open, close and re-open the pop-ups as often as you want and you can position them anywhere on the screen.

To launch the pop-ups and see the data, just click on the buttons you'll find find in these tasks.
The buttons appear at the top of each task, and look like these examples:

Finally, take note of any task specific instructions once you are in the assessment. For example you may be asked to enter a date in a certain format or to enter a number to a certain number of decimal places.

Remember you can practise the BPP questions in this question bank in an online environment on our dedicated AAT Online page. On the same page is a link to the current AAT Sample Assessment(s) as well.

If you have any comments about this book, please email nisarahmed@bpp.com or write to Nisar Ahmed, AAT Head of Programme, BPP Learning Media Ltd, BPP House, Aldine Place, London W12 8AA.

Question bank

Chapter 1 – Drafting financial statements

Task 1.1

Given below is the trial balance for Paparazzi Ltd as at 30 June 20X2.

	£'000	£'000
Land and buildings: Cost	2,100	
Plant and machinery: Cost	1,050	
Motor vehicles: Cost	1,000	
Retained earnings at 1 July 20X1		1,131
Share capital		2,500
Share premium		300
Trade receivables	2,500	
Trade payables		1,400
Inventories at 1 July 20X1	690	
Accruals		50
Prepayments	40	
Sales		14,700
Purchases	10,780	
Land and buildings: Accumulated depreciation 30 June 20X2		280
Plant and machinery: Accumulated depreciation 30 June 20X2		194
Motor vehicles: Accumulated depreciation 30 June 20X2		404
Bank	567	
7% bank loan (repayable 20X9)		1,200
Allowance for doubtful debts 30 June 20X2		92
Dividend paid	120	
Interest paid	84	
Distribution costs	1,200	
Administrative expenses	2,120	
	22,251	22,251

Further information:

- The inventories at 30 June 20X2 cost £710,000

- The corporation tax charge for the year is estimated at £130,000

(a) **Draft the statement of profit or loss and other comprehensive income for Paparazzi Ltd for the year ended 30 June 20X2.**

Paparazzi Ltd

Statement of profit or loss and other comprehensive income for the year ended 30 June 20X2

	£'000
Revenue	
Cost of sales	
Gross profit	
Distribution costs	
Administrative expenses	
Profit/(loss) from operations	
Finance costs	
Profit/(loss) before tax	
Tax	
Profit/(loss) for the period from continuing operations	

Working

Cost of sales	£'000
Opening inventories	
Purchases	
Closing inventories	

(b) **Draft the statement of financial position for Paparazzi Ltd as at 30 June 20X2**

(Complete the left hand column by writing in the correct line item from the list provided)

Paparazzi Ltd

Statement of financial position as at 30 June 20X2

	£'000
Assets	
Non-current assets:	
▼	
Current assets:	
▼	
▼	
▼	
Total assets	
Equity and liabilities	
Equity:	
▼	
▼	
▼	
Total equity	
Non-current liabilities:	
▼	
Current liabilities:	
▼	
▼	
Total liabilities	
Total equity and liabilities	

Picklist for line items:

Bank loan
Cash and cash equivalents
Inventories
Property, plant and equipment
Retained earnings
Share capital
Share premium
Tax liabilities
Trade and other payables
Trade and other receivables

Workings

Property, plant and equipment	£'000
Land and buildings – Cost	
Plant and equipment – Cost	
Motor vehicles – Cost	
Accumulated depreciation – land and buildings	
Accumulated depreciation – plant and equipment	
Accumulated depreciation – motor vehicles	

Trade and other receivables	£'000
Trade and other receivables	
Allowance for doubtful debts	
Prepayments	

Retained earnings	£'000
Retained earnings at 1 July 20X1	
Total profit for the year	
Dividends paid	

Trade and other payables	£'000
Trade payables	
Accruals	

Task 1.2

You have been asked to help with the preparation of the financial statements of Bathlea Ltd for the year ended 30 September 20X8. The extended trial balance for the year ended 30 September 20X8, is set out below.

The following further information has been supplied.

- The tax charge for the year has been calculated as £11,000.

- Depreciation has been charged on all assets for the year and included in the trial balance figures for distribution costs and administrative expenses.

- The interest on the long-term loan is charged at 12% per annum and is paid monthly in arrears. The charge for the first eleven months of the year is included in the trial balance.

- A customer owing Bathlea Ltd £10,000 went into liquidation on 2 October 20X8. This has not been accounted for.

BATHLEA LIMITED: EXTENDED TRIAL BALANCE 30 SEPTEMBER 20X8

Description	Trial balance		Adjustments		Statement of profit or loss		Statement of financial position	
	Debit £'000	Credit £'000	Debit £'000	Credit £'000	Debit £'000	Credit £'000	Debit £'000	Credit £'000
Land and buildings – cost	300						300	
Fixtures and fittings – cost	220						220	
Motor vehicles – cost	70						70	
Office equipment – cost	80						80	
Land and buildings – accumulated depreciation		65						65
Fixtures and fittings – accumulated depreciation		43						43
Motor vehicles – accumulated depreciation		27						27
Office equipment – accumulated depreciation		35						35
Sales		3,509				3,509		
Purchases	1,691				1,691			
Inventories	200		250	250	200	250	250	
Receivables	370						370	
Allowance for irrecoverable debts		5						5
Prepayments			10				10	
Bank overdraft		3						3
Payables		350						350
Accruals				9				9
Distribution costs	860		7	10	857			
Administrative expenses	890		2		892			
Interest charges	11				11			
Interim dividend	15						15	
Share capital		500						500
Retained earnings		70						70
Long-term loan		100						100
Profit (loss)					108			108
Total	4,707	4,707	269	269	3,759	3,759	1,315	1,315

(a) **Draft the statement of profit or loss and other comprehensive income for Bathlea Ltd for the year ended 30 September 20X8.**

Bathlea Limited

Statement of profit or loss and other comprehensive income for the year ended 30 September 20X8

	£'000
Revenue	
Cost of sales	
Gross profit	
Distribution costs	
Administrative expenses	
Profit/(loss) from operations	
Finance cost	
Profit/(loss) before tax	
Tax	
Profit/(loss) for the period from continuing operations	

Workings

Cost of sales	£'000
Opening inventories	
Purchases	
Closing inventories	

Administrative expenses	£'000
Administrative expenses	
Irrecoverable debts	

(b) **Draft the statement of financial position for Bathlea Ltd as at 30 September 20X8**

(Complete the left hand column by writing in the correct line item from the list provided)

Bathlea Limited

Statement of financial position as at 30 September 20X8

	£'000
Assets	
Non-current assets	
▼	
Current assets	
▼	
▼	
Total assets	
Equity and liabilities	
Equity	
▼	
▼	
Total equity	
Non-current liabilities	
▼	
Current liabilities	
▼	
▼	
▼	
Total liabilities	
Total equity and liabilities	

Picklist for line items:

Bank overdraft
Cash and cash equivalents
Inventories
Long-term loan
Property, plant and equipment
Retained earnings
Share capital
Tax liabilities
Trade and other payables
Trade and other receivables

Workings

Property, plant and equipment	£'000
Land and buildings – Cost	
Fixtures and fittings – Cost	
Motor vehicles – Cost	
Office equipment – Cost	
Land and buildings – Accumulated depreciation	
Fixtures and fittings – Accumulated depreciation	
Motor vehicles – Accumulated depreciation	
Office equipment – Accumulated depreciation	

Trade and other receivables	£'000
Trade and other receivables	
Allowance for irrecoverable debts	
Irrecoverable debt	
Prepayments	

Retained earnings	£'000
Retained earnings at 1 October 20X7	
Total profit for the year	
Dividends paid	

Trade and other payables	£'000
Trade and other payables	
Accruals: trial balance	
Additional interest accrual	

Task 1.3

The directors of Howardsend Ltd have asked you to prepare the financial statements of the company for the year ended 30 September 20X6. An extended trial balance (ETB) as at 30 September 20X6 has been taken from the computerised accounting system. Some of the balances need to be adjusted. The ETB is on the next page.

Additional data

- Credit purchases relating to September 20X6 amounting to £2,403,000 had not been entered into the accounts at the year end.

- An allowance for doubtful debts is to be maintained at 2% of trade receivables. The doubtful debts expense is included in administrative expenses.

- The inventories at the close of business on 30 September 20X6 cost £8,134,000.

- The company employed an advertising agency during the year to promote a new product. The cost of the advertising campaign was agreed at £57,000, but no invoices have yet been received for this expense and no adjustment has been made for it in the ETB. This is to be included in distribution costs.

- Interest on the long-term loan for the last six months of the year has not been included in the accounts in the trial balance. Interest is charged at 7% per annum.

- The corporation tax charge for the year has been calculated as £1,382,000.

- Land that had cost £9,600,000 has been revalued by professional valuers at £11,600,000. No adjustment has yet been made in the balances in the ETB. The revaluation is to be included in the financial statements for the year ended 30 September 20X6.

- All the operations are continuing operations.

HOWARDSEND LTD
EXTENDED TRIAL BALANCE AS AT 30 SEPTEMBER 20X6

Description	Trial balance		Adjustments		Statement of profit or loss		Statement of financial position	
	Debit £'000	Credit £'000	Debit £'000	Credit £'000	Debit £'000	Credit £'000	Debit £'000	Credit £'000
Inventories at 1 October 20X5	7,158				7,158			
Administration expenses	9,086		90		9,176			
Interest	350				350			
Sales		53,821				53,821		
Accruals				214				214
Purchases	24,407				24,407			
Allowance for doubtful receivables		53						53
Distribution costs	12,092		124		12,216			
Long-term loan		10,000						10,000
Ordinary share capital		8,000						8,000
Share premium		1,000						1,000
Cash at bank	579						579	
Property, plant and equipment – cost	57,149						57,149	
Property, plant and equipment – accum depn		14,523						14,523
Trade receivables	6,600						6,600	
Trade payables		2,577						2,577
Final dividend paid for 20X5	960						960	
Interim dividend paid for 20X6	480						480	
Retained earnings		28,887						28,887
Profit for the year					514			514
TOTAL	118,861	118,861	214	214	53,821	53,821	65,768	65,768

(a) **Draft the statement of profit or loss and other comprehensive income for Howardsend Ltd for the year ended 30 September 20X6.**

Howardsend Ltd

Statement of profit or loss and other comprehensive income for the year ended 30 September 20X6

	£'000
Revenue	
Cost of sales	_____
Gross profit	
Distribution costs	
Administrative expenses	_____
Profit/(loss) from operations	
Finance costs	_____
Profit/(loss) before tax	
Tax	_____
Profit/(loss) for the period from continuing operations	
Other comprehensive income	
Gain on revaluation	_____
Total comprehensive income for the year	_____

Workings

(Complete the left hand column by writing in the correct narrative from the list provided)

Cost of sales	£'000
▼	
▼	
▼	

Picklist for narratives:

Accruals
Closing inventories
Opening inventories
Prepayments
Purchases

Distribution costs	£'000
▼	
▼	

Picklist for narratives:

Accruals
Allowance for doubtful debts
Distribution costs
Prepayments

Administrative expenses	£'000
▼	
▼	

Picklist for narratives:

Accruals
Administrative expenses
Allowance for doubtful debts
Prepayments

(b) **Draft the statement of financial position for Howardsend Ltd as at 30 September 20X6.**

(Complete the left hand column by writing in the correct line item from the list provided)

Howardsend Ltd

Statement of financial position as at 30 September 20X6

	£'000
Assets	
Non-current assets	
▼	
Current assets	
▼	
▼	
▼	
Total assets	
Equity and liabilities	
Equity	
▼	
▼	
▼	
▼	
Total equity	
Non-current liabilities	
▼	
Current liabilities	
▼	
▼	
Total liabilities	
Total equity and liabilities	

Picklist for line items:

Cash and cash equivalents
Inventories
Long-term loan
Property, plant and equipment
Retained earnings
Revaluation reserve
Share capital
Share premium
Tax liabilities
Trade and other payables
Trade and other receivables

Workings

(Complete the left hand column by writing in the correct narrative from the list provided.)

Property, plant and equipment		£'000
	▼	
	▼	
	▼	

Picklist for narratives:

Property, plant and equipment – Accumulated depreciation
Property, plant and equipment – Cost
Revaluation

Trade and other receivables		£'000
	▼	
	▼	

Picklist for narratives:

Accruals: trial balance
Additional distribution costs accrual
Additional distribution costs prepaid
Additional interest accrual
Allowance for doubtful debts
Prepayments
Trade payables
Trade receivables

Retained earnings		£'000
	▼	
	▼	
	▼	

Picklist for narratives:

Dividends paid
Other comprehensive income for the year
Retained earnings at 1 October 20X5
Revaluation
Total comprehensive income for the year
Total profit for the year

Trade and other payables		£'000
	▼	
	▼	
	▼	
	▼	

Picklist for narratives:

Accruals: trial balance
Additional distribution costs accrual
Additional distribution costs prepaid
Additional interest accrual
Allowance for doubtful debts
Dividends
Prepayments
Tax liabilities
Trade payables
Trade receivables

Task 1.4

You have been asked to help prepare the financial statements of Benard Ltd for the year ended 31 October 20X7. The company's trial balance as at 31 October 20X7 is shown below.

Benard Ltd

Trial balance as at 31 October 20X7

	Debit £'000	Credit £'000
Share capital		12,000
Trade and other payables		3,348
Property, plant and equipment – cost	58,463	
Property, plant and equipment – accumulated depreciation as at 31 October 20X7		27,974
Trade and other receivables	6,690	
Accruals		387
7% bank loan repayable 20Y2		16,000
Cash at bank	1,184	
Retained earnings as at 1 November 20X6		12,345
Interest	560	
Sales		50,197
Purchases	34,792	
Distribution costs	6,654	
Administrative expenses	4,152	
Inventories as at 1 November 20X6	8,456	
Dividends paid	1,300	
	122,251	122,251

Further information

- The sales figure in the trial balance does not include the credit sales for October 20X7 of £3,564,000.

- The inventories at the close of business on 31 October 20X7 cost £9,786,000.

- The company paid £48,000 insurance costs in June 20X7, which covered the period from 1 July 20X7 to 30 June 20X8. This was included in administrative expenses in the trial balance.

- Interest on the bank loan for the last six months of the year has not been included in the accounts in the trial balance.

- The corporation tax charge for the year has been calculated as £1,254,000.

- All of the operations are continuing operations.

(a) **Draft the statement of profit or loss and other comprehensive income for Benard Ltd for the year ended 31 October 20X7.**

Benard Ltd

Statement of profit or loss and other comprehensive income for the year ended 31 October 20X7

	£'000
Revenue	
Cost of sales	
Gross profit	
Distribution costs	
Administrative expenses	
Profit/(loss) from operations	
Finance costs	
Profit/(loss) before tax	
Tax	
Profit/(loss) for the period from continuing operations	

Workings

(Complete the left hand column by writing in the correct narrative from the list provided.)

Cost of sales		£'000
	▼	
	▼	
	▼	

Picklist for narratives:

Accruals
Closing inventories
Credit sales for October 20X7
Opening inventories
Prepayments
Purchases

Administrative expenses	£'000
▼	
▼	

Picklist for Narratives:

Accruals
Administrative expenses
Prepayments

(b) **Draft the statement of financial position for Benard Ltd as at 31 October 20X7**

(Complete the left hand column by writing in the correct line item from the list provided.)

Benard Ltd

Statement of financial position as at 31 October 20X7

	£'000
Assets	
Non-current assets	
▼	
Current assets	
▼	
▼	
▼	
Total assets	
Equity and liabilities	
Equity	
▼	
▼	
Total equity	

	£'000
Non-current liabilities	
▼	
Current liabilities	
▼	
▼	
Total liabilities	
Total equity and liabilities	

Picklist for line items:

Bank loan
Cash and cash equivalents
Inventories
Property, plant and equipment
Retained earnings
Share capital
Tax payable
Trade and other payables
Trade and other receivables

Workings

(Complete the left hand column by writing in the correct narrative from the list provided.)

Trade and other receivables	£'000
▼	
▼	
▼	

Picklist for narratives:

Accruals: trial balance
Administrative expenses accrual
Administrative expenses prepaid
Additional interest accrual
Credit sales for October 20X7
Prepayments
Trade and other payables
Trade and other receivables

Retained earnings		£'000
	▼	
	▼	
	▼	

Picklist for narratives:

Dividends paid
Other comprehensive income for the year
Retained earnings at 1 November 20X6
Total comprehensive income for the year
Total profit for the year

Trade and other payables		£'000
	▼	
	▼	
	▼	

Picklist for narratives:

Accruals: trial balance
Administrative expenses accrual
Administrative expenses prepayment
Additional interest accrual
Credit sales for October 20X7
Dividends
Prepayments
Tax payable
Trade and other payables
Trade and other receivables

Task 1.5

You have been asked to help prepare the financial statements of Laxdale Ltd for the year ended 31 October 20X8. The company's trial balance as at 31 October 20X8 is shown below.

Laxdale Ltd

Trial balance as at 31 October 20X8

	Debit £'000	Credit £'000
Share capital		25,000
Trade and other payables		2,798
Land and buildings – cost	35,152	
Land and buildings – accumulated depreciation at 1 November 20X7		7,000
Plant and equipment – cost	12,500	
Plant and equipment – accumulated depreciation at 1 November 20X7		7,400
Trade and other receivables	5,436	
Accruals		436
8% bank loan repayable 20Y2		15,000
Cash at bank	9,774	
Retained earnings		9,801
Interest	600	
Sales		58,411
Purchases	41,620	
Distribution costs	5,443	
Administrative expenses	4,789	
Inventories as at 1 November 20X7	9,032	
Dividends paid	1,500	
	125,846	125846

Further information

- The inventories at the close of business on 31 October 20X8 were valued at £7,878,000.

- Depreciation is to be provided for the year to 31 March 20X1 as follows:

Buildings	2% per annum	Straight line basis
Plant and equipment balance basis	20% per annum	Reducing (diminishing)

Depreciation is apportioned as follows:

	%
Cost of sales	40
Distribution costs	40
Administrative expenses	20

Land, which is non-depreciable, is included in the trial balance at a cost of £15,152,000.

- The company began a series of television adverts for the company's range of products on 1 October 20X8 at a cost of £45,000. The adverts were to run for three months and were to be paid for in full at the end of December 20X8. Advertising expenses are included in distribution costs.

- Interest on the bank loan for the last six months of the year has not been included in the accounts in the trial balance.

- The corporation tax charge for the year has been calculated as £970,000.

- All of the operations are continuing operations.

(a) **Draft the statement of profit or loss and other comprehensive income for Laxdale Ltd for the year ended 31 October 20X8.**

Laxdale Ltd

Statement of profit or loss and other comprehensive income for the year ended 31 October 20X8

	£'000
Revenue	
Cost of sales	
Gross profit	
Distribution costs	
Administrative expenses	
Profit/(loss) from operations	
Finance costs	
Profit/(loss) before tax	
Tax	
Profit/(loss) for the period from continuing operations	

Workings

(Complete the left hand column by writing in the correct narrative from the list provided.)

Cost of sales		£'000
	▼	
	▼	
	▼	
	▼	

Picklist for narratives:

Accruals
Closing inventories
Depreciation
Opening inventories
Prepayments
Purchases

Distribution costs		£'000
	▼	
	▼	
	▼	

Picklist for narratives:

Accruals
Depreciation
Distribution costs
Prepayments

Administrative expenses	£'000
▼	
▼	

Picklist for narratives:

Accruals
Administrative expenses
Depreciation
Prepayments

(b) **Draft the statement of financial position for Laxdale Ltd as at 31 October 20X8.**

(Complete the left hand column by writing in the correct line item from the list provided.)

Laxdale Ltd

Statement of financial position as at 31 October 20X8

	£'000
Assets	
Non-current assets	
▼	_____
Current assets	
▼	
▼	
▼	_____
	_____
Total assets	_____
Equity and liabilities	
Equity	
▼	
▼	_____
Total equity	_____

	£'000
Non-current liabilities	
	————
Current liabilities	
	————
	————
Total liabilities	
Total equity and liabilities	════

Picklist for line items:

Bank loan
Cash and cash equivalents
Inventories
Property, plant and equipment
Retained earnings
Share capital
Tax liabilities
Trade and other payables
Trade and other receivables

Workings

(Complete the left hand column by writing in the correct narrative from the list provided.)

Property, plant and equipment	£'000
▽	
▽	
▽	
▽	

Picklist for narratives:

Accumulated depreciation – land and buildings
Accumulated depreciation – plant and equipment
Land and buildings – Cost
Plant and equipment – Cost

Retained earnings		£'000
	▼	
	▼	
	▼	

Picklist for narratives:

Dividends paid
Other comprehensive income for the year
Retained earnings at 1 November 20X7
Total comprehensive income for the year
Total profit for the year

Trade and other payables		£'000
	▼	
	▼	
	▼	
	▼	

Picklist for narratives:

Accruals: trial balance
Additional distribution costs accrual
Additional distribution costs prepaid
Additional interest accrual
Dividends
Prepayments
Tax payable
Trade and other payables
Trade and other receivables

BPP
LEARNING MEDIA

Task 1.6

You have been asked to help prepare the financial statements of Cappielow Ltd for the year ended 31 March 20X1. The company's trial balance as at 31 March 20X1 is shown below.

Cappielow Ltd

Trial balance as at 31 March 20X1

	Debit	Credit
	£'000	£'000
Share capital		10,000
Revaluation reserve at 1 April 20X0		2,000
Trade and other payables		1,347
Property, plant and equipment – cost/value	36,780	
Property, plant and equipment – accumulated depreciation at 31 March 20X1		19,876
Trade and other receivables	2,133	
Accruals		129
6% bank loan repayable 20X6		12,000
Cash at bank	7,578	
Retained earnings at 1 April 20X0		2,595
Interest	720	
Sales		35,547
Purchases	27,481	
Distribution costs	1,857	
Administrative expenses	2,235	
Inventories as at 1 April 20X0	3,790	
Dividends paid	920	
	83,494	83,494

Further information:

- The inventories at the close of business on 31 March 20X1 were valued at £4,067,000.

- Depreciation has already been provided on property, plant and equipment for the year ended 31 March 20X1.

- On 31 March 20X1 items of plant with a cost of £12,750,000 and accumulated depreciation of £3,100,000 were found to have a fair value less costs of disposal of £8,500,000 and a value in use of £8,200,000. Any adjustment should be included in cost of sales.

- Land, which is non-depreciable, is included in the trial balance at a value of £5,150,000. It is to be revalued at £7,500,000 and this revaluation is to be included in the financial statements for the year ended 31 March 20X1.

- The company hired some office copiers for the period 1 March to 30 June 20X1. The contract price for the four months was £164,000 and this was paid in full on 3 March.

- The company sourced extra warehousing space, for the storage of goods prior to their sale, for a period of three months from 1 February to 30 April 20X1. The invoice for the full three months of £114,000 was paid on 16 April. No entry has been made in the accounts for this transaction.

- The corporation tax charge for the year has been calculated as £874,000.

- On 15 April 20X1 one of the company's customers went into liquidation. Trade receivables at 31 March 20X1 include a balance of £95,000 owed by this customer. The directors have been advised that they are unlikely to receive any of this amount.

- All of the operations are continuing operations.

(a) **Draft the statement of profit or loss and other comprehensive income for Cappielow Ltd for the year ended 31 March 20X1.**

(b) **Draft the statement of changes in equity for Cappielow Ltd for the year ended 31 March 20X1.**

(c) **Draft the statement of financial position for Cappielow Ltd as at 31 March 20X1.**

Note. Additional notes and disclosures are not required.

Cappielow Ltd

Statement of profit or loss and other comprehensive income for the year ended 31 March 20X1

	£'000
Revenue	
Cost of sales	
Gross profit	
Distribution costs	
Administrative expenses	
Profit/(loss) from operations	
Finance costs	
Profit/(loss) before tax	
Tax	
Profit/(loss) for the period from continuing operations	
Other comprehensive income for the year	
Gain on revaluation of land	
Total comprehensive income for the year	

Workings

(Complete the left hand column by writing in the correct narrative from the list provided.)

Cost of sales	£'000
▼	
▼	
▼	
▼	

Picklist for narratives:

Accruals
Closing inventories
Impairment loss
Opening inventories
Prepayment
Purchases

Distribution costs		£'000
	▼	
	▼	

Picklist for narratives:

Accruals
Irrecoverable debt
Distribution costs
Prepayment

Administrative expenses		£'000
	▼	
	▼	
	▼	

Picklist for narratives:

Accruals
Administrative expenses
Irrecoverable debt
Impairment loss
Prepayment

Cappielow Ltd

Statement of changes in equity for the year ended 31 March 20X1

	Share capital £'000	Other reserves £'000	Retained earnings £'000	Total equity £'000
Balance at 1 April 20X0				
Changes in equity for 20X1				
Total comprehensive income				
Dividends				
Balance at 31 March 20X1				

Cappielow Ltd

Statement of financial position as at 31 March 20X1

(Complete the left hand column by writing in the correct line item from the list provided)

	£'000
Assets	
Non-current assets:	
▼	
Current assets:	
▼	
▼	
▼	
Total assets	
Equity and liabilities:	
Equity	
▼	
▼	
▼	
Total equity	
Non-current liabilities:	
▼	
Current liabilities:	
▼	
▼	
Total liabilities	
Total equity and liabilities	

Picklist for line items:

Bank loan
Cash and cash equivalents
Inventories
Property, plant and equipment
Retained earnings
Revaluation reserve
Share capital
Tax payable
Trade and other payables
Trade and other receivables

Workings

(Complete the left hand column by writing in the correct narrative from the list provided.)

Property, plant and equipment	£'000
▼	
▼	
▼	

Picklist for narratives:

Impairment loss
Property, plant and equipment: Accumulated depreciation
Property, plant and equipment: Cost/value

Trade and other receivables	£'000
▼	
▼	
▼	

Picklist for narratives:

Accruals: trial balance
Administrative expenses accrued
Administrative expenses prepaid
Irrecoverable debt
Distribution costs accrued
Distribution costs prepaid
Trade and other payables
Trade and other receivables

Revaluation reserve		£'000
	▼	
	▼	

Picklist for narratives:

Dividends paid
Other comprehensive income for the year
Retained reserves at 1 April 20X0
Revaluation reserve at 1 April 20X0
Total comprehensive income for the year
Total profit for the year

Retained earnings		£'000
	▼	
	▼	
	▼	

Picklist for narratives:

Dividends paid
Other comprehensive income for the year
Retained earnings at 1 April 20X0
Revaluation reserve at 1 April 20X0
Total comprehensive income for the year
Total profit for the year

Trade and other payables	£'000
 ▼	
▼	
▼	

Picklist for narratives:

Accruals: trial balance
Administrative expenses accrued
Administrative expenses prepaid
Irrecoverable debt
Distribution costs accrued
Distribution costs prepaid
Dividends
Tax payable
Trade and other payables
Trade and other receivables

Task 1.7

You have been asked to help prepare the financial statements of Pine Ltd for the year ended 31 March 20X1. The company's trial balance as at 31 March 20X1 is shown below.

Pine Ltd

Trial balance as at 31 March 20X1

	Debit £'000	Credit £'000
Share capital		50,000
Revaluation reserve at 1 April 20X0		12,000
Trade and other payables		5,342
Land & buildings – value/cost	81,778	
accumulated depreciation at 1 April 20X0		14,000
Plant and equipment – cost	24,000	
accumulated depreciation at 1 April 20X0		8,000
Trade and other receivables	9,886	
Accruals		517
4% bank loan repayable 20X8		16,000
Cash and cash equivalents	1,568	
Retained earnings at 1 April 20X0		7,945
Interest paid	640	
Sales		80,908
Purchases	53,444	
Distribution costs	9,977	
Administrative expenses	6,755	
Inventories at 1 April 20X0	5,064	
Dividends paid	1,600	
	194,712	194,712

Further information:

- The inventories at the close of business on 31 March 20X1 cost £7,004,000.

- Land, which is not depreciated, is included in the trial balance at a value of £41,778,000. It is to be revalued at £51,000,000 and this revaluation is to be included in the financial statements for the year ended 31 March 20X1.

- Depreciation is to be provided for the year to 31 March 20X1 as follows:

  Buildings   5% per annum   Straight line basis

  Plant and equipment   25% per annum   Diminishing (reducing) balance basis

  Depreciation is apportioned as follows:

	%
Cost of sales	60
Distribution costs	30
Administrative expenses	10

- Trade receivables include a debt of £24,000 which is to be written off. Irrecoverable (bad) debts are to be classified as administrative expenses.

- Distribution costs of £160,000 owing at 31 March 20X1 are to be provided for.

- The corporation tax charge for the year has been calculated as £1,254,000.

- All of the operations are continuing operations.

(a) **Draft the statement of profit or loss and other comprehensive income for Pine Ltd for the year ended 31 March 20X1.**

(b) **Draft the statement of changes in equity for Pine Ltd for the year ended 31 March 20X1.**

(c) **Draft the statement of financial position for Pine Ltd as at 31 March 20X1.**

Pine Ltd

Statement of profit or loss and other comprehensive income for the year ended 31 March 20X1

	£'000
Revenue	
Cost of sales	
Gross profit	
Distribution costs	
Administrative expenses	
Profit from operations	
Finance costs	

	£'000
Profit before tax	
Tax	
Profit for the period from continuing operations	
Other comprehensive income for the year	
Total comprehensive income for the year	

Workings

(Complete the left hand column by writing in the correct narrative from the list provided.)

Cost of sales	£'000
▼	
▼	
▼	
▼	

Picklist for narratives:

Accruals
Closing inventories
Depreciation
Opening inventories
Prepayments
Purchases

Distribution costs	£'000
▼	
▼	
▼	

Picklist for narratives:

Accruals
Irrecoverable debt
Depreciation
Distribution costs
Prepayments

Administrative expenses	£'000
▽	
▽	
▽	

Picklist for narratives:

Accruals
Administrative expenses
Irrecoverable debt
Depreciation
Prepayments

Pine Ltd

Statement of changes in equity for the year ended 31 March 20X1

	Share capital £'000	Other reserves £'000	Retained earnings £'000	Total equity £'000
Balance at 1 April 20X0				
Changes in equity for 20X1				
Total comprehensive income				
Dividends				
Issue of share capital				
Balance at 31 March 20X1				

Pine Ltd

Statement of financial position as at 31 March 20X1

(Complete the left hand column by writing in the correct line item from the list provided)

	£'000
Assets	
Non-current assets:	
▼	
Current assets:	
▼	
▼	
▼	
Total assets	
Equity and liabilities:	
Equity	
▼	
▼	
▼	
Total equity	
Non-current liabilities:	
▼	
Current liabilities:	
▼	
▼	
Total liabilities	
Total equity and liabilities	

Picklist for line items:

Bank loan
Cash and cash equivalents
Inventories
Property, plant and equipment
Retained earnings
Revaluation reserve
Share capital
Tax liability
Trade and other payables
Trade and other receivables

Workings

(Complete the left hand column by writing in the correct narrative from the list provided.)

Property, plant and equipment		£'000
	▼	
	▼	
	▼	
	▼	

Picklist for narratives:

Accumulated depreciation – land and buildings
Accumulated depreciation – plant and equipment
Land and buildings – value
Plant and equipment – cost

Trade and other receivables		£'000
	▼	
	▼	

Picklist for narratives:

Accruals: trial balance
Additional distribution costs accrual
Additional distribution costs prepaid
Irrecoverable debts
Prepayments
Trade and other payables
Trade and other receivables

Revaluation reserve		£'000
	▼	
	▼	

Picklist for narratives:

Dividends paid
Other comprehensive income for the year
Retained reserves at 1 April 20X0
Revaluation reserve at 1 April 20X0
Total comprehensive income for the year
Total profit for the year

Retained earnings		£'000
	▼	
	▼	
	▼	

Picklist for narratives:

Dividends paid
Other comprehensive income for the year
Retained earnings at 1 April 20X0
Revaluation reserve at 1 April 20X0
Total comprehensive income for the year
Total profit for the year

Trade and other payables		£'000
	▼	
	▼	
	▼	

Picklist for narratives:

Accruals: trial balance
Additional distribution costs accrued
Additional distribution costs prepaid
Irrecoverable debts
Dividends
Prepayments
Taxation liability
Trade and other payables
Trade and other receivables

Chapter 2 – The statement of cash flows

Task 2.1

An extract from a company's statement of profit or loss for the year ended 31 December 20X1 is given:

	£
Revenue	560,000
Cost of sales	300,000
Gross profit	260,000
Other expenses	160,000
Profit from operations	100,000

Other expenses include £20,000 of depreciation. Interest paid was £10,000. The tax paid for the year was £25,000.

Extracts from the statement of financial position are also given below:

	20X1 £	20X0 £
Inventories	30,000	25,000
Trade receivables	40,000	42,000
Trade payables	28,000	32,000

Prepare a reconciliation of profit from operations to net cash from operating activities using the indirect method.

Reconciliation of profit from operations to net cash from operating activities

	£
Profit from operations	
Depreciation	
Increase/decrease in inventories	
Increase/decrease in trade receivables	
Increase/decrease in trade payables	
Cash generated from operations	
Interest paid	
Tax paid	
Net cash from operating activities	

Task 2.2

Given below is an extract from a company's statement of financial position:

	Year ended 31 March	
	20X2	20X1
	£'000	£'000
Trade payables	340	380
Corporation tax	100	94
Accrued interest	8	13

The statement of profit or loss shows that interest payable for the year was £32,400 and the corporation tax charge was £98,000.

Calculate the figures that would appear in the statement of cash flows for:

(a) **Interest paid**

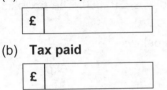

£

(b) **Tax paid**

£

Task 2.3

An extract from a company's statement of financial position is given below:

	Year ended 30 June	
	20X2	20X1
	£'000	£'000
Property, plant and equipment at cost	1,340	1,250
Less: accumulated depreciation	(560)	(480)
	780	770

During the year items with a cost of £140,000 and net carrying amount of £98,000 were sold at a loss of £23,000.

Calculate the figures for:

(a) **Cash paid to acquire property, plant and equipment during the year**

£

(b) **Proceeds of the sale of property, plant and equipment in the year**

£

(c) **The depreciation charge for the year**

£

Task 2.4

During the year ended 30 April 20X2 a company made a profit of £110,000. On 1 May 20X1 there were already 500,000 £1 ordinary shares in issue. On that date the company issued a further 200,000 ordinary shares at a price of £1.40 per share.

During the year the company revalued some of its non-current assets upwards by £70,000. An ordinary dividend of £35,000 was paid.

Share capital and reserves at 1 May 20X1 (before accounting for the share issue) were as follows:

	£
£1 ordinary shares	500,000
Share premium	100,000
Revaluation reserve	30,000
Retained earnings	180,000
	810,000

Draft a statement of changes in equity for the year ended 30 April 20X2.

Statement of changes in equity for the year ended 30 April 20X2

	Share capital £	Share premium £	Revaluation reserve £	Retained earnings £	Total equity £
Balance at 1 May 20X1					
Changes in equity					
Total comprehensive income					
Dividends					
Issue of share capital					
Balance at 30 April 20X2					

Task 2.5

You are presented with the following information for Evans.

Evans

Statement of profit or loss for the year ended 31 October 20X1

	£'000
Continuing operations	
Revenue	2,000
Cost of sales	(1,350)
Gross profit	650
Gain on disposal of non-current assets	10
Distribution costs	(99)
Administrative expenses	(120)
Profit from operations	441
Finance costs	(23)
Profit before tax	418
Tax	(125)
Profit for the period from continuing operations	293

Evans

Statements of financial position as at 31 October

	20X1		20X0	
	£'000	£'000	£'000	£'000
Assets				
Non-current assets				
Property, plant and equipment		1,180		1,010
Current assets				
Inventories	486		505	
Trade receivables	945		657	
Cash	2		10	
		1,433		1,172
Total assets		2,613		2,182
Equity and liabilities				
Equity				
Share capital	1,200		1,000	
Share premium	315		270	
Retained earnings	363		110	
		1,878		1,380

BPP
LEARNING MEDIA

	20X1		20X0	
	£'000	£'000	£'000	£'000
Non-current liabilities				
12% bank loan		50		150
Current liabilities				
Trade payables	560		546	
Tax payable	125		106	
		685		652
Total liabilities		735		802
Total equity and liabilities		2,613		2,182

Additional information for the year ended 31 October 20X1

- Vehicles which had cost £155,000 were sold during the year when their net carrying amount was £65,000.

- The total depreciation charge for the year was £190,000.

- There were no prepaid or accrued expenses at the beginning or end of the year.

- Dividends of £40,000 were paid during the year.

(a) **Prepare a reconciliation of profit from operations to net cash from operating activities for Evans Ltd for the year ended 31 October 20X1.**

Reconciliation of profit from operations to net cash from operating activities

	£'000
Profit from operations	
Adjustments for:	
Depreciation	
Gain on disposal of property, plant and equipment	
Adjustment in respect of inventories	
Adjustment in respect of trade receivables	
Adjustment in respect of trade payables	
Cash generated by operations	
Interest paid	
Tax paid	
Net cash from operating activities	

(b) **Prepare the statement of cash flows for Evans Ltd for the year ended 31 October 20X1.**

Evans Ltd

Statement of cash flows for the year ended 31 October 20X1

	£'000
Net cash from operating activities	
Investing activities	
Purchase of property, plant and equipment	
Proceeds on disposal of property, plant and equipment	
Net cash used in investing activities	
Financing activities	
Proceeds of share issue	
Repayment of bank loan	
Dividends paid	
Net cash from financing activities	
Net increase/(decrease) in cash and cash equivalents	
Cash and cash equivalents at the beginning of the year	
Cash and cash equivalents at the end of the year	

Workings

Proceeds on disposal of property, plant and equipment (PPE)	£'000
Carrying amount of PPE sold	
Gain on disposal	

Purchase of property, plant and equipment (PPE)	£'000
PPE at start of year	
Depreciation charge	
Carrying amount of PPE sold	
PPE at end of year	
Total PPE additions	

(c) **Draft the statement of changes in equity for Evans Ltd for the year ended 31 October 20X1.**

Evans Ltd

Statement of changes in equity for the year ended 31 October 20X1

	Share capital £'000	Other reserves £'000	Retained earnings £'000	Total equity £'000
Balance at 1 November 20X0				
Changes in equity				
Profit for the year				
Dividends				
Issue of share capital				
Balance at 31 October 20X1				

Task 2.6

For the year ended 31 October 20X7 you have been asked to prepare:

- A reconciliation between profit from operations and net cash from operating activities.
- A statement of cash flows for Lochnagar Ltd.

The statements of financial position of Lochnagar Ltd for the past two years and the most recent statement of profit or loss are set out as follows:

Lochnagar Ltd

Statement of profit or loss for the year ended 31 October 20X7

	£'000
Continuing operations	
Revenue	22,400
Cost of sales	(12,320)
Gross profit	10,080
Gain on disposal of property, plant and equipment	224
Distribution costs	(4,704)
Administrative expenses	(2,240)
Profit from operations	3,360
Finance costs – interest on loans	(91)
Profit before tax	3,269
Tax	(1,344)
Profit for the period from continuing operations	1,925

Lochnagar Ltd

Statements of financial position as at 31 October

	20X7	20X6
Assets	£'000	£'000
Non-current assets		
Property, plant and equipment	25,171	24,100
Current assets		
Inventories	3,696	2,464
Trade and other receivables	3,360	2,464
Cash and cash equivalents	0	129
	7,056	5,057
Total assets	32,227	29,157
Equity and liabilities		
Equity		
Share capital	2,200	2,000
Share premium	800	500
Retained earnings	24,990	23,065
Total equity	27,990	25,565
Non-current liabilities		
Bank loans	1,300	800
Current liabilities		
Trade and other payables	1,232	1,848
Tax liability	1,344	944
Bank overdraft	361	0
	2,937	2,792
Total liabilities	4,237	3,592
Total equity and liabilities	32,227	29,157

Further information

- The total depreciation charge for the year was £3,545,000.

- Property, plant and equipment costing £976,000 with accumulated depreciation of £355,000 was sold in the year at a profit of £224,000.

- All sales and purchases were on credit. Other expenses were paid for in cash.

(a) **Prepare a reconciliation of profit from operations to net cash from operating activities for Lochnagar Ltd for the year ended 31 October 20X7.**

(Complete the left hand column by writing in the correct line item from the list provided.)

Lochnagar Ltd

Reconciliation of profit from operations to net cash from operating activities for the year ended 31 October 20X7

	£'000
▼	
Adjustments for:	
▼	
▼	
▼	
▼	
▼	
Cash generated by operations	
▼	
▼	
Net cash from operating activities	

Picklist for line items:

Adjustment in respect of inventories
Adjustment in respect of trade payables
Adjustment in respect of trade receivables
Depreciation
Gain on disposal of property, plant and equipment
Interest paid
New bank loans
Proceeds on disposal of property, plant and equipment
Profit after tax
Profit before tax
Profit from operations
Purchases of property, plant and equipment
Tax paid

(b) **Prepare the statement of cash flows for Lochnagar Ltd for the year ended 31 October 20X7.**

(Complete the left hand column by writing in the correct line item from the list provided.)

Lochnagar Ltd

Statement of cash flows for the year ended 31 October 20X7

	£'000
Net cash from operating activities	
Investing activities	
▼	
▼	
Net cash used in investing activities	
Financing activities	
▼	
▼	
Net cash from financing activities	
Net increase/(decrease) in cash and cash equivalents	
Cash and cash equivalents at the beginning of the year	
Cash and cash equivalents at the end of the year	

Picklist for line items:

Adjustment in respect of inventories
Adjustment in respect of trade payables
Adjustment in respect of trade receivables
New bank loans
Proceeds of share issue
Proceeds on disposal of property, plant and equipment
Purchases of property, plant and equipment

Workings

(Complete the left hand column by writing in the correct narrative from the list provided.)

Proceeds on disposal of property, plant and equipment (PPE)	£'000
▼	
▼	

Picklist for narratives:

Carrying amount of PPE sold
Depreciation charge
Gain on disposal
PPE at end of year
PPE at start of year

Purchases of property, plant and equipment (PPE)	£'000
PPE at start of year	
▼	
▼	
▼	
Total PPE additions	

Picklist for narratives:

Carrying amount of PPE sold
Depreciation charge
Gain on disposal of PPE
PPE at end of year

Task 2.7

You have been asked to prepare the statement of cash flows for Thehoose Ltd, for the year ended 31 March 20X9. The most recent statement of profit or loss and statements of financial position of Thehoose Ltd for the past two years are set out below.

Thehoose Ltd

Statement of profit or loss for the year ended 31 March 20X9

	£'000
Continuing operations	
Revenue	37,680
Cost of sales	(22,608)
Gross profit	15,072
Gain on disposal of property, plant and equipment	376
Distribution costs	(6,782)
Administrative expenses	(3,014)
Profit from operations	5,652
Finance costs	(280)
Profit before tax	5,372
Tax	(1,484)
Profit for the period from continuing operations	3,888

Thehoose Ltd

Statements of financial position as at 31 March

	20X9	20X8
	£'000	£'000
Non-current assets		
Property, plant and equipment	27,570	21,340
Current assets		
Inventories	5,426	4,069
Trade and other receivables	3,768	4,145
Cash and cash equivalents	335	0
	9,529	8,214
Total assets	37,099	29,554
Equity and liabilities		
Equity		
Share capital	4,500	3,000
Share premium	3,000	2,000
Retained earnings	21,854	17,966
Total equity	29,354	22,966
Non-current liabilities		
Bank loans	4,000	1,500
Current liabilities		
Trade and other payables	2,261	4,069
Tax liability	1,484	887
Bank overdraft	–	132
	3,745	5,088
Total liabilities	7,745	6,588
Total equity and liabilities	37,099	29,554

Further information:

- The total depreciation charge for the year was £3,469,000.
- Property, plant and equipment costing £764,000, with accumulated depreciation of £347,000, were sold in the year.
- All sales and purchases were on credit. Other expenses were paid for in cash.

(a) **Prepare a reconciliation of profit from operations to net cash from operating activities for Thehoose Ltd for the year ended 31 March 20X9.**

(Complete the left hand column by writing in the correct line item from the list provided.)

Thehoose Ltd

Reconciliation of profit from operations to net cash from operating activities for the year ended 31 March 20X9

		£'000
	▼	
Adjustments for:		
	▼	
	▼	
	▼	
	▼	
	▼	
Cash generated by operations		
	▼	
	▼	
Net cash from operating activities		

Picklist for line items:

Adjustment in respect of inventories
Adjustment in respect of trade payables
Adjustment in respect of trade receivables
Depreciation
Gain on disposal of property, plant and equipment
Interest paid
New bank loans
Proceeds on disposal of property, plant and equipment
Profit after tax
Profit before tax
Profit from operations
Purchases of property, plant and equipment
Tax paid

(b) **Prepare the statement of cash flows for Thehoose Ltd for the year ended 31 March 20X9.**

(Complete the left hand column by writing in the correct line item from the list provided.)

Thehoose Ltd

Statement of cash flows for the year ended 31 March 20X9

	£'000
Net cash from operating activities	
Investing activities	
▼	
▼	
Net cash used in investing activities	
Financing activities	
▼	
▼	
Net cash from financing activities	
Net increase/(decrease) in cash and cash equivalents	
Cash and cash equivalents at the beginning of the year	
Cash and cash equivalents at the end of the year	

Picklist for line items:

Adjustment in respect of inventories
Adjustment in respect of trade payables
Adjustment in respect of trade receivables
Dividends paid
New bank loans
Proceeds of share issue
Proceeds on disposal of property, plant and equipment
Purchases of property, plant and equipment

Workings

(Complete the left hand column by writing in the correct narrative from the list provided.)

Proceeds on disposal of property, plant and equipment (PPE)	£'000
▼	
▼	

Picklist for narratives:

Carrying amount of PPE sold
Depreciation charge
Gain on disposal
PPE at end of year
PPE at start of year

Purchases of property, plant and equipment (PPE)	£'000
PPE at start of year	
▼	
▼	
▼	
Total PPE additions	

Picklist for narratives:

Carrying amount of PPE sold
Depreciation charge
Gain on disposal of PPE
PPE at end of year

Task 2.8

You have been asked to prepare a statement of cash flows and a statement of changes in equity for Adlington Ltd for the year ended 31 October 20X9. The most recent statement of profit or loss and statements of financial position of the company for the past two years are set out below.

Adlington Ltd

Statement of profit or loss for the year ended 31 October 20X9

	£'000
Continuing operations	
Revenue	45,500
Cost of sales	(27,300)
Gross profit	18,200
Gain on disposal of property, plant and equipment	455
Distribution costs	(6,825)
Administrative expenses	(5,005)
Profit from operations	6,825
Finance costs – interest on loan	(595)
Profit before tax	6,230
Tax	(1,757)
Profit for the period from continuing operations	4,473

Adlington Ltd

Statements of financial position as at 31 October

Assets	20X9	20X8
Non-current assets	£'000	£'000
Property, plant and equipment	31,989	22,246
Current assets		
Inventories	6,552	4,914
Trade and other receivables	4,550	4,641
Cash and cash equivalents	450	0
	11,552	9,555
Total assets	43,541	31,801
Equity and liabilities		
Equity		
Share capital	10,000	8,000
Share premium	4,000	3,000
Retained earnings	15,462	11,489
Total equity	29,462	22,489
Non-current liabilities		
Bank loan	8,500	3,000
Current liabilities		
Trade and other payables	3,822	4,368
Tax liabilities	1,757	658
Bank overdraft	–	1,286
	5,579	6,312
Total liabilities	14,079	9,312
Total equity plus liabilities	43,541	31,801

Additional data

- The total depreciation charged for the year was £4,398,000.

- Property, plant and equipment costing £568,000 with accumulated depreciation of £226,000 was sold in the year.

- All sales and purchases were on credit. Other expenses were paid for in cash.

- A dividend of £500,000 was paid during the year.

(a) **Prepare a reconciliation of profit from operations to net cash from operating activities for Adlington Ltd for the year ended 31 October 20X9.**

(Complete the left hand column by writing in the correct line item from the list provided.)

Reconciliation of profit from operations to net cash from operating activities for the year ended 31 October 20X9

	£'000
▼	
Adjustments for:	
▼	
▼	
▼	
▼	
▼	
Cash generated from operations	
▼	
▼	
Net cash from operating activities	

Picklist for line items:

Adjustment in respect of inventories
Adjustment in respect of trade payables
Adjustment in respect of trade receivables
Depreciation
Gain on disposal of property, plant and equipment
Interest paid
New bank loans
Proceeds on disposal of property, plant and equipment
Profit after tax
Profit before tax
Profit from operations
Purchases of property, plant and equipment
Tax paid

(b) **Prepare the statement of cash flows for Adlington Ltd for the year ended 31 October 20X9.**

(Complete the left hand column by writing in the correct line item from the list provided.)

Adlington Ltd

Statement of cash flows for the year ended 31 October 20X9

	£'000
Net cash from operating activities	
Investing activities	
▼	
▼	
Net cash used in investing activities	
Financing activities	
▼	
▼	
▼	
Net cash from financing activities	
Net increase/(decrease) in cash and cash equivalents	
Cash and cash equivalents at the beginning of the year	
Cash and cash equivalents at the end of the year	

Picklist for line items:

Adjustment in respect of inventories
Adjustment in respect of trade payables
Adjustment in respect of trade receivables
Dividends paid
New bank loans
Proceeds of share issue
Proceeds on disposal of property, plant and equipment
Purchases of property, plant and equipment

Workings

(Complete the left hand column by writing in the correct narrative from the list provided.)

Proceeds on disposal of property, plant and equipment (PPE)	£'000
▼	
▼	

Picklist for narratives:

Carrying amount of PPE sold
Depreciation charge
Gain on disposal
PPE at end of year
PPE at start of year

Purchases of property, plant and equipment (PPE)	£'000
PPE at start of year	
▼	
▼	
▼	
Total PPE additions	

Picklist for narratives:

Carrying amount of PPE sold
Depreciation charge
Gain on disposal of PPE
PPE at end of year

(c) **Draft the statement of changes in equity for Adlington Ltd for the year ended 31 October 20X9.**

(Complete the left hand column by writing in the correct line item from the list provided.)

Adlington Ltd

Statement of changes in equity for the year ended 31 October 20X9

	Share capital	Other reserves	Retained earnings	Total equity
	£'000	£'000	£'000	£'000
Balance at 1 November 20X8				
Changes in equity for 20X9				
Profit for the year				
Dividends				
Issue of share capital				
Balance at 31 October 20X9				

Task 2.9

You have been asked to prepare the statement of cash flows and statement of changes in equity for Forthbank Ltd for the year ended 31 March 20X1.

The most recent statement of profit or loss and statement of financial position (with comparatives for the previous year) of Forthbank Ltd are set out below.

Forthbank Ltd – Statement of profit or loss for the year ended 31 March 20X1

Continuing operations	£'000
Revenue	54,000
Cost of sales	(32,400)
Gross profit	21,600
Dividends received	650
Loss on disposal of property, plant and equipment	(110)
Distribution costs	(11,420)
Administrative expenses	(4,860)
Profit from operations	5,860
Finance costs	(301)
Profit before tax	5,559
Tax	(1,113)
Profit for the period from continuing operations	4,446

Forthbank Ltd – Statement of financial position as at 31 March 20X1

	20X1	20X0
	£'000	£'000
Assets		
Non-current assets		
Property, plant and equipment	26,660	19,140
Current assets		
Inventories	5,832	4,860
Trade and other receivables	5,400	4,320
Cash and cash equivalents	587	0
	11,819	9,180
Total assets	38,479	28,320
Equity and liabilities		
Equity		
Share capital	8,000	6,000
Share premium	3,000	2,000
Retained earnings	18,826	14,840
Total equity	29,826	22,840
Non-current liabilities		
Bank loans	4,300	800
	4,300	800
Current liabilities		
Trade payables	3,240	3,564
Tax liabilities	1,113	908
Bank overdraft	0	208
	4,353	4,680
Total liabilities	8,653	5,480
Total equity and liabilities	38,479	28,320

Further information:

- The total depreciation charge for the year was £3,366,000.

- Property, plant and equipment costing £812,000 with accumulated depreciation of £475,000 was sold in the year.

- All sales and purchases were on credit. Other expenses were paid for in cash.

- A dividend of £460,000 was paid during the year.

(a) **Prepare a reconciliation of profit from operations to net cash from operating activities for Forthbank Ltd for the year ended 31 March 20X1.**

(Complete the left hand column by writing in the correct line item from the list provided.)

Reconciliation of profit from operations to net cash from operating activities

		£'000
▼		
Adjustments for:		
▼		
▼		
▼		
▼		
▼		
▼		
Cash generated by operations		
▼		
▼		
Net cash from operating activities		

Picklist for line items:

Adjustment in respect of inventories
Adjustment in respect of trade payables
Adjustment in respect of trade receivables
Depreciation
Dividends received
Loss on disposal of property, plant and equipment
Interest paid
New bank loans
Proceeds on disposal of property, plant and equipment
Profit after tax

Profit before tax
Profit from operations
Purchases of property, plant and equipment
Tax paid

(b) **Prepare the statement of cash flows for Forthbank Ltd for the year ended 31 March 20X1.**

(Complete the left hand column by writing in the correct line item from the list provided.)

Forthbank Ltd

Statement of cash flows for the year ended 31 March 20X1

	£'000
Net cash from operating activities	
Investing activities	
▼	
▼	
▼	
Net cash used in investing activities	
Financing activities	
▼	
▼	
▼	
Net cash from financing activities	
Net increase/(decrease) in cash and cash equivalents	
Cash and cash equivalents at the beginning of the year	
Cash and cash equivalents at the end of the year	

Picklist for line items:

Adjustment in respect of inventories
Adjustment in respect of trade payables
Adjustment in respect of trade receivables
Dividends paid
Dividends received
New bank loans
Proceeds of share issue
Proceeds on disposal of property, plant and equipment
Purchases of property, plant and equipment

Workings

(Complete the left hand column by writing in the correct narrative from the list provided.)

Proceeds on disposal of property, plant and equipment (PPE)	£'000
▼	
▼	

Picklist for Narratives:

Carrying amount of PPE sold
Depreciation charge
Loss on disposal
PPE at end of year
PPE at start of year

Purchases of property, plant and equipment (PPE)	£'000
PPE at start of year	
▼	
▼	
▼	
Total PPE additions	

Picklist for narratives:

Carrying amount of PPE sold
Depreciation charge
Loss on disposal of PPE
PPE at end of year

(c) **Draft the statement of changes in equity for Forthbank Ltd for the year ended 31 March 20X1.**

Forthbank Ltd

Statement of changes in equity for the year ended 31 March 20X1

	Share capital £'000	Other reserves £'000	Retained earnings £'000	Total equity £'000
Balance at 1 April 20X0				
Changes in equity for 20X1				
Profit for the year				
Dividends				
Issue of share capital				
Balance at 31 March 20X1				

Chapter 3 – Accounting standards and The Conceptual Framework – written tasks

Task 3.1

The accounting equation of a company is as follows:

Assets £1,200 – Liabilities £800 = Equity £400

The company subsequently makes two transactions.

- It purchases inventories costing £120 on credit
- It sells these inventories for £180 cash

(a) **Explain what is meant by 'assets', 'liabilities' and 'equity'.**

(b) **Explain the effect of each transaction on the elements in the statement of financial position.**

(c) **State the accounting equation for the company after the two transactions have taken place.**

(d) **Draft a simple statement of profit or loss for the two transactions.**

Task 3.2

The purpose (objective) of financial statements is to provide financial information about the reporting entity that is useful in making decisions about providing resources to the entity. Financial statements provide, among other things, information about the equity of the company.

Prepare brief notes to answer the following questions:

(a) **According to the IASB's *Conceptual Framework for Financial Reporting*, who are the most important (primary) users of financial statements (general purpose financial reports)?**

(b) **Explain how the financial statements might be used by a user who is interested in finding out how well a company has managed working capital.**

(c) **What is meant by 'equity'? How is it related to other elements in the accounting equation?**

Task 3.3

The accounting equation is:

Assets – Liabilities = Equity

(a) **Define the following elements of financial statements**

    (i)   **Assets**
    (ii) **Liabilities**
    (iii) **Equity**

(b) **Explain why inventories are an asset of a company.**

Task 3.4

The IASB's *Conceptual Framework for Financial Reporting* explains that relevance and faithful representation are the two fundamental qualitative characteristics of useful financial information. It also sets out and explains four further qualities which enhance the usefulness of information that is relevant and faithfully represented.

(a) **Briefly explain what is meant by:**

    (i)   **Relevance**
    (ii) **Faithful representation**

    according to the *Conceptual Framework for Financial Reporting*.

(b) **State the four enhancing qualitative characteristics of useful financial information.**

Task 3.5

(a) **What is the objective of general purpose financial reporting according to the IASB *Conceptual Framework for Financial Reporting*?**

(b) **Give THREE reasons why users might be interested in the information contained in financial statements.**

Task 3.6

Financial performance of a company is assessed using the statement of profit or loss and other comprehensive income and/or the statement of cash flows.

A statement of profit or loss and other comprehensive income is prepared on the accruals basis, whereas the statement of cash flows is prepared on the basis of past cash flows.

Explain the following terms and their importance to the user:

(a) **Accruals basis**
(b) **Cash flow basis**

Task 3.7

You have a friend who is a shareholder in a small private company. She has been looking at the company's latest financial statements and is slightly confused by some of the terms used in the statement of financial position, in particular by the terms labelled 'current'. On checking the internet she has found out that these terms are defined in something called IAS 1, but she has been unable to find any further information.

Write short notes to explain how IAS 1 *Presentation of Financial Statements* defines the following terms:

(a) **Current assets**
(b) **Current liabilities**

Task 3.8

You have been asked to help prepare the financial statements of Sandringham Ltd for the year ended 30 September 20X4 and to advise the directors on the accounting treatment of certain items.

Prepare brief notes to answer the following questions that have been asked by the directors of Sandringham Ltd. Where appropriate, make reference to relevant accounting standards.

(a) (i) **Why is an adjustment made for closing inventories in the financial statements?**

(ii) **How should inventories be valued in the financial statements?**

(b) (i) **When would an impairment review of non-current assets be necessary?**

(ii) **What would you do in an impairment review?**

Task 3.9

Brondby Ltd is about to enter into two leases for items of equipment. The terms of the first lease require the company to make lease payments of £5,000 per annum with a lease term of five years. The fair value of the equipment is £20,000 and its economic life is six years. The second lease is for a term of two years and Brondby Ltd is required to make lease payments of £200 per month. The fair value of this item of equipment is £9,000 and its economic life is seven years.

The directors of Brondby Ltd understand that the accounting treatment of each lease will depend upon whether it is to be classified as a finance lease or as an operating lease, but are unsure as to the requirements of IAS 17 *Leases*, both in terms of when a lease should be classified as a finance lease or as an operating lease, and how the two types of lease should be accounted for.

Prepare brief notes for the directors of Brondby Ltd to cover the following:

(a) **When should a lease be classified as a finance lease and when should it be classified as an operating lease according to IAS 17 *Leases*?**

(b) (i) **Explain how a finance lease is accounted for in the financial statement of the lessee at the beginning of the lease term only.**

(ii) **Explain how an operating lease is accounted for in the financial statements of the lessee.**

(c) **Which of the two leases Brondby Ltd is about to enter into would be classified as a finance lease, if any?**

Task 3.10

You have been asked to help prepare the financial statements of Merched Ltd for the year ended 31 March 20X3. Legal proceedings have been started against the company because of faulty products supplied to a customer. The company's lawyers advise that it is probable that the entity will be found liable for damages of £250,000.

Explain how you would treat the probable damages arising from the legal proceedings in the financial statements. Refer, where relevant, to accounting standards.

Task 3.11

Houghton Ltd owns and operates a department store. During the year, the directors decided to offer refunds to dissatisfied customers, provided that these were claimed within three months of the date the goods were purchased. There are large notices explaining this policy on every floor of the store. Since the policy was introduced, refunds have been claimed on roughly 2% of all sales.

Prepare brief notes for the directors of Houghton Ltd to answer the following questions:

(a) **When should a provision be recognised, according to IAS 37 *Provisions, Contingent Liabilities and Contingent Assets*?**

(b) **How should the policy of refunding customers be treated in the financial statements for the year?**

(c) **How should the policy of refunding customers be disclosed in the notes to the financial statements?**

···

Task 3.12

Talland Ltd purchases goods for resale. The directors of the company would like you to clarify the accounting treatment of inventories and when to recognise revenue arising from the sale of goods. Answer the following queries of the directors.

(a) **What are inventories according to IAS 2 *Inventories*? How are inventories measured? What is included in the cost of inventories?**

(b) **What is revenue according to IAS 18 *Revenue*? How should it be measured? When should revenue be recognised?**

···

Task 3.13

The directors of Lavendar plc are considering acquiring a subsidiary. They are unclear about the criteria for an entity to be a parent of a subsidiary, and would like you to clarify this for them. They would like to write off any goodwill that arises on the acquisition of the subsidiary immediately, and have asked for your opinion on the correct accounting treatment.

Prepare brief notes to answer the following questions that have been asked by the directors of Lavendar plc:

(a) **What are the criteria for an entity being the parent of a subsidiary?**

(b) **Explain the accounting treatment that has to be adopted for the goodwill in the consolidated statement of financial position of Lavendar plc**

Note. Your answer should make reference to relevant accounting standards.

···

Chapter 4 – Accounting standards – objective test questions

Task 4.1

IAS 1 *Presentation of Financial Statements* requires some items to be disclosed as separate line items in the financial statements and others to be disclosed in the notes.

1   Depreciation
2   Revenue
3   Closing inventories
4   Finance cost
5   Dividends

Which two of the above have to be shown as line items in the statement of profit or loss and other comprehensive income, rather than in the notes to the financial statements?

1 and 4	
3 and 5	
2 and 3	
2 and 4	

Task 4.2

Salmon Ltd has incurred a substantial Irrecoverable debt amounting to 15% of its profit before tax. In accordance with IAS 1 *Presentation of Financial Statements*, how should this item be presented in Salmon Ltd's statement of profit or loss and other comprehensive income and/or notes to the financial statements?

Not disclosed separately and treated as a distribution cost	
Disclosed as an extraordinary item	
Not disclosed separately and treated as an administrative expense	
Its nature and amount disclosed separately	

Task 4.3

A decrease in trade receivables is deducted from operating profit in the reconciliation of profit from operations to net cash from operating activities.

Is this statement True or False?

True	
False	

Task 4.4

Which of these transactions would be reported in a statement of cash flows?

1   A bonus issue of shares
2   Dividends paid

1 only	
2 only	
Both 1 and 2	
Neither 1 nor 2	

Task 4.5

The components of the cost of a major item of equipment are given below.

	£
Purchase price	780,000
Import duties	117,000
Site preparation	30,000
Installation	28,000
General overheads	50,000
	1,005,000

What amount should be recognised as the cost of the asset, according to IAS 16 *Property, Plant and Equipment*?

£888,000	
£897,000	
£955,000	
£1,005,000	

Task 4.6

A property was purchased on 1 April 20X0 for £160,000. Depreciation policy is to depreciate properties over a period of 40 years. On 1 April 20X2 the property was revalued to £200,000.

What is the depreciation charge for the year ended 31 March 20X3?

£4,000	
£4,211	
£5,000	
£5,263	

Task 4.7

A machine was purchased on 1 January 20X0 for £80,000 and was depreciated over a period of 10 years using the straight-line method. On 1 January 20X2 it was decided that the machine had a total useful life of just 7 years.

What is the depreciation charge for the year ending 31 December 20X2?

£9,143	
£11,429	
£12,800	
£18,286	

Task 4.8

On 1 January 20X0 a building was purchased for £240,000. At that date its useful life was 50 years. On 1 January 20X4 it was revalued to £460,000 with no change in estimated useful life. On 31 December 20X5 the building was sold for £500,000.

What is the profit on disposal?

£40,000	
£58,400	
£60,000	
£288,800	

Task 4.9

Internally generated goodwill should be measured at fair value.

Is this statement True or False?

True	
False	

Task 4.10

An asset has a carrying amount of £125,000. Its fair value less costs of disposal is £120,000 and its value in use is £130,000, so the asset should be measured at £120,000.

Is this statement True or False?

True	
False	

Task 4.11

Fowey Ltd has four assets which the directors consider may have become impaired.

	Carrying amount	Fair value less costs of disposal	Value in use
	£	£	£
(i)	10,000	12,000	14,000
(ii)	8,000	9,000	5,800
(iii)	7,000	3,800	7,200
(iv)	9,000	4,300	5,200

Which of the above assets will be impaired according to IAS 36 *Impairment of Assets*?

(i) only	
(ii) only	
(iii) only	
(iv) only	

Task 4.12

During June 20X6, a company made the following purchases of inventory.

1 June	25 units @	£140 per unit
15 June	15 units @	£160 per unit

On 30 June it sold 30 units at a price of £150 per unit. The company uses the first-in, first-out (FIFO) method of valuation.

What is the value of closing inventories at 30 June 20X6?

£1,400	
£1,475	
£1,500	
£1,600	

Task 4.13

Bovey Ltd holds three distinct types of inventory in its warehouse at the end of its accounting year, which are valued as follows:

Product	FIFO (cost) £	LIFO (cost) £	NRV £
(i)	11,300	13,400	12,800
(ii)	7,600	4,200	5,900
(iii)	15,200	17,000	18,400
	34,100	34,600	37,100

At what value should inventories be stated in Bovey Ltd's financial statements according to IAS 2 *Inventories*?

£32,400	
£34,000	
£34,100	
£34,600	

Task 4.14

A company estimated that its corporation tax liability for the year ended 30 June 20X1 was £113,000. During the year to 30 June 20X2 the amount actually paid to Her Majesty's Revenue and Customs (HMRC) was £108,000. The estimate for the corporation tax liability for the year ended 30 June 20X2 is £129,000.

What amounts should be recognised in the financial statements for the year ended 30 June 20X2?

Tax expense (profit or loss)	Tax payable (statement of financial position)	
£124,000	£124,000	
£124,000	£129,000	
£129,000	£129,000	
£134,000	£129,000	

Task 4.15

A company leases some plant on 1 January 20X4. The cash price of the plant is £9,000, and the company leases it for four years, paying four annual instalments of £3,000 beginning on 31 December 20X4.

The company uses the sum-of-the-digits method to allocate interest.

What is the interest charge for the year ended 31 December 20X5?

£750	
£500	
£900	
£1,000	

Task 4.16

A company leases some plant on 1 January 20X4. The cash price is £9,000, and the company is to pay four annual instalments of £3,000, beginning on 1 January 20X4.

The company uses the sum-of-the-digits method to allocate interest.

What is the interest charge for the year ended 31 December 20X5?

£750	
£500	
£900	
£1,000	

....

Task 4.17

An asset is hired under a finance lease with a deposit of £30,000 on 1 January 20X1 plus 8 six monthly payments in arrears of £20,000 each. The fair value of the asset is £154,000. The finance charge is to be allocated using the sum-of-the-digits method.

What is the finance charge for the year ending 31 December 20X3?

£7,000	
£8,000	
£10,000	
£11,000	

....

Task 4.18

CS acquired a machine, using a finance lease, on 1 January 20X4. The machine had an expected useful life of 12,000 operating hours, after which it would have no residual value.

The finance lease was for a five-year term with rentals of £20,000 per year payable in arrears. The cost price of the machine was £80,000 and the implied interest rate is 7.93% per year. CS used the machine for 2,600 hours in 20X4 and 2,350 hours in 20X5

The actuarial method is used to allocate interest to accounting periods over the lease term.

What are the current liability and the non-current liability figures required by IAS 17 *Leases* **to be shown in CS's statement of financial position at 31 December 20X5?**

Current liability	Non-current liability	
£25,908	£35,967	
£51,605	£35,812	
£15,908	£35,967	
£35,908	£15,397	

Task 4.19

A company leases an asset on 1 January 20X1. The terms of the lease are to pay a deposit immediately of £575 followed by seven annual instalments of £2,000 payable in arrears. The present value of minimum lease payments is £10,000.

The interest rate implicit in the lease is 11% and the actuarial method is used to allocate interest to accounting periods over the lease term.

What is the current finance lease liability in the statement of financial position for the year ended 31 December 20X1?

£931	
£2,000	
£963	
£1,069	

Task 4.20

An asset with a fair value of £15,400 is acquired under a finance lease on 1 January 20X1 with a deposit on that date of £4,000 and four further annual payments on 31 December each year. The interest rate implicit in the lease is 15% and the actuarial method is used to allocate interest to accounting periods over the lease term.

What is the total lease obligation (liability) at 31 December 20X1?

£7,400	
£9,110	
£10,250	
£13,110	

Task 4.21

Trent Ltd entered into a finance lease agreement on 1 April 20X5. The fair value of the asset was £76,000 and Trent Ltd agreed to make four annual payments of £25,000 starting on 31 March 20X6. The rate of interest implicit in the lease is 12%. Trent Ltd uses the actuarial method to account for finance lease interest.

What is the finance charge to profit or loss relating to the lease for the year ended 31 March 20X6?

£6,120	
£9,120	
£9,600	
£25,000	

Task 4.22

At 30 April 20X7 Ellison Ltd has the following two legal claims outstanding:

1   A legal action against the company filed in February 20X7. Ellison Ltd has been advised that it is probable that the liability will materialise.

2   A legal action taken by the company against another entity, started in March 20X4. Ellison Ltd has been advised that it is probable that it will win the case.

According to IAS 37 *Provisions, Contingent Liabilities and Contingent Assets*, how should the company report these legal actions in its financial statements for the year ended 30 April 20X7?

Legal action 1	Legal action 2	
Disclose in a note to the financial statements	No disclosure	
Recognise a provision	No disclosure	
Recognise a provision	Disclose in a note to the financial statements	
Recognise a provision	Recognise the income	

Task 4.23

Which of the following events after the end of the reporting period would normally be classified as adjusting, according to IAS 10 *Events After the Reporting Period?*

Destruction of a major non-current asset	
Discovery of error or fraud	
Issue of shares	
Purchases of a major non-current asset	

Task 4.24

Teign Ltd prepares its financial statements to 30 September each year. The following events took place between 30 September and the date on which the financial statements were authorised for issue.

(i)   The company made a major purchase of plant and machinery.
(ii)   A customer who owed the company money at 30 September was declared bankrupt.

Which of the above is likely to be classified as an adjusting event according to IAS 10 *Events After the Reporting Period?*

(i) only	
(ii) only	
Both	
Neither of them	

Task 4.25

On 1 September 20X9 Usk Ltd sold goods to Chertsey Ltd. The two companies have agreed that Chertsey Ltd can return any items that are still unsold at 30 November 20X9. All the goods remained in the inventories of Chertsey Ltd at 30 September 20X9.

Usk Ltd should not recognise any revenue from this transaction in its financial statements for the year ended 30 September 20X9.

Is this statement True or False?

True	
False	

Task 4.26

Wensley plc holds 25% of the voting power in Hawes Ltd and appoints one of its four directors.

The consolidated statement of profit or loss of Wensley plc should include 25% of Hawes Ltd's profit or loss for the year as a separate line item.

Is this statement True or False?

True	
False	

Task 4.27

Erewash Ltd has rights to variable returns from its involvement in Amber Ltd and has the ability to affect those returns through its power over Amber Ltd. In relation to Erewash Ltd, Amber Ltd is:

An associate	
A parent	
A simple investment	
A subsidiary	

Task 4.28

IFRS 3 *Business Combinations* identifies key requirements of the acquisition method.

(i)   Identifying the acquirer

(ii) Determining the acquisition date

(iii) Recognising and measuring the identifiable assets acquired, liabilities assumed and any non-controlling interest in the acquiree

(iv) Recognising and measuring goodwill or a gain from a bargain purchase

Which of the above statements are key requirements of the acquisition method?

Elements (i), (ii) and (iii) only	
Elements (ii), (iii) and (iv) only	
Elements (i), (ii) and (iv) only	
All of the above	

Task 4.29

Beadnell plc acquired 100% of the issued share capital and voting rights of Catton Ltd on 1 January 20X0.

The consolidated cost of sales of Beadnell plc and its subsidiary undertaking for the year ended 31 December 20X0, before taking into account any adjustments required in respect of the information below, is £200,000.

Additional data

During the year Beadnell plc sold goods which had cost £40,000 to Catton Ltd for £50,000. 60% of these goods still remain in inventories at the end of the year.

The consolidated cost of sales for the year ending 31 December 20X0 will be:

£144,000	
£150,000	
£156,000	
£160,000	

Chapter 5 – The consolidated statement of financial position

Task 5.1

On 1 January 20X1 X plc purchased 75% of the ordinary share capital of Y Ltd when the retained earnings of Y Ltd stood at £240,000. At 31 December 20X1 the summarised statements of financial position of the two companies were as follows.

	X plc	Y Ltd
Assets	£'000	£'000
Property, plant and equipment	800	400
Investment in Y Ltd	350	–
Current assets	170	130
	1,320	530
Equity and liabilities		
Share capital	800	200
Retained earnings	420	280
	1,220	480
Current liabilities	100	50
	1,320	530

Draft a consolidated statement of financial position for X plc and its subsidiary as at 31 December 20X1.

Consolidated statement of financial position as at 31 December 20X1

	£'000
Assets	
Goodwill	
Property, plant and equipment	
Current assets	
Equity and liabilities	
Share capital	
Retained earnings	
Non-controlling interest	
Current liabilities	

Workings

Goodwill	£'000
Price paid	
Share capital – attributable to X plc	
Retained earnings – attributable to X plc	

Retained earnings	£'000
X plc	
Y Ltd – attributable to X plc	

Non-controlling interest (NCI)	£'000
Share capital – attributable to NCI	
Retained earnings – attributable to NCI	

....

Task 5.2

Fertwrangler Ltd has one subsidiary, Voncarryon Ltd, which it acquired on 1 April 20X2. The statement of financial position of Voncarryon Ltd as at 31 March 20X3 is set out below.

Voncarryon Ltd
Summarised statement of financial position as at 31 March 20X3

	£'000
Non-current assets	3,855
Current assets	4,961
Total assets	8,816
Equity	
Share capital	2,000
Share premium	1,000
Retained earnings	1,770
	4,770
Non-current liabilities	1,500
Current liabilities	2,546
Total equity and liabilities	8,816

Further information

- The share capital of Voncarryon Ltd consists of ordinary shares of £1 each. There have been no changes to the balances of share capital and share premium during the year. No dividends were paid by Voncarryon Ltd during the year.

- Fertwrangler acquired 1,200,000 shares in Voncarryon Ltd on 1 April 20X2 at a cost of £3,510,000.

- At 1 April 20X2 the balance on the retained earnings reserve of Voncarryon Ltd was £1,350,000.

- The fair value of the non-current assets of Voncarryon Ltd at 1 April 20X2 was £4,455,000. The book value of the assets at 1 April 20X2 was £4,055,000. The revaluation has not been reflected in the books of Voncarryon Ltd.

- Goodwill arising on consolidation had suffered an impairment loss of £66,000 by 31 March 20X3.

- At 31 March 20X3 the balance on the retained earnings reserve of Fertwrangler Ltd was £5,610,000.

- Non-controlling interest is measured at the proportionate share of the fair value of Voncarryon's net assets.

(a) **Calculate the goodwill figure relating to the acquisition of Voncarryon Ltd that will appear in the consolidated statement of financial position of Fertwrangler Ltd as at 31 March 20X3.**

£ [   ]

(b) **Calculate the non-controlling interest figure that will appear in the consolidated statement of financial position of Fertwrangler Ltd at 31 March 20X3.**

£ [   ]

(c) **Calculate the balance on the consolidated retained earnings reserve that will appear in the consolidated statement of financial position of Fertwrangler Ltd at 31 March 20X3.**

£ [   ]

Task 5.3

Bell plc has one subsidiary, Clive Ltd, and one investment in an associate company, Grant Ltd. The summarised statements of financial position of Clive Ltd and Grant Ltd as at 31 March 20X5 are set out below.

Statements of financial position as at 31 March 20X5

	Clive Ltd £'000	Grant Ltd £'000
Assets		
Property, plant and equipment	32,504	18,465
Current assets	11,585	4,852
Total assets	44,089	23,317
Equity and liabilities		
Equity		
Share capital	20,000	10,000
Share premium	5,000	–
Retained earnings	12,930	9,000
Total equity	37,930	19,000
Current liabilities	6,159	4,317
Total equity and liabilities	44,089	23,317

Further information

- The share capital of Clive Ltd consists of ordinary shares of £1 each. There have been no changes to the balances of share capital and share premium during the year. No dividends were paid by Clive Ltd during the year.

- Bell plc acquired 12,000,000 shares in Clive Ltd on 1 April 20X4 at a cost of £25,160,000.

- At 1 April 20X4 the balance on the retained earnings reserve of Clive Ltd was £10,600,000.

- The fair value of the property, plant and equipment of Clive Ltd at 1 April 20X4 was £33,520,000. The book value of the property, plant and equipment at 1 April 20X4 was £30,520,000. The revaluation has not been reflected in the books of Clive Ltd. There were no other differences between fair values and book values as at 1 April 20X4.

- The share capital of Grant Ltd consists of ordinary shares of £1 each. There have been no changes to the balance of share capital during the year. No dividends were paid by Grant Ltd during the year.

- Bell plc acquired 2,500,000 shares in Grant Ltd on 1 April 20X4 at a cost of £5,000,000.

- At 1 April 20X4 the balance on the retained earnings reserve of Grant Ltd was £8,000,000.

- The fair value of the net assets of Grant Ltd was £18,000,000, the same as the book value as at this date.

- Goodwill arising on the acquisition of both investments was reviewed for impairment at 31 March 20X5. The directors estimate that the impairment loss amounted to £200,000 for Clive Ltd and £50,000 for Grant Ltd.
- Non-controlling interests are measured as the proportionate share of the fair value of the subsidiary's net assets.

(a) **Calculate the goodwill figure relating to the acquisition of Clive Ltd that will appear in the consolidated statement of financial position of Bell plc as at 31 March 20X5.**

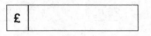

£

(b) **Calculate the amount of the investment in the associate, Grant Ltd, that will appear in the consolidated statement of financial position of Bell plc as at 31 March 20X5.**

£

(c) **Define an 'associate' making reference to relevant accounting standards.**

Task 5.4

The Managing Director of Dumyat plc has asked you to prepare the statement of financial position for the group. Dumyat plc has one subsidiary, Devon Ltd. The statements of financial position of the two companies as at 31 October 20X7 are set out below.

Statements of financial position as at 31 October 20X7

	Dumyat plc	Devon Ltd
Assets	£'000	£'000
Non-current assets		
Property, plant and equipment	65,388	31,887
Investment in Devon Ltd	26,000	
	91,388	31,887
Current assets		
Inventories	28,273	5,566
Trade and other receivables	11,508	5,154
Receivable from Devon Ltd	4,000	0
Cash and cash equivalents	2,146	68
	45,927	10,788
Total assets	137,315	42,675

Equity and liabilities	£'000	£'000
Equity		
Share capital	25,000	12,000
Share premium	12,000	4,000
Retained earnings	55,621	17,092
Total equity	92,621	33,092
Non-current liabilities		
Long-term loans	25,000	4,000
Current liabilities		
Trade and other payables	13,554	1,475
Payable to Dumyat plc	0	4,000
Tax liabilities	6,140	108
	19,694	5,583
Total liabilities	44,694	9,583
Total equity and liabilities	137,315	42,675

You have been given the following further information.

- The share capital of Devon Ltd consists of ordinary shares of £1 each. Ownership of these shares carries voting rights in Devon Ltd. There have been no changes to the balances of share capital and share premium during the year. No dividends were paid or proposed by Devon Ltd during the year.

- Dumyat plc acquired 9,000,000 shares in Devon Ltd on 1 November 20X6.

- At 1 November 20X6 the balance of retained earnings of Devon Ltd was £12,052,000.

- The fair value of the non-current assets of Devon Ltd at 1 November 20X6 was £28,800,000. The book value of the non-current assets at 1 November 20X6 was £25,800,000. The revaluation has not been recorded in the books of Devon Ltd (ignore any effect on the depreciation for the year).

- The directors of Dumyat plc have concluded that goodwill has not been impaired during the year.

- The non-controlling interest is measured at the proportionate share of the fair value of Devon Ltd's net assets.

Draft a consolidated statement of financial position for Dumyat plc and its subsidiary as at 31 October 20X7.

Dumyat plc
(Complete the left hand column by writing in the correct line item from the list provided.)
Consolidated statement of financial position as at 31 October 20X7

	£'000
Assets	
Non-current assets:	
▼	
▼	
Current assets:	
▼	
▼	
▼	
Total assets	
Equity and liabilities	
Equity	
▼	
▼	
▼	
Non-controlling interest	
Total equity	
Non-current liabilities:	
▼	
Current liabilities:	
▼	
▼	
Total liabilities	
Total equity and liabilities	

Picklist for line items:

Cash and cash equivalents
Goodwill
Inventories
Long term loans
Property, plant and equipment
Retained earnings
Share capital
Share premium
Tax payable
Trade and other payables
Trade and other receivables

Workings

(Complete the left hand column by writing in the correct narrative from the list provided.)

Goodwill		£'000
	▼	
	▼	
	▼	
	▼	
	▼	

Picklist for narratives:

Price paid
Retained earnings – attributable to Dumyat plc
Revaluation reserve – attributable to Dumyat plc
Share capital – attributable to Dumyat plc
Share premium – attributable to Dumyat plc

Retained earnings		£'000
	▼	
	▼	

Picklist for narratives:

Devon Ltd – attributable to Dumyat plc
Dumyat plc
Revaluation

Non-controlling interest (NCI)	£'000
▼	
▼	
▼	
▼	

Picklist for narratives:

Current assets – attributable to NCI
Non-current assets – attributable to NCI
Price paid
Retained earnings – attributable to NCI
Revaluation reserve – attributable to NCI
Share capital – attributable to NCI
Share premium – attributable to NCI

Task 5.5

The Managing Director of Tolsta plc has asked you to prepare the statement of financial position for the group. Tolsta plc has one subsidiary, Balallan Ltd. The statements of financial position of the two companies as at 31 October 20X8 are set out below.

Statements of financial position as at 31 October 20X8

	Tolsta plc £'000	Balallan Ltd £'000
Assets		
Non-current assets		
Property, plant and equipment	47,875	31,913
Investment in Balallan Ltd	32,000	
	79,875	31,913
Current assets		
Inventories	25,954	4,555
Trade and other receivables	14,343	3,656
Cash and cash equivalents	1,956	47
	42,253	8,258
Total assets	122,128	40,171
Equity and liabilities		
Equity		
Share capital	45,000	12,000
Share premium	12,000	6,000
Retained earnings	26,160	11,340
Total equity	83,160	29,340
Non-current liabilities		
Long-term loans	20,000	7,000
Current liabilities		
Trade and other payables	14,454	3,685
Tax liabilities	4,514	146
	18,968	3,831
Total liabilities	38,968	10,831
Total equity and liabilities	122,128	40,171

Further information

- The share capital of Balallan Ltd consists of ordinary shares of £1 each. Ownership of these shares carries voting rights in Balallan Ltd. There have been no changes to the balances of share capital and share premium during the year. No dividends were paid or proposed by Balallan Ltd during the year.

- Tolsta plc acquired 8,000,000 shares in Balallan Ltd on 1 November 20X7.

- At 1 November 20X7 the balance of retained earnings of Balallan Ltd was £9,750,000.

- The fair value of the non-current assets of Balallan Ltd at 1 November 20X7 was £31,100,000. The book value of the non-current assets at 1 November 20X7 was £26,600,000. The revaluation has not been recorded in the books of Balallan Ltd (ignore any effect on the depreciation for the year).

- Included in Trade and other receivables for Tolsta plc and in Trade and other payables for Balallan Ltd is an inter-company transaction for £2,000,000 that took place in early October 20X8.

- The directors of Tolsta plc have concluded that goodwill has been impaired by £2,100,000 during the year.

- The non-controlling interest is measured as the proportionate share of the fair value of Balallan Ltd's net assets.

Draft a consolidated statement of financial position for Tolsta plc and its subsidiary as at 31 October 20X8.

Tolsta plc

Consolidated statement of financial position as at 31 October 20X8

	£'000
Assets	
Non-current assets:	
Intangible assets: goodwill	
Property, plant and equipment	———
	———
Current assets:	
Inventories	
Trade and other receivables	
Cash and cash equivalents	———
	———
Total assets	———
Equity and liabilities	
Equity	
Share capital	
Share premium	
Retained earnings	———
Non-controlling interest	———
Total equity	———
Non-current liabilities:	
Long-term loan	———
Current liabilities:	
Trade and other payables	
Tax liabilities	———
	———
Total liabilities	———
Total equity and liabilities	———

Workings

(Complete the left hand column by writing in the correct narrative from the list provided.)

Goodwill	£'000
▼	
▼	
▼	
▼	
▼	
▼	

Picklist for narratives:

Impairment
Price paid
Retained earnings – attributable to Tolsta plc
Revaluation reserve – attributable to Tolsta plc
Share capital – attributable to Tolsta plc
Share premium – attributable to Tolsta plc

Retained earnings	£'000
▼	
▼	
▼	

Picklist for narratives:

Balallan Ltd – attributable to Tolsta plc
Impairment
Revaluation
Tolsta plc

Non-controlling interest (NCI)		£'000
	▼	
	▼	
	▼	
	▼	

Picklist for narratives:

Current assets – attributable to NCI
Impairment
Non-current assets – attributable to NCI
Price paid
Retained earnings – attributable to NCI
Revaluation reserve – attributable to NCI
Share capital – attributable to NCI
Share premium – attributable to NCI

Task 5.6

Ard plc has one subsidiary, Ledi Ltd. The summarised statements of financial position of the two companies as at 31 March 20X9 are set out below.

Summarised statements of financial position as at 31 March 20X9

	Ard plc	Ledi Ltd
Assets	£'000	£'000
Non-current assets		
Property, plant and equipment	45,210	27,480
Investment in Ledi Ltd	23,000	
	68,210	27,480
Current assets	32,782	10,835
Total assets	100,992	38,315
Equity and liabilities		
Equity		
Share capital	50,000	20,000
Retained earnings	21,526	9,740
Total equity	71,526	29,740
Non-current liabilities	14,000	4,000
Current liabilities	15,466	4,575
Total equity and liabilities	100,992	38,315

Further information

- The share capital of Ledi Ltd consists of ordinary shares of £1 each. Ownership of these shares carries voting rights in Ledi Ltd. There have been no changes to the balances of share capital and share premium during the year. No dividends were paid or proposed by Ledi Ltd during the year.

- Ard plc acquired 12,000,000 shares in Ledi Ltd on 1 April 20X8.

- On 1 April 20X8 the balance of retained earnings of Ledi Ltd was £7,640,000.

- Included in Trade and other receivables for Ard plc and in Trade and other payables for Ledi Ltd is an inter-company transaction for £3,000,000 that took place in early March 20X9.

- The directors of Ard plc have concluded that goodwill has been impaired by £1,600,000 during the year.

Draft a consolidated statement of financial position for Ard plc and its subsidiary as at 31 March 20X9.

Ard plc

Consolidated statement of financial position as at 31 March 20X9

	£'000
Assets	
Non-current assets:	
Intangible assets: goodwill	
Property, plant and equipment	
Current assets	
Total assets	
Equity and liabilities	
Equity	
Share capital	
Retained earnings	
Non-controlling interest	
Total equity	
Non-current liabilities	
Current liabilities	
Total liabilities	
Total equity and liabilities	

Workings

(Complete the left hand column by writing in the correct narrative from the list provided).

Goodwill	£'000
▼	
▼	
▼	
▼	

Picklist for narratives:

Impairment
Price paid
Retained earnings – attributable to Ard plc
Share capital – attributable to Ard plc

Retained earnings		£'000
	▼	
	▼	
	▼	

Picklist for narratives:

Ard plc
Impairment
Ledi Ltd – attributable to Ard plc

Non-controlling interest (NCI)		£'000
	▼	
	▼	

Picklist for narratives:

Current assets – attributable to NCI
Impairment
Non-current assets – attributable to NCI
Price paid
Retained earnings – attributable to NCI
Share capital – attributable to NCI

Task 5.7

The Managing Director of Glebe plc has asked you to prepare the statement of financial position for the group. Glebe plc acquired 70% of the issued share capital of Starks Ltd on 1 April 20X0. At that date Starks Ltd had issued share capital of £10,000,000 and retained earnings of £11,540,000.

The summarised statements of financial position of the two companies as at 31 March 20X1 are set out below.

	Glebe plc	Starks Ltd
	£'000	£'000
Assets		
Investment in Starks Ltd	18,000	
Non-current assets	36,890	25,600
Current assets	22,364	7,835
Total assets	77,254	33,435
Equity and liabilities		
Equity		
Share capital	40,000	10,000
Retained earnings	12,249	16,650
Total equity	52,249	26,650
Non-current liabilities	13,000	5,000
Current liabilities	12,005	1,785
Total liabilities	25,005	6,785
Total equity and liabilities	77,254	33,435

Additional data

- The fair value of the non-current assets of Starks Ltd at 1 April 20X0 was £26,300,000. The book value of the non-current assets at 1 April 20X0 was £23,900,000. The revaluation has not been recorded in the books of Starks Ltd (ignore any effect on the depreciation for the year).

- The directors of Glebe plc have concluded that goodwill has been impaired by £400,000 during the year.

- Glebe plc has decided non-controlling interests will be valued at their proportionate share of net assets.

Draft a consolidated statement of financial position for Glebe plc and its subsidiary as at 31 March 20X1.

Glebe plc

Consolidated statement of financial position as at 31 March 20X1

	£'000
Assets	
Non-current assets:	
Intangible assets: goodwill	
Property, plant and equipment	
Current assets:	
Total assets	
Equity and liabilities	
Equity	
Share capital	
Retained earnings	
Non-controlling interest	
Total equity	
Non-current liabilities:	
Current liabilities:	
Total liabilities	
Total equity and liabilities	

Workings

(Complete the left hand column by writing in the correct narrative from the list provided.)

Goodwill	£'000
▼	
▼	
▼	
▼	
▼	

Picklist for narratives:

Impairment
Price paid
Retained earnings – attributable to Glebe plc
Revaluation reserve – attributable to Glebe plc
Share capital – attributable to Glebe plc

Retained earnings		£'000
	▼	
	▼	
	▼	

Picklist for narratives:

Glebe plc
Impairment
Revaluation
Starks Ltd – attributable to Glebe plc

Non-controlling interest (NCI)		£'000
	▼	
	▼	
	▼	

Picklist for narratives:

Current assets – attributable to NCI
Impairment
Non-current assets – attributable to NCI
Price paid
Retained earnings – attributable to NCI
Revaluation reserve – attributable to NCI
Share capital – attributable to NCI

Chapter 6 – The consolidated statement of profit or loss

Task 6.1

P plc has owned 7,000 of the 10,000 ordinary shares in S Ltd since 1 April 20X0. The statements of profit or loss for each company for the year ended 31 March 20X2 are given below.

Statements of profit or loss for the year ended 31 March 20X2

	P plc £'000	S Ltd £'000
Continuing operations		
Revenue	4,600	2,210
Cost of sales	(2,700)	(1,320)
Gross profit	1,900	890
Other income – dividend from S Ltd	70	–
Operating expenses	(870)	(430)
Profit before tax	1,100	460
Tax	(300)	(120)
Profit for the period from continuing operations	800	340

Draft a consolidated statement of profit or loss income for P plc and its subsidiary for the year ended 31 March 20X2.

Consolidated statement of profit or loss for the year ended 31 March 20X2

	£'000
Continuing operations	
Revenue	
Cost of sales	
Gross profit	
Other income	
Operating expenses	
Profit before tax	
Tax	
Profit for the period from continuing operations	

	£'000
Attributable to:	
Equity holders of the parent	
Non-controlling interests	

Task 6.2

C plc purchased 60% of the shares in D Ltd a number of years ago. The statements of profit or loss for each company for the year ended 31 December 20X1 are given below.

	C plc	D Ltd
	£'000	£'000
Continuing operations		
Revenue	38,600	14,700
Cost of sales	(25,000)	(9,500)
Gross profit	13,600	5,200
Other income – dividend from D Ltd	300	–
Operating expenses	(7,700)	(2,900)
Profit before tax	6,200	2,300
Tax	(1,600)	(600)
Profit for the period from continuing operations	4,600	1,700

You are also given the following information.

- During the year C plc sold goods which had cost £4,000,000 to D Ltd for £5,000,000. All of the goods were still in the inventory of D Ltd at the year-end.

Draft a consolidated statement of profit or loss for C plc and its subsidiary for the year ended 31 December 20X1.

Consolidated statement of profit or loss for the year ended 31 December 20X1

	£'000
Continuing operations	
Revenue	
Cost of sales	
Gross profit	
Other income	
Operating expenses	
Profit before tax	
Tax	
Profit for the period from continuing operations	
Attributable to:	
Equity holders of the parent	
Non-controlling interests	

Workings

Revenue	£'000
C plc	
D Ltd	
Total inter-company adjustment	

Cost of sales	£'000
C plc	
D Ltd	
Total inter-company adjustment	

Task 6.3

The managing director of Aswall plc has asked you to prepare the draft consolidated statement of profit or loss for the group. The company has one subsidiary, Unsafey Ltd. The statements of profit or loss for the two companies for the year ended 31 March 20X4 are set out below.

Statements of profit or loss for the year ended 31 March 20X4

	Aswall plc £'000	Unsafey Ltd £'000
Continuing operations		
Revenue	32,412	12,963
Cost of sales	(14,592)	(5,576)
Gross profit	17,820	7,387
Other income – dividend from Unsafey Ltd	1,500	–
Distribution costs	(5,449)	(1,307)
Administrative expenses	(3,167)	(841)
Profit from operations	10,704	5,239
Finance costs	(1,960)	(980)
Profit before tax	8,744	4,259
Tax	(2,623)	(1,063)
Profit for the period from continuing operations	6,121	3,196

Further information:

- Aswall plc owns 75% of the ordinary share capital of Unsafey Ltd.

- During the year Unsafey Ltd sold goods which had cost £1,200,000 to Aswall plc for £1,860,000. None of the goods had been sold by Aswall plc by the end of the year.

Draft a consolidated statement of profit or loss for Aswall plc and its subsidiary for the year ended 31 March 20X4.

Aswall plc

Consolidated statement of profit or loss for the year ended 31 March 20X4

	£'000
Continuing operations	
Revenue	
Cost of sales	
Gross profit	
Other income	
Distribution costs	
Administrative expenses	
Profit from operations	
Finance costs	
Profit before tax	
Tax	
Profit for the period from continuing operations	
Attributable to:	
Equity holders of the parent	
Non-controlling interest	

Workings

Revenue	£'000
Aswall plc	
Unsafey Ltd	
Total inter-company adjustment	

Cost of sales	£'000
Aswall plc	
Unsafey Ltd	
Total inter-company adjustment	

Non-controlling interest (NCI)	£'000
Profit for the period attributable to NCI	
Unrealised profit attributable to NCI	

Task 6.4

Danube plc has one subsidiary, Inn Ltd.

Extracts from their statements of profit or loss for the year ended 31 March 20X2 are shown below:

	Danube plc £'000	Inn Ltd £'000
Continuing operations		
Revenue	15,800	5,400
Cost of sales	(8,500)	(2,800)
Gross profit	7,300	2,600
Other income	300	–
Operating expenses	(3,300)	(1,230)
Profit from operations	4,300	1,370

Additional data

- Danube plc acquired 75% of the ordinary share capital of Inn Ltd on 1 April 20X1.

- During the year Inn Ltd sold goods which had cost £600,000 to Danube plc for £1,000,000. Half of these goods still remain in the inventories of Danube plc at the end of the year.

- Other income of Danube plc included a dividend received from Inn Ltd.

- Inn ltd had paid a dividend of 400,000 on 1 March 20X2.

Draft the consolidated statement of profit or loss for Danube plc and its subsidiary up to and including the profit from operations line for the year ended 31 March 20X2.

Danube plc

Consolidated statement of profit or loss for the year ended 31 March 20X2

	£'000
Continuing operations	
Revenue	
Cost of sales	
Gross profit	
Other income	
Operating expenses	
Profit from operations	

Workings

Revenue	£'000
Danube plc	
Inn Ltd	
Total inter-company adjustment	

Cost of sales	£'000
Danube plc	
Inn Ltd	
Total inter-company adjustment	

Task 6.5

The managing director of Wewill plc has asked you to prepare the draft consolidated statement of profit or loss for the group. The company has one subsidiary, Rokyu Ltd. The statements of profit or loss for the two companies for the year ended 31 March 20X4 are set out below.

Statements of profit or loss for the year ended 31 March 20X4

	Wewill plc £'000	Rokyu Ltd £'000
Continuing operations		
Revenue	36,400	14,600
Cost of sales	(20,020)	(6,935)
Gross profit	16,830	7,665
Other income – dividend from Rokyu Ltd	860	–
Distribution costs	(6,552)	(3,358)
Administrative expenses	(4,004)	(1,898)
Profit from operations	6,684	2,409
Finance costs	(675)	(154)
Profit before tax	6,009	2,255
Tax	(1,468)	(445)
Profit for the period from continuing operations	4,541	1,810

Additional data:

- Wewill plc acquired 80% of the ordinary share capital of Rokyu Ltd on 1 April 20X3.

- During the year Wewill plc sold goods which had cost £1,000,000 to Rokyu Ltd for £1,400,000. None of the goods had been sold by Rokyu Ltd by the end of the year.

Draft a consolidated statement of profit or loss for Wewill plc and its subsidiary for the year ended 31 March 20X4.

Wewill plc

Consolidated statement of profit or loss for the year ended 31 March 20X4

	£'000
Continuing operations	
Revenue	
Cost of sales	
Gross profit	
Other income	
Distribution costs	
Administrative expenses	
Profit from operations	
Finance costs	
Profit before tax	
Tax	
Profit for the period from continuing operations	
Attributable to:	
Equity holders of the parent	
Non-controlling interest	

Workings

Revenue	£'000
Wewill plc	
Rokyu Ltd	
Total inter-company adjustment	

Cost of sales	£'000
Wewill plc	
Rokyu Ltd	
Total inter-company adjustment	

Chapter 7 – Calculating ratios

Task 7.1

Given below is a summarised statement of profit or loss and a summarised statement of financial position for a company.

Statement of profit or loss for the year ended 30 April 20X2

	£'000
Continuing operations	
Revenue	989
Cost of sales	(467)
Gross profit	522
Operating expenses	(308)
Profit from operations	214
Interest payable	(34)
Profit before tax	180
Tax	(48)
Profit for the period from continuing operations	132

Statement of financial position as at 30 April 20X2

	£'000
Non-current assets	1,200
Current assets	700
	1,900
Share capital and reserves	1,000
Non-current liabilities: Long-term loan	400
Current liabilities	500
	1,900

Calculate the following ratios to the nearest ONE DECIMAL PLACE.

(a)	Gross profit percentage		%
(b)	Operating profit percentage		%
(c)	Return on capital employed		%
(d)	Asset turnover (net assets)		times
(e)	Interest cover		times
(f)	Gearing		%

Task 7.2

Given below are extracts from a company's statement of profit or loss and statement of financial position.

Statement of profit or loss for the year ended 30 June 20X2 – extract

	£
Revenue	772,400
Cost of sales	507,400
Gross profit	265,000

Statement of financial position as at 30 June 20X2 – extract

	£
Inventories	58,600
Trade receivables	98,400
Trade payables	86,200
Bank overdraft	6,300

Calculate the following ratios to the nearest ONE DECIMAL PLACE.

(a)	Current ratio	:1
(b)	Quick (acid test) ratio	:1
(c)	Trade receivables collection period	days
(d)	Inventory turnover	times
(e)	Inventory holding period	days
(f)	Trade payables payment period	days

Task 7.3

You have been asked to calculate ratios for Midsummer Ltd in respect of its financial statements for the year ending 31 March 20X4 to assist a shareholder in his analysis of the company. The shareholder has given you Midsummer's statement of profit or loss and the summarised statement of financial position prepared for internal purposes. These are set out below.

Midsummer Ltd

Statement of profit or loss for the year ended 31 March 20X4

	£'000
Continuing operations	
Revenue	8,420
Cost of sales	(3,536)
Gross profit	4,884
Distribution costs	(1,471)
Administrative expenses	(1,224)
Profit from operations	2,189
Finance costs	(400)
Profit before tax	1,789
Tax	(465)
Profit for the period from continuing operations	1,324

Midsummer Ltd

Summarised statement of financial position as at 31 March 20X4

Assets	£'000
Non-current assets	15,132
Current assets	4,624
Total assets	19,756
Equity and liabilities	
Equity	
Share capital	6,000
Share premium	2,000
Retained earnings	4,541
Total equity	12,541
Non-current liabilities: long term loan	5,000
Current liabilities	2,215
Total liabilities	7,215
Total equity plus liabilities	19,756

(a) **State the formulae that are used to calculate each of the following ratios:**

(Write in the correct formula from the list provided)

(i) Return on capital employed	▾

Formulae:

Profit after tax/Total equity × 100

Profit from operations/Total equity × 100

Profit after tax/Total equity + Non-current liabilities × 100

Profit from operations/Total equity + Non-current liabilities × 100

(ii) Operating profit percentage	▾

Formulae:

Profit from operations/Revenue × 100

Profit from operations/Total assets × 100

Profit from operations/Total equity + Non-current liabilities × 100

Profit from operations/Finance costs × 100

(iii) Gross profit percentage	▾

Formulae:

Gross profit/Total equity × 100

Gross profit/Revenue × 100

Gross profit/Total assets × 100

Gross profit/Total assets – Current liabilities

(iv) Asset turnover (net assets)	▾

Formulae:

Revenue/Total assets – Current liabilities

Revenue/Total assets – Total liabilities

Total assets – Current liabilities/Revenue

Total assets – Total liabilities/Revenue

(v) Gearing		▼

Formulae:

Current assets/Current liabilities

Revenue/Total assets – Current liabilities

Non-current liabilities/Total equity + Non-current liabilities

Profit after tax/Number of issued ordinary shares

(vi) Interest cover		▼

Formulae:

Finance costs/Profit from operations

Finance costs/Revenue

Profit from operations/Finance costs

Revenue/Finance costs

(b) **Calculate the ratios to the nearest ONE DECIMAL PLACE.**

(i) Return on capital employed		%
(ii) Operating profit percentage		%
(iii) Gross profit percentage		%
(iv) Asset turnover (net assets)		times
(v) Gearing		%
(vi) Interest cover		%

Task 7.4

A shareholder in Drain Ltd has asked you to help her by analysing the financial statements of the company for the year ended 31 March 20X6. These are set out below.

Drain Ltd
Statement of profit or loss for the year ended 31 March 20X6

	£'000
Continuing operations	
Revenue	21,473
Cost of sales	(9,878)
Gross profit	11,595
Distribution costs	(4,181)
Administrative expenses	(3,334)
Profit from operations	4,080
Finance costs	(350)
Profit before tax	3,730
Tax	(858)
Profit for the period from continuing operations	2,872

Drain Ltd
Statement of financial position as at 31 March 20X6

	£'000
Assets	
Non-current assets	
Property, plant and equipment	27,781
Current assets	
Inventories	1,813
Trade receivables	3,000
Cash and cash equivalents	62
	4,875
Total assets	32,656
Equity and liabilities	
Equity	
Share capital	5,000
Retained earnings	20,563
	25,563
Non-current liabilities	
Bank loans	5,000
Current liabilities	
Trade and other payables	1,235
Tax liabilities	858
	2,093
Total liabilities	7,093
Total equity and liabilities	32,656

(a) **State the formulae that are used to calculate each of the following ratios:**

(Write in the correct formula from the list provided)

(i) Gross profit percentage	▼

Formulae:

Gross profit/Total equity × 100

Gross profit/Revenue × 100

Gross profit/Total assets × 100

Gross profit/Total assets – Current liabilities

(ii) Operating profit percentage	▼

Formulae:

Profit from operations/Revenue × 100

Profit from operations/Total assets × 100

Profit from operations/Total equity + Non-current liabilities × 100

Profit from operations/Finance costs × 100

(iii) Current ratio	▼

Formulae:

Total assets/Total liabilities

Current assets – Inventories/Current liabilities

Current assets/Current liabilities

Total assets – Inventories/Total liabilities

(iv) Quick (acid test) ratio	▼

Formulae:

Current assets/Current liabilities

Total assets – Inventories/Total liabilities

Total assets/Total liabilities

Current assets – Inventories/Current liabilities

(v) Inventory holding period	▼
Formulae:	
Inventories/Cost of sales × 365	
Inventories/Revenue × 365	
Cost of sales/Inventories × 365	
Revenue/Inventories × 365	
(vi) Trade receivables collection period	▼
Formulae:	
Trade payables/Cost of sales × 365	
Trade receivables/Cost of sales × 365	
Revenue/Trade receivables × 365	
Trade receivables/Revenue × 365	

(b) **Calculate the ratios to the nearest ONE DECIMAL PLACE.**

(i) Gross profit percentage		%
(ii) Operating profit percentage		%
(iii) Current ratio		:1
(iv) Quick (acid test) ratio		:1
(v) Inventory holding period		days
(vi) Trade receivables collection period		days

Task 7.5

You have been asked to calculate ratios for Route Ltd in respect of its financial statements for the year ending 31 March 20X7.

Route Ltd's statement of profit or loss and statement of financial position are set out below.

Route Ltd

Statement of profit or loss for the year ended 31 March 20X7

	£'000
Continuing operations	
Revenue	20,562
Cost of sales	(11,309)
Gross profit	9,253
Distribution costs	(4,841)
Administrative expenses	(3,007)
Profit from operations	1,405
Finance costs – interest on bank loan	(800)
Profit before tax	605
Tax	(133)
Profit for the period from continuing operations	472

Route Ltd

Statement of financial position as at 31 March 20X7

Assets	£'000
Non-current assets	
Property, plant and equipment	23,982
Current assets	
Inventories	4,012
Trade and other receivables	2,241
Cash and cash equivalents	84
	6,337
Total assets	30,319

Equity and liabilities	£'000
Equity	
Share capital	4,000
Retained earnings	9,413
Total equity	13,413
Non-current liabilities	
Bank loans	14,000
Current liabilities	
Trade and other payables	2,773
Tax liabilities	133
	2,906
Total liabilities	16,906
Total equity and liabilities	30,319

(a) **State the formulae that are used to calculate each of the following ratios:**

(Write in the correct formula from the list provided)

(i) Operating expenses/revenue percentage		▼

Formulae:

Administrative expenses/Revenue × 100

Distribution costs + administrative expenses/Revenue × 100

Distribution costs/Revenue × 100

Revenue/Distribution costs + administrative expenses × 100

(ii) Current ratio		▼

Formulae:

Total assets/Total liabilities

Current assets – Inventories/Current liabilities

Current assets/Current liabilities

Total assets – Inventories/Total liabilities

(iii) Quick (acid test) ratio	▼

Formulae:

Current assets/Current liabilities

Total assets – Inventories/Total liabilities

Total assets/Total liabilities

Current assets – Inventories/Current liabilities

(iv) Gearing ratio	▼

Formulae:

Current assets/Current liabilities

Revenue/Total assets – Current liabilities

Non-current liabilities/Total equity + Non-current liabilities

Profit after tax/Number of issued ordinary shares

(v) Interest cover	▼

Formulae:

Finance costs/Profit from operations

Finance costs/Revenue

Profit from operations/Finance costs

Revenue/Finance costs

(b) **Calculate the ratios to the nearest ONE DECIMAL PLACE.**

(i) Operating expenses/revenue percentage		%
(ii) Current ratio		:1
(iii) Quick (acid test) ratio		:1
(iv) Gearing ratio		%
(v) Interest cover		times

Task 7.6

You have been asked to calculate ratios for Orford Ltd in respect of its financial statements for the year ending 31 October 20X8.

Orford Ltd's statement of profit or loss and statement of financial position are set out below.

Orford Ltd

Statement of profit or loss for the year ended 31 October 20X8

	£'000
Continuing operations	
Revenue	4,900
Cost of sales	(2,597)
Gross profit	2,303
Distribution costs	(1,225)
Administrative expenses	(490)
Profit from operations	588
Finance costs	(161)
Profit before tax	427
Tax	(64)
Profit for the period from continuing operations	363

Orford Ltd

Statement of financial position as at 31 October 20X8

Assets	£'000
Non-current assets	
Property, plant and equipment	8,041
Current assets	
Inventories	649
Trade receivables	392
Cash and cash equivalents	0
	1,041
Total assets	9,082
Equity and liabilities	
Equity	
Share capital	2,500
Retained earnings	3,741
Total equity	6,241
Non-current liabilities	
Bank loans	2,300
Current liabilities	
Trade payables	286
Tax liabilities	64
Bank overdraft	191
	541
Total liabilities	2,841
Total equity and liabilities	9,082

(a) **State the formulae that are used to calculate each of the following ratios:**

(Write in the correct formula from the list provided)

(i) Return on shareholders' funds	▼

Formulae:

Profit after tax/Total equity × 100

Profit before tax/Total equity × 100

Profit from operations/Total equity × 100

Profit from operations/Total equity + Non-current liabilities × 100

(ii) Inventory holding period	▼

Formulae:

Inventories/Cost of sales × 365

Inventories/Revenue × 365

Cost of sales/Inventories × 365

Revenue/Inventories × 365

(iii) Trade receivables collection period	▼

Formulae:

Trade payables/Cost of sales × 365

Trade receivables/Cost of sales × 365

Revenue/Trade receivables × 365

Trade receivables/Revenue × 365

(iv) Trade payables payment period	▼

Formulae:

Trade payables/Revenue × 365

Trade payables/Cost of sales × 365

Revenue/Trade payables × 365

Cost of sales/Trade payables × 365

(v) Working capital cycle	▼

Formulae:

Current assets/Current liabilities

Current assets – Inventories/Current liabilities

Inventory days + Receivable days – Payable days

Inventory days + Receivable days + Payable days

(vi) Asset turnover (non-current assets)	
Formulae:	
Revenue/Non-current assets	
Revenue/Total assets – Current liabilities	
Non-current assets/Revenue	
Total assets – Current liabilities/Revenue	

(b) **Calculate the ratios to the nearest ONE DECIMAL PLACE.**

(i)	Return on shareholders' funds		%
(ii)	Inventory holding period		days
(iii)	Trade receivables collection period		days
(iv)	Trade payables payment period		days
(v)	Working capital cycle		days
(vi)	Asset turnover (non-current assets)		times

Task 7.7

You have been asked to calculate ratios for Tower Ltd in respect of its financial statements for the year ending 31 October 20X9.

Tower Ltd's statement of profit or loss and statement of financial position as follows:

Tower Ltd

Statement of profit or loss for the year ended 31 October 20X9

	£'000
Continuing operations	
Revenue	27,800
Cost of sales	(14,178)
Gross profit	13,622
Distribution costs	(6,950)
Administrative expenses	(3,892)
Profit from operations	2,780
Finance costs	(840)
Profit before tax	1,940
Tax	(894)
Profit for the period from continuing operations	1,046

Tower Ltd

Statement of financial position as at 31 October 20X9

Assets	£'000
Non-current assets	
Property, plant and equipment	23,016
Current assets	
Inventories	3,261
Trade receivables	1,946
Cash and cash equivalents	-
	5,207
Total assets	28,223
Equity and liabilities	
Equity	
Share capital	8,500
Retained earnings	5,037
Total equity	13,537
Non-current liabilities	
Bank loans	12,000
Current liabilities	
Trade payables	1,276
Tax liabilities	894
Bank overdraft	516
	2,686
Total liabilities	14,686
Total equity and liabilities	28,223

(a) **State the formulae that are used to calculate each of the following ratios:**

(Write in the correct formula from the list provided)

(i) Gearing	▼
Formulae:	
Current assets/Current liabilities > 100	
Revenue/Total assets – Current liabilities × 100	
Non-current liabilities/Total equity + Non-current liabilities × 100	
Profit after tax/Number of issued ordinary shares × 100	

(ii) Interest cover	▼

Formulae:

Finance costs/Profit from operations

Finance costs/Revenue

Profit from operations/Finance costs

Revenue/Finance costs

(iii) Current ratio	▼

Formulae:

Total assets/Total liabilities

Current assets – Inventories/Current liabilities

Current assets/Current liabilities

Total assets – Inventories/Total liabilities

(iv) Trade receivables collection period	▼

Formulae:

Trade payables/Cost of sales × 365

Trade receivables/Cost of sales × 365

Revenue/Trade receivables × 365

Trade receivables/Revenue × 365

(v) Trade payables payment period	▼

Formulae:

Trade payables/Revenue × 365

Trade payables/Cost of sales × 365

Revenue/Trade payables × 365

Cost of sales/Trade payables × 365

(b) **Calculate the ratios to the nearest ONE DECIMAL PLACE.**

(i)	Gearing		%
(ii)	Interest cover		times
(iii)	Current ratio		:1
(iv)	Trade receivables collection period		days
(v)	Trade payables payment period		days

Task 7.8

You have been asked to calculate ratios for Jewel Ltd in respect of its financial statements for the year ending 31 March 20X1 to assist your manager in his analysis of the company.

Jewel Ltd's statement of profit or loss and statement of financial position are set out below.

Jewel Ltd – Statement of profit or loss for the year ended 30 September 20X1

	£'000
Continuing operations	
Revenue	36,000
Cost of sales	(19,800)
Gross profit	16,200
Distribution costs	(6,840)
Administrative expenses	(6,120)
Profit from operations	3,240
Finance costs	(280)
Profit before tax	2,960
Tax	(2,094)
Profit for the period from continuing operations	866

Jewel Ltd – Statement of financial position as at 30 September 20X1

	£'000
Assets	
Non-current assets	
Property, plant and equipment	26,908
Current assets	
Inventories	2,376
Trade receivables	3,960
Cash and cash equivalents	787
	7,123
Total assets	34,031
Equity and liabilities	
Equity	
Share capital	12,000
Retained earnings	14,155
Total equity	26,155
Non-current liabilities	
Bank loans	4,000
	4,000
Current liabilities	
Trade payables	1,782
Tax liabilities	2,094
	3,876
Total liabilities	7,876
Total equity and liabilities	34,031

(a) **State the formulae that are used to calculate each of the following ratios:**

(Write in the correct formula from the list provided)

(i) Gross profit percentage	▼

Formulae:

Gross profit/Revenue × 100

Gross profit/Total assets × 100

Gross profit/Total equity × 100

Gross profit/Total equity + Non-current liabilities × 100

(ii) Operating profit percentage	▼

Formulae:

Profit from operations/Finance costs × 100

Profit from operations/Revenue × 100

Profit from operations/Total assets × 100

Profit from operations/Total equity + Non-current liabilities × 100

(iii) Return on shareholders' funds	▼

Formulae:

Profit after tax/Total equity × 100

Profit before tax/Total equity × 100

Profit from operations/Total equity × 100

Profit from operations/Total equity + Non-current liabilities × 100

(iv) Quick (acid test) ratio	▼

Formulae:

Current assets/Current liabilities

Total assets/Total liabilities

Current assets – Inventories/Current liabilities

Total assets – Inventories/Total liabilities

(v)	Operating expenses/revenue percentage		▼

Formulae:

Administrative expenses/Revenue × 100

Distribution costs + Administrative expenses/Revenue × 100

Distribution costs/Revenue × 100

Revenue/Distribution costs + Administrative expenses × 100

(b) **Calculate the ratios to the nearest ONE DECIMAL PLACE.**

(i)	Gross profit percentage		%
(ii)	Operating profit percentage		%
(iii)	Return on shareholders' funds		%
(iv)	Quick (acid test) ratio		:1
(v)	Operating expenses/revenue percentage		%

Chapter 8 – Interpreting financial statements

Task 8.1

Given below is a range of financial ratios for two companies that both operate in the retail trade.

	Rigby Ltd	Rialto Ltd
Gross profit percentage	60%	32%
Operating profit percentage	28%	10%
Asset turnover	0.80 times	2.2 times
ROCE	22%	22%
Current ratio	2.0	1.8
Quick ratio	1.2	0.4
Inventory turnover	4.8 times	10.3 times
Trade receivables collection period	41 days	3 days
Trade payables payment period	62 days	70 days
Gearing	33%	50%
Interest cover	16 times	5 times

(a) **Comment upon what the ratios indicate about each business.**

(b) **One of the businesses is a supermarket and the other is a jeweller who supplies some goods on credit to long standing customers. Identify which business is which.**

....

Task 8.2

Duncan Tweedy wishes to invest some money in one of two private companies. He has obtained the latest financial statements for Byrne Ltd and May Ltd prepared for internal purposes. As part of his decision making process he has asked you to assess the relative profitability of the two companies, based on the following ratios.

	Byrne Ltd	May Ltd
Return on capital employed	21.5%	32.1%
Gross profit percentage	59.0%	67.0%
Operating profit percentage	25.0%	36.0%

Prepare a report for Duncan Tweedy that:

(a) **Uses each ratio to comment on the relative profitability of the companies, and**
(b) **Concludes, with reasons, which company is the more profitable.**

....

Task 8.3

A colleague has asked you to take over an assignment. He has been helping a shareholder of Youngernst Ltd to understand the financial statements of the company for the past two years. The shareholder is interested in finding out how well the company has managed working capital. Your colleague has obtained the financial statements of Youngernst Ltd for the past two years and has calculated the following ratios:

Ratio	20X3	20X2
Current ratio	2.8:1	2.3:1
Quick (acid test) ratio	0.6:1	1.1:1
Trade receivables collection period	48 days	32 days
Trade payables payment period	27 days	30 days
Inventory holding period	84 days	67 days

Prepare notes for a meeting with the shareholder that include

(a) **Your comments on the change in the ratios of Youngernst Ltd over the two years, including an analysis of whether the change in each of the ratios shows that the management of the components of working capital has improved or deteriorated.**

(b) **A brief overall conclusion, based on the ratios above.**

Task 8.4

Madge Keygone is the managing director of Asbee Ltd. She has just returned from a meeting with one of the company's major shareholders. The shareholder was concerned about the current ratio, quick ratio, inventory holding period and trade receivables collection period and how they compared with the industry averages. Madge did not understand the shareholder's concern and has asked you to help her. She has calculated these ratios from the summarised financial statements of Asbee Ltd and has obtained the industry averages from computerised databases. These are set out below.

	Asbee Ltd	Industry average
Current ratio	2.3:1	1.9:1
Quick (acid test) ratio	0.8:1	0.9:1
Inventory holding period	176 days	98 days
Trade receivables collection period	51 days	47 days

Prepare a letter for Madge Keygone that includes the following.

(a) **Comments about how the ratios for Asbee Ltd compare with the industry averages and what this tells you about the company.**

(b) **A conclusion, based on the ratios above, as to whether the shareholder is right to be concerned.**

Task 8.5

Leopold Scratchy plans to invest in shares in a private company. He has identified two companies that might be suitable, Partridge Ltd and Carington Ltd. He has obtained the latest financial statements of the companies in order to learn more about the risk inherent in, and return provided by, a potential investment in these companies. You have used these financial statements to compute the following ratios:

	Partridge Ltd	Carington Ltd
Gross profit percentage	59%	59%
Operating profit percentage	23%	15%
Return on shareholders' funds	38%	29%
Gearing	45%	5%

Both companies have the same number of £1 ordinary shares and approximately the same amount of shareholders' funds (share capital and reserves).

Prepare a report for Leopold Scratchy that includes:

(a) **Comments on the relative return and risk of the two companies based on the ratios above.**

(b) **A conclusion, with reasons based on the ratios above, as to which of the two companies would provide Leopold with the best return on his investment and which of the two companies would be the safer investment.**

Task 8.6

Peter Stewart is a shareholder in Hillhead Ltd. He wishes to assess the efficiency and effectiveness of the management of the company. He has asked you to assist him by analysing the financial statements of the company for the last two years. You have computed the following ratios to assist you in your analysis.

	20X2	20X1
Gross profit percentage	40.0%	45.0%
Operating profit percentage	9.5%	7.5%
Inventory holding period	86.7 days	65.7 days
Trade receivables collection period	55.9 days	40.2 days

The financial statements show that sales have risen by 14% in the period.

Prepare a report for Peter Stewart that includes:

(a) **A comment on the relative performance of the company for the two years based on the ratios calculated and what this tells you about the company.**

(b) **ONE suggestion as to how EACH of the ratios might be improved.**

Task 8.7

Nancy Charlton is considering buying shares in Limden Ltd and has asked you to assist her in determining the level of profitability and risk of the company. You have computed the following ratios in respect of Limden Ltd's financial statements for the last two years to assist you in your analysis.

	20X1	20X0
Gross profit percentage	46.0%	42.0%
Operating profit percentage	6.5%	8.0%
Return on shareholders' funds	7.4%	10.8%
Gearing	35.2%	22.4%
Interest cover	2.9 times	7.5 times

Prepare a report to Nancy that includes:

(a) **A comment on the relative performance of the company for the two years based on the ratios calculated and what this tells you about the company.**

(b) **Advice, with reasons based on the ratios you have calculated, on whether or not Nancy should invest.**

●●

Task 8.8

The directors of Knole Ltd are concerned about the company's liquidity and cash flow. At the beginning of the current year the company had a positive cash balance of nearly £500,000 but by the year end this had become an overdraft of just over £1,500,000. The directors cannot understand how this has happened.

The company purchased new plant and equipment during the year, but there should have been enough cash available to cover this expenditure. Knole Ltd is highly profitable and has been able to raise finance by increasing its bank loans and by issuing new share capital during the year.

The directors have given you the financial statements for the past two years. You have used these to prepare a reconciliation of the profit from operations to net cash from operating activities. You have also calculated some ratios. The reconciliations and the ratios are set out below.

Knole Ltd

Reconciliation of profit from operations to net cash inflow from operating activities for the year ended 31 October

	20X8	20X7
	£'000	£'000
Profit from operations	13,200	11,060
Adjustments for:		
Depreciation	4,777	3,745
Gain on disposal of property, plant and equipment	(880)	(570)
Decrease/(Increase) in inventories	(4,840)	(3,606)
Decrease/(Increase) in trade receivables	(2,640)	(1,208)
(Decrease)/Increase in trade payables	(2,420)	(1,320)
Cash generated by operations	7,197	8,101
Tax paid	(944)	(885)
Interest paid	(280)	(105)
Net cash from operating activities	5,973	7,111

Ratios	20X8	20X7
Current ratio	3.6:1	2.5:1
Quick (acid test) ratio	1.7:1	1.3:1
Gearing	7.2%	4.1%

Prepare a report for the Directors of Knole Ltd that includes:

(a) **Comments upon the change in net cash from operating activities between 20X7 and 20X8.**

(b) **A comment on the relative liquidity and financial position of the company for the two years based on the ratios calculated and what this tells you about the company.**

....

Answer bank

Answer bank

Chapter 1

Task 1.1

(a) **Paparazzi Ltd**

Statement of profit or loss and other comprehensive income for the year ended 30 June 20X2

	£'000
Revenue	14,700
Cost of sales (W)	(10,760)
Gross profit	3,940
Distribution costs	(1,200)
Administrative expenses	(2,120)
Profit/(loss) from operations	620
Finance costs	(84)
Profit/(loss) before tax	536
Tax	(130)
Profit/(loss) for the period from continuing operations	406

Workings

Cost of sales	£'000
Opening inventories	690
Purchases	10,780
Closing inventories	(710)
	10,760

(b) **Paparazzi Ltd**

Statement of financial position as at 30 June 20X2

	£'000
Assets	
Non-current assets:	
Property, plant and equipment (W)	3,272
Current assets:	
Inventories	710
Trade and other receivables (W)	2,448
Cash and cash equivalents	567
	3,725
Total assets	6,997
Equity and liabilities	
Equity:	
Share capital	2,500
Share premium	300
Retained earnings (W)	1,417
Total equity	4,217
Non-current liabilities:	
Bank loan	1,200
Current liabilities:	
Trade and other payables (W)	1,450
Tax liabilities	130
	1,580
Total liabilities	2,780
Total equity and liabilities	6,997

Workings

Property, plant and equipment	£'000
Land and buildings – Cost	2,100
Plant and equipment – Cost	1,050
Motor vehicles – Cost	1,000
Accumulated depreciation – land and buildings	(280)
Accumulated depreciation – plant and equipment	(194)
Accumulated depreciation – motor vehicles	(404)
	3,272

Trade and other receivables	£'000
Trade and other receivables	2,500
Allowance for doubtful debts	(92)
Prepayments	40
	2,448

Retained earnings	£'000
Retained earnings at 1 July 20X1	1,131
Total profit for the year	406
Dividends paid	(120)
	1,417

Trade and other payables	£'000
Trade payables	1,400
Accruals	50
	1,450

Task 1.2

(a) **Bathlea Limited**

Statement of profit or loss and other comprehensive income for the year ended 30 September 20X8

	£'000
Revenue	3,509
Cost of sales (W)	(1,641)
Gross profit	1,868
Distribution costs	(857)
Administrative expenses (W)	(902)
Profit/(loss) from operations	109
Finance cost (11 + 1)	(12)
Profit/(loss) before tax	97
Tax	(11)
Profit/(loss) for the period from continuing operations	86

Workings

Cost of sales	£'000
Opening inventories	200
Purchases	1,691
Closing inventories	(250)
	1,641

Administrative expenses	£'000
Administrative expenses	892
Irrecoverable debts	10
	902

(b) **Bathlea Limited**

Statement of financial position as at 30 September 20X8

	£'000
Assets	
Non-current assets	
Property, plant and equipment (W)	500
Current assets	
Inventories	250
Trade and other receivables (W)	365
	615
Total assets	1,115
Equity and liabilities	
Equity	
Share capital	500
Retained earnings (W)	141
Total equity	641
Non-current liabilities	
Long-term loan	100
Current liabilities	
Trade and other payables (W)	360
Tax liabilities	11
Bank overdraft	3
	374
Total liabilities	474
Total equity and liabilities	1,115

Workings

Property, plant and equipment	£'000
Land and buildings – Cost	300
Fixtures and fittings – Cost	220
Motor vehicles – Cost	70
Office equipment – Cost	80
Land and buildings – Accumulated depreciation	(65)
Fixtures and fittings – Accumulated depreciation	(43)
Motor vehicles – Accumulated depreciation	(27)
Office equipment – Accumulated depreciation	(35)
	500

Trade and other receivables	£'000
Trade and other receivables	370
Allowance for irrecoverable debts	(5)
Irrecoverable debt	(10)
Prepayments	10
	365

Retained earnings	£'000
Retained earnings at 1 October 20X7	70
Total profit for the year	86
Dividends paid	(15)
	141

Trade and other payables	£'000
Trade and other payables	350
Accruals: trial balance	9
Additional interest accrual	1
	360

Task 1.3

(a) **Howardsend Ltd**

Statement of profit or loss and other comprehensive income for the year ended 30 September 20X6

	£'000
Revenue	53,821
Cost of sales (W)	(25,834)
Gross profit	27,987
Distribution costs (W)	(12,273)
Administrative expenses (W)	(9,255)
Profit/(loss) from operations	6,459
Finance costs (7% × 10,000)	(700)
Profit/(loss) before tax	5,759
Tax	(1,382)
Profit/(loss) for the period from continuing operations	4,377
Other comprehensive income	
Gain on revaluation (11,600 – 9,600)	2,000
Total comprehensive income for the year	6,377

Workings

Cost of sales	£'000
Opening inventories	7,158
Purchases (24,407 + 2,403)	26,810
Closing inventories	(8,134)
	25,834

Distribution costs	£'000
Distribution costs	12,216
Accruals	57
	12,273

Administrative expenses	£'000
Administrative expenses	9,176
Allowance for doubtful debts (132 – 53)	79
	9,255

(b) **Howardsend Ltd**

Statement of financial position as at 30 September 20X6

	£'000
Assets	
Non-current assets	
Property, plant and equipment (W)	44,626
Current assets	
Inventories	8,134
Trade and other receivables (W)	6,468
Cash and cash equivalents	579
	15,181
Total assets	59,807
Equity and liabilities	
Equity	
Share capital	8,000
Share premium	1,000
Revaluation reserve	2,000
Retained earnings (W)	31,824
Total equity	42,824
Non-current liabilities	
Long-term loan	10,000
Current liabilities	
Trade and other payables (W)	5,601
Tax liabilities	1,382
	6,983
Total liabilities	16,983
Total equity and liabilities	59,807

Workings

Property, plant and equipment	£'000
Property, plant and equipment – Cost	57,149
Property, plant and equipment – Accumulated depreciation	(14,523)
Revaluation	2,000
	44,626

Trade and other receivables	£'000
Trade receivables	6,600
Allowance for doubtful debts (2% × 6,600)	(132)
	6,468

Retained earnings	£'000
Retained earnings at 1 October 20X5	28,887
Total profit for the year	4,377
Dividends paid	(1,440)
	31,824

Trade and other payables	£'000
Trade payables (2,577 + 2,403)	4,980
Accruals: trial balance	214
Additional distribution costs accrual	57
Additional interest accrual (7% × 10,000 × 6/12)	350
	5,601

Task 1.4

(a) **Benard Ltd**

Statement of profit or loss and other comprehensive income for the year ended 31 October 20X7

	£'000
Revenue (50,197 + 3,564)	53,761
Cost of sales (W)	(33,462)
Gross profit	20,299
Distribution costs	(6,654)
Administrative expenses (W)	(4,120)
Profit/(loss) from operations	9,525
Finance costs (560 + 560)	(1,120)
Profit/(loss) before tax	8,405
Tax	(1,254)
Profit/(loss) for the period from continuing operations	7,151

Workings

Cost of sales	£'000
Opening inventories	8,456
Purchases	34,792
Closing inventories	(9,786)
	33,462

Administrative expenses	£'000
Administrative expenses	4,152
Prepayments (48 × 8/12)	(32)
	4,120

(b) **Benard Ltd**

Statement of financial position as at 31 October 20X7

	£'000
Assets	
Non-current assets	
Property, plant and equipment (58,463 – 27,974)	30,489
Current assets	
Inventories	9,786
Trade and other receivables (W)	10,286
Cash and cash equivalents	1,184
	21,256
Total assets	51,745
Equity and liabilities	
Equity	
Share capital	12,000
Retained earnings (W)	18,196
Total equity	30,196
Non-current liabilities	
Bank loan	16,000
Current liabilities	
Trade and other payables (W)	4,295
Tax payable	1,254
	5,549
Total liabilities	21,549
Total equity and liabilities	51,745

Workings

Trade and other receivables	£'000
Trade and other receivables	6,690
Credit sales for October 20X7	3,564
Administrative expenses prepaid	32
	10,286

Retained earnings	£'000
Retained earnings at 1 November 20X6	12,345
Total profit for the year	7,151
Dividends paid	(1,300)
	18,196

Trade and other payables	£'000
Trade and other payables	3,348
Accruals: trial balance	387
Additional interest accrual	560
	4,295

Task 1.5

(a) **Laxdale Ltd**

Statement of profit or loss and other comprehensive income for the year ended 31 October 20X8

	£'000
Revenue	58,411
Cost of sales (W)	(43,342)
Gross profit	15,069
Distribution costs (W)	(6,026)
Administrative expenses (W)	(5,073)
Profit/(loss) from operations	3,970
Finance costs (8% × 15,000)	(1,200)
Profit/(loss) before tax	2,770
Tax	(970)
Profit/(loss) for the period from continuing operations	1,800

Workings

Cost of sales	£'000
Opening inventories	9,032
Purchases	41,620
Depreciation (40% × 1,420)	568
Closing inventories	(7,878)
	43,342

Distribution costs	£'000
Distribution costs	5,443
Depreciation (40% × 1,420)	568
Accruals (45 × 1/3)	15
	6,026

Administrative expenses	£'000
Administrative expenses	4,789
Depreciation (20% × 1,420)	284
	5,073

Depreciation

Buildings (2% × 35,152 – 15,152)	400
Plant and equipment (20% × 12,500 – 7,400)	1,020
	1,420

(b) **Laxdale Ltd**

Statement of financial position as at 31 October 20X8

	£'000
Assets	
Non-current assets	
Property, plant and equipment (W)	31,832
Current assets	
Inventories	7,878
Trade and other receivables	5,436
Cash and cash equivalents	9,774
	23,088
Total assets	54,920
Equity and liabilities	
Equity	
Share capital	25,000
Retained earnings (W)	10,101
Total equity	35,101
Non-current liabilities	
Bank loan	15,000
Current liabilities	
Trade and other payables (W)	3,849
Tax liabilities	970
	4,819
Total liabilities	19,819
Total equity and liabilities	54,920

Workings

Property, plant and equipment	£'000
Land and buildings – Cost	35,152
Plant and equipment – Cost	12,500
Accumulated depreciation – land and buildings (7,000 + 400)	(7,400)
Accumulated depreciation – plant and equipment (7,400 + 1,020)	(8,420)
	31,832

Retained earnings	£'000
Retained earnings at 1 November 20X7	9,801
Total profit for the year	1,800
Dividends paid	(1,500)
	10,101

Trade and other payables	£'000
Trade and other payables	2,798
Accruals: trial balance	436
Additional distribution costs accrual	15
Additional interest accrual	600
	3,849

Task 1.6

(a) **Cappielow Ltd**

Statement of profit or loss and other comprehensive income for the year ended 31 March 20X1

	£'000
Revenue	35,547
Cost of sales (W)	(28,354)
Gross profit	7,193
Distribution costs (W)	(1,933)
Administrative expenses (W)	(2,207)
Profit/(loss) from operations	3,053
Finance costs	(720)
Profit/(loss) before tax	2,333
Tax	(874)
Profit/(loss) for the period from continuing operations	1,459
Other comprehensive income for the year	
Gain on revaluation of land (7,500 – 5,150)	2,350
Total comprehensive income for the year	3,809

Workings

Cost of sales	£'000
Opening inventories	3,790
Purchases	27,481
Closing inventories	(4,067)
Impairment loss (12,750 – 3,100 – 8,500)	1,150
	28,354

Distribution costs	£'000
Distribution costs	1,857
Accruals (114 × 2/3)	76
	1,933

Administrative expenses	£'000
Administrative expenses	2,235
Prepayment (164 × ¾)	(123)
Irrecoverable debt	95
	2,207

(b) **Cappielow Ltd**

Statement of changes in equity for the year ended 31 March 20X1

	Share capital £'000	Other reserves £'000	Retained earnings £'000	Total equity £'000
Balance at 1 April 20X0	10,000	2,000	2,595	14,595
Changes in equity for 20X1				
Total comprehensive income		2,350	1,459	3,809
Dividends	0	0	(920)	(920)
Balance at 31 March 20X1	10,000	4,350	3,134	17,484

(c) **Cappielow Ltd**

Statement of financial position as at 31 March 20X1

	£'000
Assets	
Non-current assets:	
Property, plant and equipment (W)	18,104
Current assets:	
Inventories	4,067
Trade and other receivables (W)	2,161
Cash and cash equivalents	7,578
	13,806
Total assets	31,910

	£'000
Equity and liabilities:	
Equity	
Share capital	10,000
Revaluation reserve (W)	4,350
Retained earnings (W)	3,134
Total equity	17,484
Non-current liabilities:	
Bank loan	12,000
Current liabilities:	
Trade and other payables (W)	1,552
Tax payable	874
	2,426
Total liabilities	14,426
Total equity and liabilities	31,910

Workings

Property, plant and equipment	£'000
Property, plant and equipment – Cost/value (36,780 + 2,350)	39,130
Property, plant and equipment – Accumulated depreciation	(19,876)
Impairment loss	(1,150)
	18,104

Trade and other receivables	£'000
Trade and other receivables	2,133
Administrative expenses prepaid	123
Irrecoverable debt	(95)
	2,161

Revaluation reserve	£'000
Revaluation reserve at 1 April 20X0	2,000
Other comprehensive income for the year	2,350
	4,350

Retained earnings	£'000
Retained earnings at 1 April 20X0	2,595
Total profit for the year	1,459
Dividends paid	(920)
	3,134

Trade and other payables	£'000
Trade and other payables	1,347
Accruals: trial balance	129
Distribution costs accrued	76
	1,552

Task 1.7

(a) **Pine Ltd**

Statement of profit or loss and other comprehensive income for the year ended 31 March 20X1

	£'000
Revenue	80,908
Cost of sales (W)	(55,104)
Gross profit	25,804
Distribution costs (W)	(11,937)
Administrative expenses (W)	(7,379)
Profit from operations	6,488
Finance costs	(640)
Profit before tax	5,848
Tax	(1,254)
Profit for the period from continuing operations	4,594
Other comprehensive income for the year (Gain on revaluation of land (51,000 – 41,778))	9,222
Total comprehensive income for the year	13,816

Workings

Cost of sales	£'000
Opening inventories	5,064
Purchases	53,444
Depreciation (60% × 6,000)	3,600
Closing inventories	(7,004)
	55,104

Distribution costs	£'000
Distribution costs	9,977
Depreciation (30% × 6,000)	1,800
Accruals	160
	11,937

Administrative expenses	£'000
Administrative expenses	6,755
Depreciation (10% × 6,000)	600
Irrecoverable debt	24
	7,379

Depreciation

Buildings (5% × 81,778 – 41,778)	2,000
Plant and equipment (25% × (24,000 – 8,000))	4,000
	6,000

(b) **Pine Ltd**

Statement of changes in equity for the year ended 31 March 20X1

	Share capital £'000	Other reserves £'000	Retained earnings £'000	Total equity £'000
Balance at 1 April 20X0	50,000	12,000	7,945	69,945
Changes in equity for 20X1				
Total comprehensive income	0	9,222	4,594	13,816
Dividends	0	0	(1,600)	(1,600)
Issue of share capital	0	0	0	0
Balance at 31 March 20X1	50,000	21,222	10,939	82,161

(c) **Pine Ltd**

Statement of financial position as at 31 March 20X1

	£'000
Assets	
Non-current assets:	
Property, plant and equipment (W)	87,000
Current assets:	
Inventories	7,004
Trade and other receivables (W)	9,862
Cash and cash equivalents	1,568
	18,434
Total assets	105,434
Equity and liabilities:	
Equity	
Share capital	50,000
Revaluation reserve (W)	21,222
Retained earnings (W)	10,939
Total equity	82,161
Non-current liabilities:	
Bank loan	16,000
Current liabilities:	
Trade and other payables (W)	6,019
Tax liability	1,254
	7,273
Total liabilities	23,273
Total equity and liabilities	105,434

Workings

Property, plant and equipment	£'000
Land and buildings – value (81,778 + 9,222)	91,000
Plant and equipment – cost	24,000
Accumulated depreciation – land and buildings (14,000 + 2,000)	(16,000)
Accumulated depreciation – plant and equipment (8,000 + 4,000)	(12,000)
	87,000

Trade and other receivables	£'000
Trade and other receivables	9,886
Irrecoverable debts	(24)
	9,862

Revaluation reserve	£'000
Revaluation reserve at 1 April 20X0	12,000
Other comprehensive income for the year	9,222
	21,222

Retained earnings	£'000
Retained earnings at 1 April 20X0	7,945
Total profit for the year	4,594
Dividends paid	(1,600)
	10,939

Trade and other payables	£'000
Trade and other payables	5,342
Accruals: trial balance	517
Additional distribution costs accrual	160
	6,019

Answer bank

Chapter 2

Task 2.1

Reconciliation of profit from operations to net cash from operating activities

	£
Profit from operations	100,000
Depreciation	20,000
Increase in inventories (30,000 – 25,000)	(5,000)
Decrease in trade receivables (40,000 – 42,000)	2,000
Decrease in trade payables (28,000 – 32,000)	(4,000)
Cash generated from operations	113,000
Interest paid	(10,000)
Tax paid	(25,000)
Net cash from operating activities	78,000

Task 2.2

(a)

£	37,400

	£
Opening balance	13,000
Profit or loss	32,400
Closing balance	(8,000)
	37,400

(b)

£	92,000

	£
Opening balance	94,000
Profit or loss	98,000
Closing balance	(100,000)
	92,000

Task 2.3

(a)

£	230,000

	£'000
Opening balance	1,250
Disposals	(140)
Closing balance	(1,340)
Cash paid to acquire PPE	(230)

(b)

£	75,000

	£'000
Net carrying amount	98
Loss on disposal	(23)
	75

(c)

£	122,000

	£'000
Opening balance	480
Disposals (140 – 98)	(42)
Closing balance	(560)
	(122)

Task 2.4

Statement of changes in equity for the year ended 30 April 20X2

	Share capital £	Share premium £	Revaluation reserve £	Retained earnings £	Total equity £
Balance at 1 May 20X1	500,000	100,000	30,000	180,000	810,000
Changes in equity					
Total comprehensive income			70,000	110,000	180,000
Dividends				(35,000)	(35,000)
Issue of share capital (200,000 × 1.4)	200,000	80,000			280,000
Balance at 30 April 20X2	700,000	180,000	100,000	255,000	1,235,000

Task 2.5

(a) **Evans**

Reconciliation of profit from operations to net cash from operating activities for the year ended 31 October 20X1

	£'000
Profit from operations	441
Adjustments for:	
Depreciation	190
Gain on disposal of property, plant and equipment	(10)
Adjustment in respect of inventories (505 – 486)	19
Adjustment in respect of trade receivables (945 – 657)	(288)
Adjustment in respect of trade payables (560 – 546)	14
Cash generated by operations	366
Interest paid	(23)
Tax paid	(106)
Net cash from operating activities	237

(b) **Evans Ltd**

Statement of cash flows for the year ended 31 October 20X1

	£'000
Net cash from operating activities	237
Investing activities	
Purchase of property, plant and equipment (W)	(425)
Proceeds on disposal of property, plant and equipment (W)	75
Net cash used in investing activities	(350)
Financing activities	
Proceeds of share issue (1,200 – 1,000) + (315 – 270)	245
Repayment of bank loan (150 – 50)	(100)
Dividends paid	(40)
Net cash from financing activities	105
Net increase/(decrease) in cash and cash equivalents	(8)
Cash and cash equivalents at the beginning of the year	10
Cash and cash equivalents at the end of the year	2

Workings

Proceeds on disposal of property, plant and equipment (PPE)	£'000
Carrying amount of PPE sold	65
Gain on disposal	10
	75

Purchases of property, plant and equipment (PPE)	£'000
PPE at start of year	1,010
Depreciation charge	(190)
Carrying amount of PPE sold	(65)
PPE at end of year	(1,180)
Total PPE additions	(425)

(c) **Evans Ltd**

Statement of changes in equity for the year ended 31 October 20X1

	Share capital £'000	Share premium £'000	Retained earnings £'000	Total equity £'000
Balance at 1 November 20X0	1,000	270	110	1,380
Changes in equity				
Profit for the year			293	293
Dividends			(40)	(40)
Issue of share capital	200	45	–	245
Balance at 31 October 20X1	1,200	315	363	1,878

Task 2.6

(a) **Lochnagar Ltd**

Reconciliation of profit from operations to net cash from operating activities for the year ended 31 October 20X7

	£'000
Profit from operations	3,360
Adjustments for:	
Depreciation	3,545
Gain on disposal of property, plant and equipment	(224)
Adjustment in respect of inventories (3,696 – 2,464)	(1,232)
Adjustment in respect of trade receivables (3,360 – 2,464)	(896)
Adjustment in respect of trade payables (1,232 – 1,848)	(616)
Cash generated by operations	3,937
Interest paid	(91)
Tax paid	(944)
Net cash from operating activities	2,902

(b) **Lochnagar Ltd**

Statement of cash flows for the year ended 31 October 20X7

	£'000
Net cash from operating activities	2,902
Investing activities	
Purchases of property, plant and equipment (W)	(5,237)
Proceeds on disposal of property, plant and equipment (W)	845
Net cash used in investing activities	(4,392)
Financing activities	
Proceeds of share issue	500
New bank loans (1,300 – 800)	500
Net cash from financing activities	1,000
Net increase/(decrease) in cash and cash equivalents	(490)
Cash and cash equivalents at the beginning of the year	129
Cash and cash equivalents at the end of the year	(361)

Workings

Proceeds on disposal of property, plant and equipment (PPE)	£'000
Carrying amount of PPE sold	621
Gain on disposal	224
	845

Purchases of property, plant and equipment (PPE)	£'000
PPE at start of year	24,100
Depreciation charge	(3,545)
Carrying amount of PPE sold	(621)
PPE at end of year	(25,171)
Total PPE additions	(5,237)

Task 2.7

(a) **Thehoose Ltd**

Reconciliation of profit from operations to net cash from operating activities for the year ended 31 March 20X9

	£'000
Profit from operations	5,652
Adjustments for:	
Depreciation	3,469
Gain on disposal of property, plant and equipment	(376)
Adjustment in respect of inventories (5,426 – 4,069)	(1,357)
Adjustment in respect of trade receivables (4,145 – 3,768)	377
Adjustment in respect of trade payables (4,069 – 2,261)	(1,808)
Cash generated by operations	5,957
Interest paid	(280)
Tax paid	(887)
Net cash from operating activities	4,790

(b) **Thehoose Ltd**

Statement of cash flows for the year ended 31 March 20X9

	£'000
Net cash from operating activities	4,790
Investing activities	
Purchases of property, plant and equipment (W)	(10,116)
Proceeds on disposal of property, plant and equipment (W)	793
Net cash used in investing activities	(9,323)
Financing activities	
Proceeds of share issue: (4,500 + 3,000) – (3,000 + 2,000)	2,500
New bank loans: 4,000 – 1,500	2,500
Net cash from financing activities	5,000
Net increase/(decrease) in cash and cash equivalents	467
Cash and cash equivalents at the beginning of the year	(132)
Cash and cash equivalents at the end of the year	335

Workings

Proceeds on disposal of property, plant and equipment (PPE)	£'000
Carrying amount of PPE sold	417
Gain on disposal	376
	793

Purchases of property, plant and equipment (PPE)	£'000
PPE at start of year	21,340
Depreciation charge	(3,469)
Carrying amount of PPE sold	(417)
PPE at end of year	(27,570)
Total PPE additions	10,116

Task 2.8

(a) **Reconciliation of profit from operations to net cash from operating activities for the year ended 31 October 20X9**

	£'000
Profit from operations	6,825
Adjustments for:	
Depreciation	4,398
Gain on disposal of property, plant and equipment	(455)
Adjustment in respect of inventories (6,552 – 4,914)	(1,638)
Adjustment in respect of trade receivables (4,641 – 4,550)	91
Adjustment in respect of trade payables (4,368 – 3,822)	(546)
Cash generated by operations	8,675
Tax paid	(658)
Interest paid	(595)
Net cash from operating activities	7,422

(b) **Adlington Ltd**

Statement of cash flows for the year ended 31 October 20X9

	£'000
Net cash from operating activities	7,422
Investing activities	
Purchases of property, plant and equipment (W)	(14,483)
Proceeds on disposal of property, plant and equipment (W)	797
Net cash used in investing activities	(13,686)
Financing activities	
Proceeds of share issue: (10,000 + 4,000) – (8,000 + 3,000)	3,000
New bank loans: 8,500 – 3,000	5,500
Dividends paid	(500)
Net cash from financing activities	8,000
Net increase/(decrease) in cash and cash equivalents	1,736
Cash and cash equivalents at the beginning of the year	(1,286)
Cash and cash equivalents at the end of the year	450

Workings

Proceeds on disposal of property, plant and equipment (PPE)	£'000
Carrying amount of PPE sold	342
Gain on disposal	455
	797

Purchases of property, plant and equipment (PPE)	£'000
PPE at start of year	22,246
Depreciation charge	(4,398)
Carrying amount of PPE sold	(342)
PPE at end of year	(31,989)
Total PPE additions	14,483

BPP
LEARNING MEDIA

(c) **Adlington Ltd**

Statement of changes in equity for the year ended 31 October 20X9

	Share capital £'000	Other reserves £'000	Retained earnings £'000	Total equity £'000
Balance at 1 November 20X8	8,000	3,000	11,489	22,489
Changes in equity for 20X9				
Profit for the year	0	0	4,473	4,473
Dividends	0	0	(500)	(500)
Issue of share capital	2,000	1,000	0	3,000
Balance at 31 October 20X9	10,000	4,000	15,462	29,462

Task 2.9

(a) **Forthbank Ltd**

Reconciliation of profit from operations to net cash from operating activities

	£'000
Profit from operations	5,860
Adjustments for:	
Depreciation	3,366
Dividends received	(650)
Loss on disposal of property, plant and equipment	110
Adjustment in respect of inventories (5,832 – 4,860)	(972)
Adjustment in respect of trade receivables (5,400 – 4,320)	(1,080)
Adjustment in respect of trade payables (3,240 – 3,564)	(324)
Cash generated by operations	6,310
Tax paid	(908)
Interest paid	(301)
Net cash from operating activities	5,101

(b) **Forthbank Ltd**

Statement of cash flows for the year ended 31 March 20X1

	£'000
Net cash from operating activities	5,101
Investing activities	
Purchases of property, plant and equipment (W)	(11,223)
Proceeds on disposal of property, plant and equipment (W)	227
Dividends received	650
Net cash used in investing activities	(10,346)
Financing activities	
Proceeds of share issue (11,000 – 8,000)	3,000
New bank loans (4,300 – 800)	3,500
Dividends paid	(460)
Net cash from financing activities	6,040
Net increase/(decrease) in cash and cash equivalents	795
Cash and cash equivalents at the beginning of the year	(208)
Cash and cash equivalents at the end of the year	587

Workings

Proceeds on disposal of property, plant and equipment (PPE)	£'000
Carrying amount of PPE sold	337
Loss on disposal	(110)
	227

Purchases of property, plant and equipment (PPE)	£'000
PPE at start of year	19,140
Depreciation charge	(3,366)
Carrying amount of PPE sold	(337)
PPE at end of year	(26,660)
Total PPE additions	(11,223)

(c) **Forthbank Ltd**

Statement of changes in equity for the year ended 31 March 20X1

	Share Capital £'000	Other Reserves £'000	Retained Earnings £'000	Total Equity £'000
Balance at 1 April 20X0	6,000	2,000	14,840	22,840
Changes in equity for 20X1				
Profit for the year	0	0	4,446	4,446
Dividends	0	0	(460)	(460)
Issue of share capital	2,000	1,000	0	3,000
Balance at 31 March 20X1	8,000	3,000	18,826	29,826

Chapter 3

Note. Based on the information available at the time this book was written, we anticipate that the tasks in this section would be human marked in the real assessment.

Task 3.1

(a) Definitions:

- Assets are resources controlled by the entity as a result of past events and from which future economic benefits are expected to flow to the entity.

- Liabilities are present obligations of the entity arising from past events, the settlement of which is expected to result in an outflow of resources embodying economic benefits from the entity.

- Equity is the owners' residual interest in the assets of the entity after deducting all its liabilities.

(b) Transaction 1 would increase inventories, an asset, by £120 and also increase trade payables, a liability, by £120.

Transaction 2 would decrease the asset inventories by £120, but increase the asset cash by £180. Thus there would be a net increase in assets of £60. In the other half of the statement of financial position, equity would increase by £60, being the profit made on the sale.

(c) The accounting equation after the two transactions would be:

ASSETS LESS LIABILITIES = EQUITY

(i) £1,320 – £920   = £400

(ii) £1,380 – £920   = £460

(d) **Statement of profit or loss**

	£
Sales	180
Cost of sales	(120)
Gross profit	60

....

Task 3.2

(a) The IASB *Conceptual Framework* states that **existing and potential investors, lenders and other creditors** are the primary users of general purpose financial reports (financial statements).

These are the people who **provide capital** (finance) to an entity, either in the form of share capital (equity) as owners, or in the form of loans.

(b) The statement of financial position shows the current assets and current liabilities of the company for the current year and the preceding year and the notes to the financial statements provide further information (for example, total receivables are analysed into trade receivables, other receivables and prepayments). The user can observe the movements in working capital and can also calculate ratios that measure working capital management. He or she can also interpret this information in the context of the financial statements as a whole. For example, the statement of profit or loss and other comprehensive income (with comparative figures) shows whether revenue and expenses are increasing or decreasing, which may help to explain any unusual movements in working capital. The statement of cash flows will provide additional information on liquidity and should help him or her to assess the extent to which the directors' management of working capital is affecting the company's cash flows.

(c) The IASB's *Conceptual Framework* defines equity as the residual amount found by deducting all of the entity's liabilities from all of the entity's assets. It consists of the capital that the owners have invested, plus accumulated profits, less dividends (or other amounts) paid to the owners. This can be expressed as:

Assets less liabilities = equity

Equity = contributions from owners plus income less expenses less distributions to owners

Income (profits or gains) is increases in equity (net assets) other than contributions from owners. Expenses are decreases in equity (net assets) other than distributions to owners.

Task 3.3

(a) The IASB's *Conceptual Framework* defines the elements of financial statements as follows.

(i) Assets are resources controlled by an entity as a result of past events and from which future economic benefits are expected to flow to the entity.

(ii) Liabilities are present obligations of an entity arising from past events, the settlement of which is expected to result in an outflow of resources embodying economic benefits from the entity.

(iii) Equity is the owners' residual interest in the assets of an entity after deducting all its liabilities.

(b) Inventories are an asset because:

- They are the result of a past event (the purchase of goods); and

- The purchase of inventories gives rise to future economic benefits because it results in a future inflow of cash when the inventories are sold.

Task 3.4

(a) (i) Information is relevant if it is capable of making a difference in the decisions made by users.

(ii) If financial information faithfully represents the economic phenomena that it purports to represent, it is

- Complete;
- Neutral; and
- Free from error.

(b) The four enhancing qualitative characteristics of useful financial information are:

- Comparability
- Verifiability
- Timeliness
- Understandability

Task 3.5

(a) The objective of general purpose financial reporting is to provide financial information about the reporting entity that is useful to existing and potential investors, lenders and other creditors in making decisions about providing resources to the entity.

(b) The introduction to the *Conceptual Framework* lists the following decisions that users may need to make, based on the information in general purpose financial statements prepared for external users:

- To decide when to buy, hold or sell an equity investment.

- To assess the stewardship or accountability of management.

- To assess the ability of the entity to pay and provide other benefits to its employees.

- To assess the security for amounts lent to the entity.

- To determine taxation policies.

- To determine distributable profits and dividends.

- To prepare and use national income statistics.

- To regulate the activities of entities.

Tutorial note: Candidates only needed to give THREE of the above.

Task 3.6

(a) **Accruals basis**

Accrual accounting shows the effects of transactions and other events and circumstances on a reporting entity's economic resources and claims in the periods in which those effects occur, even if the resulting cash receipts and payments occur in a different period.

This is important to users because information about an entity's economic resources and claims and changes in these during a period is more useful in assessing an entity's past and future performance than information based solely on cash receipts and payments during that period.

(b) **Cash flow basis**

Information about a reporting entity's cash flows shows users how the reporting entity obtains and spends cash, including information about its borrowing and repayment of debt, cash dividends paid to investors and other factors that may affect its liquidity or solvency. Cash flow information helps users to understand a reporting entity's operations and its financing and investing activities.

Information about a reporting entity's cash flows during a period also helps users to assess the entity's ability to generate cash in the future.

Task 3.7

(a) An asset is a current asset if:

- It is cash or a cash equivalent (a short term investment or deposit that can be easily converted into cash); or

- The entity expects to collect, sell or consume it within its normal operating cycle; or

- It is held primarily for trading and is expected to be realised (received) within twelve months after the reporting period.

(b) A liability is a current liability if:

- The entity expects to settle it in its normal operating cycle; or

- It is held primarily for trading and is due to be settled (paid) within twelve months after the reporting period.

Task 3.8

(a) Inventories

(i) Financial statements are prepared on an accruals basis. This means that costs are matched with the revenues to which they relate. In addition, IAS 2 *Inventories* states that the carrying amount of inventories is recognised as an expense in the period in which the related revenue is recognised. Closing inventories are therefore recognised as an asset in the statement of financial position and carried forward to the next period, when they will be sold and the revenue will be recognised.

(ii) Closing inventories are valued at the lower of cost and net realisable value.

(b) Impairment

(i) IAS 36 *Impairment of Assets* requires an impairment review to be carried out if there is any indication that an asset has become impaired. An asset is impaired if its carrying amount is greater than its recoverable amount. IAS 36 also states that certain assets should be reviewed for impairment annually, even if there is no indication of impairment. These assets are goodwill acquired in a business combination and intangible assets with indefinite lives.

(ii) When an asset is reviewed for impairment, its carrying amount is compared with its recoverable amount. Recoverable amount is the higher of fair value less costs of disposal and value in use.

Task 3.9

(a) A lease is classified as a finance lease if it is a lease that transfers substantially all the risks and rewards incidental to ownership of an asset to the lessee.

A lease is classified as an operating lease if it does not transfer substantially all the risks and rewards of ownership of an asset to the lessee.

(b) (i) If an entity leases an asset under a finance lease, it recognises the lease as an asset in the statement of financial position. It also recognises a liability for the outstanding lease payments. The asset and the liability are measured at the fair value of the leased asset, or the present value of the minimum lease payments (if this is lower).

(ii) If an entity leases an asset under an operating lease, the lease payments are charged to profit or loss on a straight line basis unless another systematic basis is more appropriate. The leased asset is not recognised in the statement of financial position.

(c) The first lease has a term (five years) which is for the major part of the useful life of the equipment (six years). The present value of the minimum lease payments is unknown, but from the information provided it is likely to amount to substantially all of the fair value of the leased asset (total lease payments of £25,000 compared with a fair value of £20,000). This indicates that the first lease should be classified as a finance lease.

The second lease is for only a small part of the total useful life of the equipment (two years out of seven). Again, the present value of the minimum lease payments is unknown, but total lease payments are £4,800 (£200 × 24) which is only just over 50% of the fair value of the item (the present value of the minimum lease payments would be less than £4,800). This indicates that the second lease is an operating lease.

Task 3.10

The treatment of the damages claim is governed by IAS 37 *Provisions, Contingent Liabilities and Contingent Assets*. According to IAS 37 a provision should be recognised when:

(a) An entity has a present obligation (legal or constructive) as a result of a past event.

(b) It is probable that a transfer of economic benefits will be required to settle the obligation.

(c) A reliable estimate can be made of the obligation.

For a provision to be recognised, the circumstances must meet each of these three criteria. In the case of the damages claim there is a present obligation (a) to pay damages. The lawyer has stated that this transfer of economic benefits is probable (b). In addition the amount of the claim has been estimated reliably (c) at £250,000, so a provision for this amount should be recognised in the financial statements.

Task 3.11

(a) IAS 37 *Provisions, Contingent Liabilities and Contingent Assets* states that a provision should be recognised when:

- An entity has a present obligation as a result of a past event. The obligation can be either legal or constructive; and

- It is probable that an outflow of resources embodying economic benefits will be required to settle the obligation; and

- A reliable estimate can be made of the amount of the obligation.

(b) Houghton Ltd has a constructive obligation to make the refunds because it has publicised its policy, leading its customers to expect that it will refund purchases. (The past obligating event is the sale of the product).

It is also probable that the company will actually have to make some refunds (an outflow of resources embodying economic benefits) in the next reporting period (refunds have already been claimed).

Although the precise amount of future claims is unknown it should be possible to make a reasonable estimate based on past experience. (IAS 37 explains that it is almost always possible to make a reliable estimate.)

Therefore Houghton Ltd should recognise a provision, based on its best estimate of the cost of refunds relating to goods sold in the last three months of the year.

(c) IAS 37 requires disclosure of the following information for each class of provision:

- The carrying amount at the beginning and end of the period
- Additional provisions made in the period
- Amounts used during the period
- Unused amounts reversed during the period

There should also be a narrative note giving:

- A brief description of the nature of the obligation and expected timing of any resulting transfers of economic benefit.

- An indication of the uncertainties about the amount or timing of those transfers of economic benefit.

Task 3.12

(a) Inventories are assets held by an entity that are for sale in the ordinary course of business.

IAS 2 *Inventories* requires inventories to be recognised in the financial statements at the lower of cost and net realisable value.

The cost of inventories should include the purchase price, import duties and other taxes, and transport, handling and other costs directly attributable to the acquisition of the finished goods. Essentially, all costs incurred in bringing the inventories to their present location and condition can be included.

(b) IAS 18 *Revenue* defines revenue as the 'gross inflows of economic benefits received and receivable by the entity on its own account'.

IAS 18 states that revenue should be measured at the 'fair value of the consideration received or receivable'.

Revenue from the sale of goods should be recognised when the following conditions have been satisfied:

(i) The entity has transferred to the buyer the significant risks and rewards of ownership of the goods

(ii) The entity retains neither continuing managerial involvement nor effective control over the goods sold

(iii) The amount of revenue can be measured reliably

(iv) It is probable that economic benefits associated with the transaction will flow to the entity and

(v) The costs incurred or to be incurred in respect of the transaction can be measured reliably.

Task 3.13

(a) IFRS 10 *Consolidated Financial Statements* explains that an entity that has an investment in another entity should determine whether it is a parent by assessing whether it controls that other entity.

IFRS 10 states that an investor controls an investee if and only if the investor has all the following:

- Power over the investee

- Exposure, or rights, to variable returns from its involvement with the investee; and

- The ability to use its power over the investee to affect the amount of the investor's returns.

An investor has power over an investee when it has existing rights that give it the current ability to direct its relevant activities (the activities that significantly affect its returns). The most common form of rights that give power are voting rights, where an investor holds more than half the voting rights in its investee. However, an investor may have other rights that give it power over its investee, even if it does not hold a majority of the voting rights. For example, it may have the right to appoint or remove the entity's board of directors, or other management personnel, or it may have legal or contractual rights to direct the entity's activities.

(b) IFRS 3 *Business Combinations* states that goodwill acquired in a business combination should be carried in the statement of financial position at cost less any impairment losses. The cost of goodwill is the difference between the cost of the investment and the fair value of the identifiable assets and liabilities acquired. Goodwill is not amortised, but must be reviewed for impairment annually. Therefore the directors of Lavendar cannot write off the goodwill on acquisition immediately.

Chapter 4

Task 4.1

1 and 4	
3 and 5	
2 and 3	
2 and 4	✓

Task 4.2

Not disclosed separately and treated as a distribution cost	
Disclosed as an extraordinary item	
Not disclosed separately and treated as an administrative expense	
Its nature and amount disclosed separately	✓

Task 4.3

True	
False	✓

A decrease in trade receivables means that less cash has been 'tied up' in working capital.

Task 4.4

1 only	
2 only	✓
Both 1 and 2	
Neither 1 nor 2	

Task 4.5

£888,000	
£897,000	
£955,000	✓
£1,005,000	

General overheads should not be included in the cost of an item of property, plant and equipment.

....

Task 4.6

£4,000	
£4,211	
£5,000	
£5,263	✓

£200,000 ÷ 38 = £5,263

....

Task 4.7

£9,143	
£11,429	
£12,800	✓
£18,286	

Carrying amount at 1 January 20X2	=	£80,000 – (2 × 8,000)
	=	£64,000
Remaining useful life at 1 January 20X2	=	7 – 2 years
	=	5 years
Depreciation charge y/e 31 December 20X2	=	$\dfrac{£64,000}{5}$
	=	£12,800

....

Task 4.8

£40,000	
£58,400	
£60,000	✓
£288,800	

	£
Carrying amount at 31 December 20X5	
£460,000 – (2 × £460,000/46 years)	440,000
Disposal proceeds	500,000
Profit on disposal	60,000

Task 4.9

True	
False	✓

IAS 38 *Intangible Assets* prohibits the recognition of internally generated goodwill.

Task 4.10

True	
False	✓

According to IAS 36 *Impairment of Assets*, an asset is impaired if its recoverable amount is lower than its carrying amount. An asset's recoverable amount is the higher of fair value less costs of disposal or value in use. This asset has a recoverable amount of £130,000, so it is not impaired and should continue to be measured at its carrying amount of £125,000.

Task 4.11

(i) only	
(ii) only	
(iii) only	
(iv) only	✓

IAS 36 states that an asset is impaired if its carrying amount exceeds its recoverable amount. Recoverable amount is the higher of fair value less costs of disposal and value in use.

....

Task 4.12

£1,400	
£1,475	
£1,500	✓
£1,600	

- The items sold are assumed to be the 25 units purchased on 1 June and 5 units purchased on 15 June.

- Therefore the items in inventory are 10 units purchased on 15 June.

- Net realisable value is lower than cost, so the value of inventories is: $10 \times 150 = £1,500$

....

Task 4.13

£32,400	✓
£34,000	
£34,100	
£34,600	

	£'000
Inventories	
Product I (Cost: FIFO)	11,300
Product II (NRV)	5,900
Product III (Cost: FIFO)	15,200
	32,400

Task 4.14

Tax expense (profit or loss)	Tax payable (statement of financial position)	
£124,000	£124,000	
£124,000	£129,000	✓
£129,000	£129,000	
£134,000	£129,000	

	£
Expense for current year	129,000
Less adjustment in respect of prior period	(5,000)
Tax expense in profit or loss	124,000
Tax payable (liability)	129,000

....

Task 4.15

£750	
£500	
£900	✓
£1,000	

$^3/_{10} \times £3,000 = £900$

....

Task 4.16

£750	
£500	
£900	
£1,000	✓

$^2/_6 \times £3,000 = £1,000$

....

Task 4.17

£7,000	✓
£8,000	
£10,000	
£11,000	

	£
Deposit	30,000
Instalments (8 × £20,000)	160,000
	190,000
Fair value	154,000
Interest	36,000

Sum-of-the-digits = $\dfrac{8 \times 9}{2}$ = 36

6 months to	June X1	$^8/_{36}$ × £36,000		
	Dec X1	$^7/_{36}$ × £36,000		
	June X2	$^6/_{36}$ × £36,000		
	Dec X2	$^5/_{36}$ × £36,000		
	June X3	$^4/_{36}$ × £36,000	=	£4,000
	Dec X3	$^3/_{36}$ × £36,000	=	£3,000
				£7,000

Task 4.18

Current liability	Non-current liability	
£25,908	£35,967	
£51,605	£35,812	
£15,908	£35,967	✓
£35,908	£15,397	

	£
Cost 1.1.X4	80,000
Interest 7.93%	6,344
Instalment	(20,000)
Balance 31.12.X4	66,344
Interest 7.93%	5,261
Instalment	(20,000)
Balance 31.12.X5	51,605
Interest 7.93%	4,092
Instalment	(20,000)
Balance 31.12.X6	35,697
Current liability (51,605 – 35,697) =	15,908
Non-current liability	35,697
Total balance at 31.12.X5	51,605

Task 4.19

£931	
£2,000	
£963	
£1,069	✓

Working

		Capital £		Interest £	Cash (memo) £
1.1.X	Asset	10,000			
1.1.X1	Deposit	(575)			
		9,425			
1.1.X1 – 31.12.X1	Interest		× 11% =	1,037	
31.12.X1	Instalment 1	(963)		(1,037)	2,000
Balance at 31.12.X1		8,462			
1.1.X2 – 31.12.X2	Interest		× 11% =	931	
31.12.X2	Instalment 2	(1,069)		(931)	2,000
Balance at 31.12.X2		7,393			

Task 4.20

£7,400	
£9,110	✓
£10,250	
£13,110	

Using the actuarial method, the liability at 31 December 20X1 is:

	£
Fair value	15,400
Less deposit	(4,000)
	11,400
Interest (11,400 × 15%)	1,710
Payment 31 December 20X1	(4,000)
	9,110

Task 4.21

£6,120	
£9,120	✓
£9,600	
£25,000	

Finance charge of £9,120 (76,000 × 12%)

Task 4.22

Legal action 1	Legal action 2	
Disclose in a note to the financial statements	No disclosure	
Recognise a provision	No disclosure	
Recognise a provision	Disclose in a note to the financial statements	✓
Recognise a provision	Recognise the income	

Task 4.23

A	Destruction of a major non-current asset	
B	Discovery of error or fraud	✓
C	Issue of shares	
D	Purchases of a major non-current asset	

Task 4.24

(i) only	
(ii) only	✓
Both	
Neither of them	

Task 4.25

True	✓
False	

Usk Ltd has not yet transferred the significant risks and rewards of ownership of the goods and cannot recognise revenue (IAS 18 *Revenue*).

Task 4.26

True	✓
False	

Hawes Ltd is an associate of Wensley plc.

Task 4.27

An associate	
A parent	
A simple investment	
A subsidiary	✓

Erewash Ltd **controls** Amber Ltd. An investor controls an investee when it is exposed, or has rights, to variable returns from its involvement with the investee and has the ability to affect those returns through its power over the investee (IFRS 10).

Task 4.28

Elements (i), (ii) and (iii) only	
Elements (ii), (iii) and (iv) only	
Elements (i), (ii) and (iv) only	
All of the above	✓

Task 4.29

£144,000	
£150,000	
£156,000	✓
£160,000	

	£
Consolidated cost of sales	200,000
Less intra-group sales	(50,000)
Unrealised profit (50,000 – 40,000 × 60%)	6,000
	156,000

Chapter 5

Task 5.1

Consolidated statement of financial position as at 31 December 20X1

	£'000
Assets	
Goodwill (W)	20
Property, plant and equipment (800 + 400)	1,200
Current assets (170 + 130)	300
	1,520
Equity and liabilities	
Share capital	800
Retained earnings (W)	450
	1,250
Non-controlling interest (W)	120
	1,370
Current liabilities (100 + 50)	150
	1,520

Workings

Goodwill	£'000
Price paid	350
Share capital – attributable to X plc (75% × 200)	(150)
Retained earnings – attributable to X plc (75% × 240)	(180)
	20

Retained earnings	£'000
X plc	420
Y Ltd – attributable to X plc (75% × (280 – 240))	30
	450

Non-controlling interest (NCI)	£'000
Share capital – attributable to NCI (25% × 200)	50
Retained earnings – attributable to NCI (25% × 280)	70
	120

Task 5.2

(a) **Goodwill**

£	594,000

	£'000	£'000
Price paid		3,510
Share capital – attributable to parent (60% × 2,000)	1,200	
Share premium – attributable to parent (60% × 1,000)	600	
Retained earnings – attributable to parent (60% × 1,350)	810	
Fair value adjustment – attributable to parent (60% × 400)	240	
		(2,850)
		660
Less impairment		(66)
		594

Working

Group structure

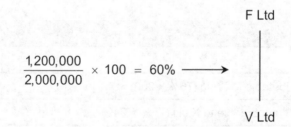

$$\frac{1,200,000}{2,000,000} \times 100 = 60\%$$

F Ltd

V Ltd

(b) **Non-controlling interest**

£	2,068,000

	£'000
Share capital – attributable to NCI (40% × 2,000)	800
Share premium – attributable to NCI (40% × 1,000)	400
Retained earnings – attributable to NCI (40% × 1,770)	708
Fair value adjustment – attributable to NCI (40% × 400)	160
	2,068

(c) **Consolidated retained earnings reserve**

£	5,796,000

	£'000	£'000
Fertwrangler Ltd		5,610
Voncarryon Ltd:		
At 31 March 20X3	1,770	
At acquisition	(1,350)	
	420	
Attributable to parent (60%)		252
Impairment of goodwill		(66)
		5,796

. . . .

Task 5.3

(a)

£	1,800,000

Goodwill relating to the acquisition of Clive Ltd at 31 March 20X5

	£'000	£'000
Price paid		25,160
Share capital – attributable to parent (60% × 20,000)	12,000	
Share premium – attributable to parent (60% × 5,000)	3,000	
Retained earnings – attributable to parent (60% × 10,600)	6,360	
Fair value adjustment – attributable to parent (60% × 3,000)	1,800	
		(23,160)
		2,000
Less impairment		(200)
		1,800

(b)

£	5,200,000

Investment in associate

	£'000
Cost	5,000
Bell plc's share of post-acquisition profit (25% × 1,000)	250
Less goodwill written off (W)	(50)
	5,200

Alternative calculation (proof)

	£'000
Bell plc's share of net assets at year end (25% × 19,000)	4,750
Add goodwill (W)	450
	5,200

Working: Goodwill

	£'000
Cost of investment/price paid	5,000
Share capital – attributable to Bell plc (25% × 10,000)	(2,500)
Retained earnings – attributable to Bell plc (25% × 8,000)	(2,000)
	500
Less impairment loss	(50)
	450

(c) IAS 28 *Investments in Associates and Joint Ventures* defines an associate as an investment over which the investor has significant influence. Significant influence is the power to participate in the financial and operating policy decisions of the investee but is not control or joint control of those policies.

Task 5.4

Dumyat plc

Consolidated statement of financial position as at 31 October 20X7

	£'000
Assets	
Non-current assets:	
Goodwill (W)	2,711
Property, plant and equipment (65,388 + 31,887 + 3,000)	100,275
	102,986
Current assets:	
Inventories (28,273 + 5,566)	33,839
Trade and other receivables (11,508 + 5,154)	16,662
Cash and cash equivalents (2,146 + 68)	2,214
	52,715
Total assets	155,701
Equity and liabilities	
Equity	
Share capital	25,000
Share premium	12,000
Retained earnings (W)	59,401
	96,401
Non-controlling interest (W)	9,023
Total equity	105,424
Non-current liabilities:	
Long-term loans (25,000 + 4,000)	29,000
Current liabilities:	
Trade and other payables (13,554 + 1,475)	15,029
Tax payable (6,140 + 108)	6,248
	21,277
Total liabilities	50,277
Total equity and liabilities	155,701

Workings

Note: **Group structure**

Dumyat plc owns 75% of Devon Ltd (9,000,000/12,000,000).

Goodwill	£'000
Price paid	26,000
Share capital – attributable to Dumyat plc (75% × 12,000)	(9,000)
Share premium – attributable to Dumyat plc (75% × 4,000)	(3,000)
Retained earnings – attributable to Dumyat plc (75% × 12,052)	(9,039)
Revaluation reserve – attributable to Dumyat plc (75% × 3,000)	(2,250)
	2,711

Retained earnings	£'000
Dumyat plc	55,621
Devon Ltd – attributable to Dumyat plc (75% × (17,092 – 12,052))	3,780
	59,401

Non-controlling interest (NCI)	£'000
Share capital – attributable to NCI (25% × 12,000)	3,000
Share premium – attributable to NCI (25% × 4,000)	1,000
Retained earnings – attributable to NCI (25% × 17,092)	4,273
Revaluation reserve – attributable to NCI (25% × 3,000)	750
	9,023

Task 5.5

Tolsta plc

Consolidated statement of financial position as at 31 October 20X8

	£'000
Assets	
Non-current assets:	
Intangible assets: goodwill (W)	8,400
Property, plant and equipment (47,875 + 31,913 + 4,500)	84,288
	92,688
Current assets:	
Inventories	30,509
Trade and other receivables (14,343 + 3,656 – 2,000)	15,999
Cash and cash equivalents	2,003
	48,511
Total assets	141,199
Equity and liabilities	
Equity	
Share capital	45,000
Share premium	12,000
Retained earnings (W)	25,120
	82,120
Non-controlling interest (W)	11,280
Total equity	93,400
Non-current liabilities:	
Long-term loan	27,000
Current liabilities:	
Trade and other payables (14,454 + 3,685 – 2,000)	16,139
Tax liabilities	4,660
	20,799
Total liabilities	47,799
Total equity and liabilities	141,199

Workings

Note: **Group structure**

Tolsta plc owns 2/3 of Balallan Ltd (8,000,000/12,000,000).

Goodwill	£'000
Price paid	32,000
Share capital – attributable to Tolsta plc (2/3 × 12,000)	(8,000)
Share premium – attributable to Tolsta plc (2/3 × 6,000)	(4,000)
Retained earnings – attributable to Tolsta plc (2/3 × 9,750)	(6,500)
Revaluation reserve – attributable to Tolsta plc (2/3 × 4,500)	(3,000)
Impairment	(2,100)
	8,400

Retained earnings	£'000
Tolsta plc	26,160
Balallan Ltd – attributable to Tolsta plc (2/3% × (11,340 – 9,750))	1,060
Impairment	(2,100)
	25,120

Non-controlling interest (NCI)	£'000
Share capital – attributable to NCI (1/3 × 12,000)	4,000
Share premium – attributable to NCI (1/3 × 6,000)	2,000
Retained earnings – attributable to NCI (1/3 × 11,340)	3,780
Revaluation reserve – attributable to NCI (1/3 × 4,500)	1,500
	11,280

Task 5.6

Ard plc

Consolidated statement of financial position as at 31 March 20X9

	£'000
Assets	
Non-current assets:	
Intangible assets: goodwill (W)	4,816
Property, plant and equipment	72,690
Current assets (32,782 + 10,835 – 3,000)	40,617
Total assets	118,123
Equity and liabilities	
Equity	
Share capital	50,000
Retained earnings (W)	21,186
Non-controlling interest (W)	11,896
Total equity	83,082
Non-current liabilities	18,000
Current liabilities (15,466 + 4,575 – 3,000)	17,041
Total liabilities	35,041
Total equity and liabilities	118,123

Workings

Note: **Group structure**

Ard plc owns 60% of Ledi Ltd (12,000,000/20,000,000).

Goodwill	£'000
Price paid	23,000
Share capital – attributable to Ard plc (60% × 20,000)	(12,000)
Retained earnings – attributable to Ard plc (60% × 7,640)	(4,584)
Impairment	(1,600)
	4,816

Retained earnings	£'000
Ard plc	21,526
Ledi Ltd – attributable to Ard plc (60% × (9,740 – 7,640))	1,260
Impairment	(1,600)
	21,186

Non-controlling interest (NCI)	£'000
Share capital – attributable to NCI (40% × 20,000)	8,000
Retained earnings – attributable to NCI (40% × 9,740)	3,896
	11,896

Task 5.7

Glebe plc

Consolidated statement of financial position as at 31 March 20X1

	£'000
Assets	
Non-current assets:	
Intangible assets: goodwill (W)	842
Property, plant and equipment (36,890 + 25,600 + 2,400)	64,890
Current assets:	30,199
Total assets	95,931
Equity and liabilities	
Equity	
Share capital	40,000
Retained earnings (W)	15,426
Non-controlling interest (W)	8,715
Total equity	64,141
Non-current liabilities:	18,000
Current liabilities:	13,790
Total liabilities	31,790
Total equity and liabilities	95,931

Workings

Goodwill	£'000
Price paid	18,000
Share capital – attributable to Glebe plc (70% × 10,000)	(7,000)
Retained earnings – attributable to Glebe plc (70% × 11,540)	(8,078)
Revaluation reserve – attributable to Glebe plc (70% × 2,400)	(1,680)
Impairment	(400)
	842

Retained earnings	£'000
Glebe plc	12,249
Starks Ltd – attributable to Glebe plc (70% × (16,650 – 11,540))	3,577
Impairment	(400)
	15,426

Non-controlling interest (NCI)	£'000
Share capital – attributable to NCI (30% × 10,000)	3,000
Retained earnings – attributable to NCI (30% × 16,650)	4,995
Revaluation reserve – attributable to NCI (30% × 2,400)	720
	8,715

Chapter 6

Task 6.1

Consolidated statement of profit or loss for the year ended 31 March 20X2

	£'000
Continuing operations	
Revenue	6,810
Cost of sales	4,020
Gross profit	2,790
Other income	0
Operating expenses	1,300
Profit before tax	1,490
Tax	420
Profit for the period from continuing operations	1,070
Attributable to:	
Equity holders of the parent	968
Non-controlling interests (30% × 340)	102
	1,070

Task 6.2

Consolidated statement of profit or loss for the year ended 31 December 20X1

	£'000
Continuing operations	
Revenue (W)	48,300
Cost of sales (W)	30,500
Gross profit	17,800
Other income	0
Operating expenses	10,600
Profit before tax	7,200
Tax	2,200
Profit for the period from continuing operations	5,000
Attributable to:	
Equity holders of the parent	4,320
Non-controlling interests (1,700 × 40%)	680
	5,000

Working

Revenue	£'000
C plc	38,600
D Ltd	14,700
Total inter-company adjustment	(5,000)
	48,300

Cost of sales	£'000
C plc	25,000
D Ltd	9,500
Total inter-company adjustment (5,000 – 1,000 unrealised profit)	(4,000)
	30,500

Task 6.3

Aswall plc

Consolidated statement of profit or loss for the year ended 31 March 20X4

	£'000
Continuing operations	
Revenue (W)	43,515
Cost of sales (W)	(18,968)
Gross profit	24,547
Other income	0
Distribution costs	(6,756)
Administrative expenses	(4,008)
Profit from operations	13,783
Finance costs	(2,940)
Profit before tax	10,843
Tax	(3,686)
Profit for the period from continuing operations	7,157
Attributable to:	
Equity holders of the parent	6,523
Non-controlling interest (W)	634
	7,157

Workings

Revenue	£'000
Aswall plc	32,412
Unsafey Ltd	12,963
Total inter-company adjustment	(1,860)
	43,515

Cost of sales	£'000
Aswall plc	14,592
Unsafey Ltd	5,576
Total inter-company adjustment (1,860 – 660 unrealised profit)	(1,200)
	18,968

Non-controlling interest (NCI)	£'000
Profit for the period attributable to NCI (25% × 3,196)	799
Unrealised profit attributable to NCI (25% × 660)	(165)
	634

Task 6.4

Danube plc

Consolidated statement of profit or loss for the year ended 31 March 20X2

	£'000
Continuing operations	
Revenue	20,200
Cost of sales	(10,500)
Gross profit	9,700
Other income	0
Operating expenses	(4,530)
Profit from operations	5,170

Workings

Revenue	£'000
Danube plc	15,800
Inn Ltd	5,400
Total inter-company adjustment	(1,000)
	20,200

Cost of sales	£'000
Danube plc	8,500
Inn Ltd	2,800
Total inter-company adjustment (1,000 – 200)	(800)
	10,500

Task 6.5

Wewill plc

Consolidated statement of profit or loss for the year ended 31 March 20X4

	£'000
Continuing operations	
Revenue (W)	49,600
Cost of sales (W)	(25,955)
Gross profit	23,645
Other income	0
Distribution costs	(9,910)
Administrative expenses	(5,902)
Profit from operations	7,833
Finance costs	(829)
Profit before tax	7,004
Tax	(1,913)
Profit for the period from continuing operations	5,091
Attributable to:	
Equity holders of the parent	4,729
Non-controlling interest (20% × 1,810)	362
	5,091

Workings

Revenue	£'000
Wewill plc	36,400
Rokyu Ltd	14,600
Total inter-company adjustment	(1,400)
	49,600

Cost of sales	£'000
Wewill plc	20,020
Rokyu Ltd	6,935
Total inter-company adjustment (1,400 – 400)	(1,000)
	25,955

Chapter 7

Task 7.1

(a)	Gross profit percentage $\dfrac{522}{989} \times 100$	52.8	%
(b)	Operating profit percentage $\dfrac{214}{989} \times 100$	21.6	%
(c)	Return on capital employed $\dfrac{214}{1,400} \times 100$	15.3	%
(d)	Asset turnover (net assets) $\dfrac{989}{1,400}$	0.7	times
(e)	Interest cover $\dfrac{214}{34}$	6.3	times
(f)	Gearing $\dfrac{400}{1,400} \times 100$	28.6	%

Task 7.2

(a)	Current ratio $\dfrac{58,600 + 98,400}{86,200 + 6,300}$	1.7	:1
(b)	Quick (acid test) ratio $\dfrac{98,400}{86,200 + 6,300}$	1.1	:1
(c)	Trade receivables collection period $\dfrac{98,400}{772,400} \times 365$	46.5	days
(d)	Inventory turnover $\dfrac{507,400}{58,600}$	8.7	times
(e)	Inventory holding period $\dfrac{58,600}{507,400} \times 365$	42.1	days
(f)	Trade payables payment period $\dfrac{86,200}{507,400} \times 365$	62.0	days

Task 7.3

(a) Formulae

(i)	Return on capital employed	$\dfrac{\text{Profit from operations}}{\text{Total equity + Non-current liabilities}} \times 100\%$
(ii)	Operating profit percentage	$\dfrac{\text{Profit from operations}}{\text{Revenue}} \times 100\%$
(iii)	Gross profit percentage	$\dfrac{\text{Gross profit}}{\text{Revenue}} \times 100\%$
(iv)	Asset turnover (net assets)	$\dfrac{\text{Revenue}}{\text{Total assets} - \text{Current liabilities}}$
(v)	Gearing	$\dfrac{\text{Non-current liabilities}}{\text{Total equity + Non-current liabilities}} \times 100\%$
(vi)	Interest cover	$\dfrac{\text{Profit from operations}}{\text{Finance costs}}$

(b) Calculations

(i)	Return on capital employed	$\dfrac{2,189}{17,541} \times 100$	12.5	%
(ii)	Operating profit percentage	$\dfrac{2,189}{8,420} \times 100$	26.0	%
(iii)	Gross profit percentage	$\dfrac{4,884}{8,420} \times 100$	58.0	%
(iv)	Asset turnover (net assets)	$\dfrac{8,420}{17,541}$	0.5	times
(v)	Gearing	$\dfrac{5,000}{17,541} \times 100$	28.5	%
(vi)	Interest cover	$\dfrac{2,189}{400}$	5.5	%

Task 7.4

(a) Formulae

(i)	Gross profit percentage	$\dfrac{\text{Gross profit}}{\text{Revenue}} \times 100\%$
(ii)	Operating profit percentage	$\dfrac{\text{Profit from operations}}{\text{Revenue}} \times 100\%$
(iii)	Current ratio	$\dfrac{\text{Current assets}}{\text{Current liabilities}}$
(iv)	Quick (acid test) ratio	$\dfrac{\text{Current assets} - \text{Inventories}}{\text{Current liabilities}}$
(v)	Inventory holding period	$\dfrac{\text{Inventories}}{\text{Cost of sales}} \times 365$
(vi)	Trade receivables collection period	$\dfrac{\text{Trade receivables}}{\text{Revenue}} \times 365$

(b) Calculations

(i)	Gross profit percentage $\dfrac{11{,}595}{21{,}473} \times 100$	54.0	%
(ii)	Operating profit percentage $\dfrac{4{,}080}{21{,}473} \times 100$	19.0	%
(iii)	Current ratio $\dfrac{4{,}875}{2{,}093}$	2.3	:1
(iv)	Quick (acid test) ratio $\dfrac{4{,}875 - 1{,}813}{2{,}093}$	1.5	:1
(v)	Inventory holding period $\dfrac{1{,}813}{9{,}878} \times 365$	67.0	days
(vi)	Trade receivables collection period $\dfrac{3{,}000}{21{,}473} \times 365$	51.0	days

Task 7.5

(a) Formulae

(i)	Operating expenses/revenue percentage	$\dfrac{\text{Dist. costs + Admin. expenses}}{\text{Revenue}} \times 100\%$
(ii)	Current ratio	$\dfrac{\text{Current assets}}{\text{Current liabilities}}$
(iii)	Quick (acid test) ratio	$\dfrac{\text{Current assets } - \text{ Inventories}}{\text{Current liabilities}}$
(iv)	Gearing ratio	$\dfrac{\text{Non-current liabilities}}{\text{Total equity + Non-current liabilities}} \times 100\%$
(v)	Interest cover	$\dfrac{\text{Profit from operations}}{\text{Finance costs}}$

(b) Calculations

(i)	Operating expenses/Revenue percentage $\dfrac{4,841+3,007}{20,562} \times 100$	38.2	%
(ii)	Current ratio $\dfrac{6,337}{2,906}$	2.2	:1
(iii)	Quick (acid test) ratio $\dfrac{2,325}{2,906}$	0.8	:1
(iv)	Gearing ratio $\dfrac{14,000}{27,413}$	51.1	%
(v)	Interest cover $\dfrac{1,405}{800}$	1.8	times

Task 7.6

(a) Formulae

(i)	Return on shareholders' funds	$\dfrac{\text{Profit after tax}}{\text{Total equity}} \times 100\%$
(ii)	Inventory holding period	$\dfrac{\text{Inventories}}{\text{Cost of sales}} \times 365$
(iii)	Trade receivables collection period	$\dfrac{\text{Trade receivables}}{\text{Revenue}} \times 365$
(iv)	Trade payables payment period	$\dfrac{\text{Trade payables}}{\text{Cost of sales}} \times 365$
(v)	Working capital cycle	Inventory days + Receivable days – Payable days
(vi)	Asset turnover (non-current assets)	$\dfrac{\text{Revenue}}{\text{Non-current assets}}$

(b) Calculations

(i)	Return on shareholders' funds $\dfrac{363}{6,241} \times 100$	5.8	%
(ii)	Inventory holding period $\dfrac{649}{2,597} \times 365$	91.2	days
(iii)	Trade receivables collection period $\dfrac{392}{4,900} \times 365$	29.2	days
(iv)	Trade payables payment period $\dfrac{286}{2,597} \times 365$	40.2	days
(v)	Working capital cycle 91.2 + 29.2 – 40.2	80.2	days
(vi)	Asset turnover (non-current assets) $\dfrac{4,900}{8,041}$	0.6	times

Task 7.7

(a) Formulae

(i)	Gearing	$\dfrac{\text{Non-current liabilities}}{\text{Total equity + Non-current liabilities}} \times 100\%$
(ii)	Interest cover	$\dfrac{\text{Profit from operations}}{\text{Finance costs}}$
(iii)	Current ratio	$\dfrac{\text{Current assets}}{\text{Current liabilities}}$
(iv)	Trade receivables collection period	$\dfrac{\text{Trade receivables}}{\text{Revenue}} \times 365$
(v)	Trade payables payment period	$\dfrac{\text{Trade payables}}{\text{Cost of sales}} \times 365$

(b) Calculations

(i)	Gearing $\dfrac{12,000}{13,537+12,000} \times 100$	47.0	%
(ii)	Interest cover $\dfrac{2,780}{840}$	3.3	times
(iii)	Current ratio $\dfrac{5,207}{2,686}$	1.9	:1
(iv)	Trade receivables collection period $\dfrac{1,946}{27,800} \times 365$	25.6	days
(v)	Trade payables payment period $\dfrac{1,276}{14,178} \times 365$	32.8	days

Task 7.8

(a) Formulae used to calculate the ratios

(i)	Gross profit percentage	$\dfrac{\text{Gross profit}}{\text{Revenue}} \times 100\%$
(ii)	Operating profit percentage	$\dfrac{\text{Profit from operations}}{\text{Revenue}} \times 100\%$
(iii)	Return on shareholders' funds	$\dfrac{\text{Profit after tax}}{\text{Total equity}} \times 100\%$
(iv)	Quick (acid test) ratio	$\dfrac{\text{Current assets} - \text{Inventories}}{\text{Current liabilities}}$
(v)	Operating expenses/revenue percentage	$\dfrac{\text{Dist. costs} + \text{Admin. expenses}}{\text{Revenue}} \times 100\%$

(b) Calculation of the ratios

(i)	Gross profit percentage $\dfrac{16,200}{36,000} \times 100$	45.0	%
(ii)	Operating profit percentage $\dfrac{3,240}{36,000} \times 100$	9.0	%
(iii)	Return on shareholders' funds $\dfrac{866}{26,155} \times 100$	3.3	%
(iv)	Quick (acid test) ratio $\dfrac{7,123 - 2,376}{3,876}$	1.2	:1
(v)	Operating expenses/revenue percentage $\dfrac{6,840 + 6,120}{36,000} \times 100$	36.0	%

Answer bank

Chapter 8

Note. Based on the information available at the time this book was written, we anticipate that the tasks in this section would be human marked in the real assessment.

Task 8.1

(a) Rigby Ltd is operating on a high gross profit percentage, relatively high operating profit percentage but a fairly low asset turnover. This indicates a low volume, high margin type of business. The ROCE is the same as that of Rialto Ltd but Rialto Ltd has low gross and operating profit percentages but high asset turnover indicating a high volume, low margin business.

In terms of working capital Rialto Ltd has a reasonable current ratio but low quick ratio indicating fairly large inventory levels although with inventory turnover of 10.3 times this inventory is being turned over much more rapidly than in Rigby Ltd. Rialto Ltd has virtually no receivables and both companies take a reasonable amount of credit from suppliers.

Rialto Ltd is more highly geared than Rigby Ltd but with interest cover of 5 times this would not appear to be a major problem.

(b) From the ratios given it would appear that Rigby Ltd is the jeweller with relatively low revenue, high profit margins and slower inventory turnover. Rialto Ltd with higher, low margin revenue and almost no receivables would appear to be the supermarket.

••

Task 8.2

REPORT

To: **Duncan Tweedy**

From: **A Technician**

Date: **October 20X3**

Subject: **Comparison of profitability of Byrne Ltd and May Ltd**

The purpose of this report is to assess the relative profitability of the two companies, Byrne Ltd and May Ltd, in order to determine which company is likely to be the better investment. This will be done by using a number of key financial ratios in order to assess the performance of each company.

(a) **Comparative profitability**

May Ltd's return on capital is significantly higher than that of Byrne Ltd. The return on capital employed for May Ltd shows that the overall return for all the providers of capital (shareholders and long term lenders) is 32.1% compared to only 21.5% for the providers of capital in Byrne Ltd. Therefore from a potential shareholder's viewpoint May provides a better overall return.

May Ltd's gross profit percentage and operating profit percentage are both also significantly higher than those of Byrne Ltd. This indicates that both May's profit after cost of sales from trading activities and its overall profit after deducting other operating expenses are a higher proportion of its sales revenue than those of Byrne Ltd. For each £1 of sales made during the reported period, May is generating more profit.

(b) **Conclusion**

The profitability ratios show us that May Ltd is using its capital base more efficiently and making more profit from each £1 of sales than Byrne Ltd. May Ltd is definitely the more profitable company (in relative terms).

Task 8.3

Notes for meeting

(a) **Comments on the changes in the ratios**

Current ratio

This seems to show that the company is in a very healthy position; the ratio has improved during the year. The company's current liabilities are covered almost three times by its current assets. Most people would regard this as more than adequate.

However, a very high current ratio can also mean that working capital is not being managed very efficiently and this is borne out by the other ratios.

Quick ratio

This has deteriorated from a satisfactory 1.1 to a slightly worrying 0.6 over the year. The fact that the fall has been so sharp is probably a cause for concern.

The fall in the quick ratio suggests that the improvement in the current ratio is mainly due to an increase in inventory levels. In addition, the high current ratio coupled with the relatively low quick ratio suggests that most of the company's current assets are in the form of inventory. These factors indicate that the company may be carrying too much inventory, which means that cash is being 'tied up' unnecessarily.

Trade receivables collection period

This has risen from 32 days to 48 days during the year, which means that customers are taking longer to pay. If sales have remained at a constant level during the year, this suggests that there may be credit control problems (customers being granted too much credit or staff failing to chase debts).

The ratio should be interpreted with caution. It is possible that this apparent increase in the collection period is due to increased sales towards the year end (as receivables at the year end would be high in relation to revenue for the year).

Trade payables payment period

This has fallen slightly during the year. If the ratio is considered in isolation there does not appear to be cause for concern (most suppliers grant a credit period of around 30 days and so 27 days appears reasonable).

However, note that at the end of the year the time taken to collect receivables is considerably longer than the time taken to pay suppliers (at the start of the year the payment period and the collection period were about the same). This may reflect poor management and could lead to cash flow problems.

Inventory holding period

This has risen significantly during the year. This increase appears to confirm what was suggested by the movements in the current ratio and quick ratio: inventory levels are very high and rising and the company is probably carrying too much inventory. Given that the quick ratio has fallen during the year, this situation may lead to cash flow problems.

The increase in inventory may not necessarily be a result of poor management. For example, the company may have received several big orders shortly before the year end and management may have deliberately purchased extra inventories in order to meet them.

(b) **Conclusion**

The overall picture given by these five ratios seems to suggest poor working capital management. The apparent increase in the level of inventory is a particular cause for concern and the company also appears to be having problems in collecting cash from customers.

Task 8.4

Sender's address

Ms Madge Keygone

Address

December 20X4

Dear Ms Keygone,

Asbee Ltd

As requested, I am writing to explain the significance of the ratios mentioned by the shareholder in your recent meeting.

(a) **Comparison with industry averages**

- The current ratio for Asbee Ltd is higher than the industry average, which suggests that the company has more current assets in relation to its current liabilities than is normal for the industry. On the face of it, this is a good sign as it indicates that Asbee Ltd has better liquidity than other companies in the same industry. On the other hand, the low quick ratio (see below) suggests that the company's current assets may largely consist of inventories and receivables, which are often difficult to convert into cash quickly. This could mean that Asbee Ltd may not be able to meet its current liabilities as they fall due and that therefore it is in a worse position than other similar companies.

- The quick ratio is slightly lower than the industry average. This suggests that Asbee Ltd has less cash and receivables in relation to its current liabilities than other companies in the industry. This means that the company's liquidity position appears to be worse than that of the rest of the industry. Asbee Ltd may have very little or no actual cash, with all or most of its quick assets made up of trade receivables.

- The inventory holding period is almost twice as long as the industry average and indicates that other companies in the industry sell inventory almost twice as quickly as Asbee Ltd. This is almost certainly one of the reasons why the current ratio is high compared to other companies. The current ratio and the inventories holding period taken together suggest that inventory levels are abnormally high. There are a number of possible reasons for this: a large number of old or obsolete items which should be written down to net realisable value; or lack of control over inventories.

- The trade receivables collection period is also longer than the industry average, suggesting that Asbee Ltd takes longer to collect amounts receivable from customers than other companies in the industry. This indicates that there are problems with the management of receivables. These may include poor credit control, failure to chase overdue amounts or an increase in the level of irrecoverable debts.

(b) **Conclusion**

The low quick ratio is probably the main reason why the shareholder is concerned. As stated above, Asbee Ltd's true liquidity could be rather worse than the quick ratio suggests. If the company has a bank overdraft rather than a positive cash balance, this would be worrying.

The shareholder is also probably concerned that too much cash has been absorbed by inventories. In addition he or she may believe that there are inventory control problems that are not being addressed.

In combination with the low quick ratio the receivables collection period suggests that the company has potential liquidity problems. Its liquidity appears to be worse than that of the rest of the industry and the shareholder will view this as a cause for concern.

I hope that this explanation has been helpful. Please do not hesitate to contact me if you have any further queries or if you require any further explanations.

Yours sincerely,

Task 8.5

REPORT

To: **Leopold Scratchy**

From: **Accounting Technician**

Subject: **Financial statements of Partridge Ltd and Carington Ltd**

Date: **June 20X5**

As requested, I have considered the risk and return of two potential investments. My analysis is based on the latest financial statements of the two companies. I have calculated four key ratios for each of the two companies.

(a) **The relative risk and return of the two companies**

Gross profit percentage

The two companies have approximately the same gross profit percentage and therefore equally profitable trading operations. A gross profit percentage of 59% appears to be reasonably healthy.

Operating profit percentage

Partridge Ltd has a much higher operating profit percentage than Carington Ltd which means that it is the more profitable of the two companies overall. As both companies have the same gross profit percentage, this indicates that Carington Ltd has higher operating expenses relative to its sales than Partridge Ltd.

Return on shareholders' funds

The return on the shareholders' funds of Partridge Ltd is considerably higher than that of Carington Ltd. This shows that Partridge Ltd would provide a much higher return to an investor relative to its total equity (capital 'owned' by equity shareholders) than Carington Ltd.

Gearing

Partridge Ltd has a high gearing ratio while Carington Ltd has a very low gearing ratio. This shows that Partridge Ltd is financed by loans (borrowings) as well as by equity capital (ordinary shares) and that loans make up quite a high percentage of its total capital employed. This contrasts with Carington Ltd, which has almost no loan finance. Partridge Ltd is a riskier investment than Carington Ltd. Interest on its loans must be paid regardless of the level of profit and this reduces the amount available for distribution to ordinary shareholders. This means that in a poor year, dividends to ordinary shareholders may be reduced or there may be no dividend at all.

(b) **Conclusion**

On the basis of the ratios calculated, an investment in Partridge Ltd would provide you with a much better return on the amount that you invest than an investment in Carington Ltd, assuming both companies maintain their current levels of profitability.

However, Partridge Ltd is much more highly geared than Carington Ltd and so Carington Ltd would be the safer investment of the two. Both companies are profitable, and while Carington Ltd appears to be less profitable overall, its return on shareholders' funds still appears to be acceptable. You may need to decide on the level of risk that you are prepared to accept, relative to the return on your investment.

I hope that these comments are helpful. Please do not hesitate to contact me if you need any further assistance.

Task 8.6

REPORT

To: Peter Stewart

From: Accounting Technician

Subject: Review of financial statements of Hillhead Ltd

Date: DD/MM/YY

As requested, I have analysed the efficiency and effectiveness of the management of Hillhead Ltd, based on four key ratios.

(a) **The relative performance of the company for the past two years**

Gross profit percentage

The gross profit margin has fallen. This means that on average the business is making less gross profit for each sale made. There could be many reasons for this fall in gross profit margin, for example, raw material prices may have increased and Hillhead Ltd has been unable to pass on these price increases to customers. Alternatively, the increase in sales suggests that management may have cut prices to try and attract new customers.

Operating profit percentage

The operating profit percentage has improved. As sales have risen and the gross profit percentage has fallen, the increase in the operating profit percentage must be as a result of lower overhead costs. Hillhead Ltd has obviously had strong control of costs during the year.

Inventory holding period

Hillhead Ltd's inventory holding period has worsened significantly. The company is taking longer to convert its inventory into cash by selling it. This suggests that it has been less efficient in managing inventory in the current year.

Trade receivables collection period

The trade receivables collection period has also worsened significantly. It could be that management allowed more credit to its customers or it may be a sign of worsening credit control or the possibility of irrecoverable debts.

(b) **Suggestions for improvement of the ratios**

Gross profit percentage

The gross profit percentage could be improved if selling prices could be increased without a corresponding increase in costs. Alternatively, raw materials or goods for resale could be sourced for lower prices.

Operating profit percentage

This ratio will improve if cost savings can be made and revenue remains stable. If operating expenses have reduced in the current year, there may be little scope for reducing them any further.

Inventory holding period

The long inventory holding period may indicate old or obsolete inventory, so this may need to be written off. Management needs to improve inventory ordering and purchasing/manufacture so that high levels of inventory do not build up and 'tie up' cash.

Trade receivables collection period

As the trade receivables collection period has increased, management should assess the recoverability of receivables. Credit control procedures should be tightened so that cash can be collected on a timely basis.

....

Task 8.7

REPORT

To: Nancy Charlton

From: Accounting Technician

Subject: Performance of Limden Ltd

Date: 18 June 20X1

As requested, I have analysed the financial performance of Limden Ltd, based on the ratios provided.

(a) **The relative performance of the company for the last two years**

Gross profit percentage

The gross profit percentage has improved over the two years. There are several possible reasons for this: the company may have increased its sales prices or been able to reduce its direct costs or both. Alternatively it may have changed the type of product that it sells (the sales mix), so that individual sales are more profitable than before.

Operating profit percentage

The operating profit percentage has fallen significantly. Because the gross profit percentage has improved, this suggests that selling and administrative expenses have increased during 20X1.

Return on shareholders' funds

Return on shareholders' funds has also fallen significantly. This is not surprising, given that operating profit percentage has also fallen. Less profit is being generated relative to the shareholders' investment in the company. This means that less profit will be available to pay dividends to shareholders.

Gearing

Gearing (the proportion of the company's finance obtained from borrowings) has increased. The company has probably taken out significant new loans during the year. The company has become a riskier investment as the increased interest payments will reduce profits available to shareholders still further.

Interest cover

Interest cover has fallen very sharply in 20X1. This is consistent with the increase in gearing and the fall in the operating profit percentage: the additional borrowings have increased finance costs and at the same time less profit is available to cover these costs. This fall in interest cover is another indication that the company has become a riskier investment.

(b) **Conclusion**

On the basis of the information provided, I advise you not to invest in this company. The company's trading operations appear to be profitable, but operating profit has decreased and the additional debt suggests that Limden Ltd would be a risky investment.

Task 8.8

REPORT

To: The Directors of Knole Ltd

From: Accounting technician

Subject: The company's liquidity and cash flow

Date:

As requested, I have examined the company's financial statements for the years ended 31 October 20X7 and 20X8 and I set out my comments below.

(a) **The change in net cash from operating activities**

Profit from operations has increased by approximately 20% in the year. However, the net cash from operating activities has decreased from £7,110,000 in 20X7 to £5,973,000 in 20X8. This means that the company has generated less cash from its operations than in the previous year, despite the increase in profit.

During the year the company took out additional bank loans and this has resulted in an increase of £175,000 in interest paid. Tax paid has increased by £59,000, presumably as a result of the increase in operating profit. Both these increases are relatively modest.

The main reason for the decrease in cash is the movement in working capital in the year, which has reduced cash by £9,900,000. Inventories have increased by £4,840,000, compared with an increase of £3,606,000 in 20X7. If sales have increased, the increase in inventories is probably needed to meet customer demand. However, it could also have been caused by slow moving items or other problems. Trade receivables have increased by £2,640,000 in the period. Again, this could be because sales have increased towards the end of the year. An alternative explanation might be that customers are being allowed more credit or taking longer to pay. Trade payables have decreased by £2,420,000 in the year. This suggests that either the company is paying its suppliers too quickly or that the suppliers have changed their credit terms.

The changes in working capital mean that the cash generated by the company's operations is 'tied up' in inventories and trade receivables. This reduces the amount of cash available for paying interest on the bank loan and tax on profits. It also reduces the cash available for investing in property, plant and equipment and other non-current assets. It is almost certainly the reason why the company moved from a positive cash balance to a bank overdraft during the year. This is particularly surprising and worrying given the significant increase in profit from operations.

(b) **The liquidity and financial position of the company**

The current ratio and the quick (or acid test) ratio have both increased significantly during the year. The current ratio is very high and shows that in theory the company can comfortably meet its current liabilities. Similarly, the quick ratio shows that despite the cash outflow during the year, in theory the company should have no problems in meeting its day to day liabilities as they fall due. (The quick ratio is used as a measure of short term liquidity because it excludes inventories, which cannot be quickly converted into cash).

Most people would consider that a current ratio of 3.6 is far too high. The ratio confirms that the company almost certainly has too much inventory. This is one of the main reasons why the company has moved from a positive cash balance to an overdraft during the year. Again, the high quick ratio and the increase in the year show that the company is almost certainly not managing its trade receivables well. Like inventories, these need to be converted into cash much more quickly. Better working capital management would probably solve the company's cash flow problems.

The gearing ratio measures the extent to which the company is financed by debt rather than equity. The gearing ratio has increased during the year, which reflects the increase in bank loans. However, it is still very low. This suggests that the company should not have any problems in raising more finance in the longer term, should it need to. Knole Ltd is profitable and the low gearing means that investors will see it as a relatively safe investment.

If you have any questions, or require any further information, please do not hesitate to contact me.

AAT AQ2013 SAMPLE ASSESSMENT 1
FINANCIAL STATEMENTS

Time allowed: 2½ hours

Task 1 (21 marks)

You have been asked to help prepare the financial statements of Bookham Ltd for the year ended 30 June 20X1. The company's trial balance as at 30 June 20X1 is shown below.

Trial balance:

	Debit £'000	Credit £'000
Sales		78,241
Purchases	36,148	
Distribution costs	7,249	
Administrative expenses	27,338	
Inventories at 1 July 20X0	6,328	
Dividends paid	600	
Interest paid	1,520	
Share capital		32,000
Retained earnings at 1July 20X0		7,462
Bank loan repayable		17,000
Trade and other payables		6,813
Corporation tax		60
Property, plant and equipment at cost	64,229	
Property, plant and equipment – accumulated depreciation at 30 June 20X1		17,867
Trade receivables	12,447	
Allowance for doubtful debts at 1July 20X0		236
Cash at bank	3,820	
	159,679	159,679

Further information:

- The share capital of the company consists of ordinary shares with a nominal value of £1.

- The inventories at the close of business on 30 June 20X1 cost £7,493,000.

- Insurance expenditure of £156,000, in respect of the period 1 May 20X1 to 30 April 20X2, was paid on 17 April 20X1. This payment is included in distribution costs in the trial balance.

- Costs of £5,000 relating to the routine servicing of photocopiers in the general administration office have been included in the cost of property, plant and equipment in the trial balance.

- The allowance for doubtful debts is to increase by £47,000. Bookham Ltd classifies doubtful debts as an administrative expense.

- The corporation tax balance of £60,000 included in the trial balance was the result of an over-estimate of the tax liability for the previous year. The corporation tax charge in respect of the profits for the current year to 30 June 20X1 is estimated to be £1,486,000.

- Land included in property, plant and equipment at a carrying amount of £14,000,000 is to be revalued at the end of the year at £19,000,000.

- All of the operations are continuing operations.

(a) **Draft the statement of profit or loss and other comprehensive income for Bookham Ltd for the year ended 30 June 20X1.**

(b) **Draft the statement of changes in equity for Bookham Ltd for the year ended 30 June 20X1.**

Note. Additional notes and disclosures are not required. You don't have to use the workings to achieve full marks on the task but any answers input into the workings tables will be taken into consideration if you make errors in the proforma.

[You will be asked to draft a statement of financial position in Task 2 using the same data.]

Bookham Ltd

Statement of profit or loss and other comprehensive income for the year ended 30 June 20X1

	£'000
Revenue	
Cost of sales	
Gross profit	
Distribution costs	
Administrative expenses	
Profit from operations	
Finance costs	
Profit before tax	
Tax	
Profit for the period from continuing operations	
Other comprehensive income for the year	
Total comprehensive income for the year	

Workings

Costs of sales	£'000
▼	
▼	
▼	

Drop-down list:

Accrual
Closing inventories
Doubtful debts adjustment
Opening inventories
Prepayment
Purchases
Service costs

Distribution costs	£'000
▼	
▼	

Drop-down list:

Accrual
Depreciation
Distribution costs
Doubtful debts adjustment
Prepayment
Service costs

Administrative expenses	£'000
▼	
▼	
▼	

Drop-down list:

Accrual
Administrative expenses
Doubtful debts adjustment
Prepayment
Service costs

Tax	£'000
▼	
▼	

Drop-down list:

Current year
Previous year

Bookham Ltd
Statement of changes in equity for the year ended 30 June 20X1

	Share capital £'000	Revaluation reserve £'000	Retained earnings £'000	Total equity £'000
Balance at 1 July 20X0				
Changes in equity				
Total comprehensive income				
Dividends				
Balance at 30 June 20X1				

Task 2 (19 marks)

This task is a continuation of the scenario in task 1 and uses the same data.

You have been asked to help prepare the financial statements of Bookham Ltd for the year ended 30 June 20X1. The company's trial balance as at 30 June 20X1 and further information are shown in Task 1 above.

Draft the statement of financial position for Bookham Ltd as at 30 June 20X1.

Note. Additional notes and disclosures are not required. You don't need to use the workings tables to achieve full marks on the task, but data entered into the workings tables will be taken into consideration if you make errors in the proforma.

Bookham Ltd – Statement of financial position as at 30 June 20X1.

	£'000
ASSETS	
Non-current assets	
▼	
Current assets	
▼	
▼	
▼	
Total assets	
EQUITY AND LIABILITIES	
Equity	
▼	
▼	
▼	
Total equity	
Non-current liabilities	
▼	
Current liabilities	
▼	
▼	
Total liabilities	
Total equity and liabilities	

Drop-down list:

Bank loans
Cash and cash equivalents
Inventories
Property, plant and equipment
Retained earnings
Revaluation reserve
Share capital
Tax liability
Trade and other payables
Trade and other receivables

Workings

Property, plant and equipment	£'000
▼	
▼	
▼	
▼	

Drop-down list:

Accumulated depreciation
Property, plant and equipment – cost
Revaluation
Servicing costs

Trade and other receivables	£'000
▼	
▼	
▼	

Drop-down list:

Accrual
Allowance for doubtful debts
Prepayment
Trade and other payables
Trade receivables

Retained earnings	£'000
▼	
▼	
▼	

Drop-down list:

Dividends paid
Profit for the year
Retained earnings at 1 July 20X0

....

Task 3 (8 marks)

In accordance with the IASB *Conceptual Framework for Financial Reporting*:

(a) Identify the TWO FUNDAMENTAL characteristics of useful information.

(b) Define the term 'income'.

....

Task 4 (14 marks)

On 1 July 20X0 Pancras Ltd leases a machine from Sherborne plc. The lease is for a term of 4 years and Pancras Ltd is required to make lease payments of £9,000 annually in arrears. The present value of the minimum lease payments is £28,000. The machine has a useful life of 5 years and would cost £30,000 if bought for cash.

Pancras Ltd prepares its financial statements to 30 June each year.

Prepare brief notes for the directors of Pancras Ltd to answer the following:

(a) Why must the lease be classified as a finance lease?

(b) Explain how the lease would be accounted for in the financial statements of Pancras Ltd, using the figures from above to illustrate your answer where possible.

....

Task 5 (17 marks)

Verwood Ltd prepares financial statements to 30 June each year. The financial statements for the year ending 30 June 20X1 were authorised for issue on 29 July 20X1.

The destruction of a major production plant by fire on 22 July 20X1 must be classified as an adjusting event in accordance with IAS 10 *Events After the Reporting Period*.

(a) **Is this statement True or False?**

True

False

The following information relates to an item of inventory held in the warehouse of Bloxworth Ltd:

Cost incurred to date £	Estimated costs of completion £	Estimated costs of sale £	Estimated selling price £
62	7	10	70

(b) **At what value should the item of inventory be stated in the company's financial statements in accordance with IAS 2 *Inventories*?**

£53

£60

£62

£69

The following information relates to Weymouth Ltd for the year ended 30 June 20X1.

Profit from operations (before deducting depreciation) £7,300.

	YE 30.6.20X1 £	YE 30.6.20X0 £
Inventories	4,200	4,700
Trade receivables	3,600	3,400
Trade payables	1,500	1,600

(c) **What is the amount of net cash generated from operating activities (prior to any tax and interest paid)?**

£6,700

£7,500

£7,700

£7,900

At the end of an accounting period. Blandford Ltd has a contingent asset where an inflow of economic benefits is **probable** and a contingent liability where the likelihood of an outflow of resources is **remote**.

(d) **Which of the following would be the correct accounting treatment for each of these items?**

Contingent asset	Contingent liability	
Recognise in the statement of financial position as an asset	Disclosure is required	☐
Recognise in the statement of financial position as an asset	No disclosure is required	☐
No asset is recognised Disclosure is required	Disclosure is required	☐
No asset is recognised Disclosure is required	No disclosure is required	☐

The directors of Dorchester Ltd are concerned that one of its machines might have become impaired. The following information applies:

	£
Carrying amount	19,600
Fair value	18,500
Costs of disposal	300
Value in use	18,400

(e) **What is the amount of impairment loss that will be recognised in the statement of profit or loss, in accordance with IAS 36 *Impairment of Assets?***

£NIL

£1,100

£1,200

£1,400

☐

(f) **The directors of Wimborne Ltd, a company that already has a number of subsidiaries, are considering buying a minority stake in Abbotsbury Ltd. In accordance with IAS 28 *Investments in Associates* and *Joint Ventures*, Wimborne Ltd will usually account for an associate in its group accounts if it owns directly or indirectly at least:**

10% of the company's voting power

20% of the company's voting power

40% of the company's voting power

50% of the company's voting power

☐

Task 6 (28 marks)

Beacon plc acquired 70% of the issued share capital and voting rights of Hill Ltd on 1 July 20X0 for £1,400,000. At that date Hill Ltd had issued share capital of £1,000,000 and retained earnings of £190,000.

Extracts of the statements of financial position for the two companies one year later at 30 June 20X1, as well as further information, are shown below.

Extracts of statements of financial position:

	Beacon plc £'000	Hill Ltd £'000
ASSETS		
Non-current assets		
Investment in Hill Ltd	1,400	
Property, plant and equipment	2,577	1,087
	3,977	1,087
Current assets		
Inventories	537	221
Trade receivables	269	145
Cash and cash equivalents	83	29
	889	395
Total assets	4,866	1,482
EQUITY AND LIABILITIES		
Equity		
Share capital	4,100	1,000
Retained earnings	370	250
Total equity	4,470	1,250
Non-current liabilities	210	140
Current liabilities		
Trade payables	156	76
Taxation	30	16
	186	92
Total liabilities	396	232
Total equity and liabilities	4,866	1,482

Further information:

- At 1 July 20X0 the fair value of the non-current assets of Hill Ltd was £200,000 more than the carrying amount. This revaluation has not been recorded in the books of Hill Ltd (ignore any effect on the depreciation for the year).

- During the year, Beacon plc sold some of its inventory to Hill Ltd for £60,000. The goods had cost Beacon plc £40,000. One-fifth of these goods were still in the inventory of Hill Ltd at 30 June 20X1. There were no inter-company balances outstanding at the end of the year in respect of this transaction in trade receivables or in trade payables.

- Beacon plc has decided that non-controlling interest will be valued at their proportionate share of net assets.

Draft the consolidated statement of financial position for Beacon plc and its subsidiary undertaking as at 30 June 20X1.

Note. You don't need to use the workings to achieve full marks on the task, however data entered into the workings tables will be taken into consideration if you make errors in the proforma.

Beacon plc
Consolidated statement of financial position as at 30 June 20X1

	£'000
ASSETS	
Non-current assets	
Goodwill	
Property, plant and equipment	
Current assets	
Inventories	
Trade receivables	
Cash and cash equivalents	
Total assets	
EQUITY AND LIABILITIES	
Equity	
Share capital	
Retained earnings	
Non-controlling interest	
Total equity	
Non-current liabilities	
Current liabilities	
Trade payables	
Taxation	
Total liabilities	
Total equity and liabilities	

Workings

Goodwill	£'000
▼	
▼	
▼	
▼	
Goodwill =	

Drop-down list:

Inter-company transaction
Price paid
Retained earnings – attributable to Beacon plc
Revaluation reserve – attributable to Beacon plc
Share capital –attributable to Beacon plc

Inventories	£'000
Consolidated inventories (prior to any company adjustment)	
Inter-company adjustment	

Retained earnings	£'000
▼	
▼	
▼	

Drop-down list:

Beacon plc (excluding any inter-company adjustment)
Hill Ltd – attributable to Beacon plc
Inter-company adjustment
Retained earnings – attributable to Beacon plc

Non-controlling interest (NCI)	£'000
▽	
▽	
▽	

Drop-down list:

Price paid
Retained earnings – attributable to NCI
Revaluation reserve – attributable to NCI
Share capital –attributable to NCI

....

Task 7 (20 marks)

You have been given the financial statements of Bridport Ltd for the year ending 30 June 20X1. You are now required to prepare financial ratios to assist your manager in his analysis of the company.

Bridport Ltd's statement of profit or loss and statement of financial position are shown below.

Bridport Ltd – Statement of profit or loss for the year ended 30 June 20X1

	£'000
Continuing Operations	
Revenue	58,914
Costs of sales	(42,126)
Gross profit	16,788
Distribution costs	(2,483)
Administrative expenses	(5,769)
Profit from operations	8,536
Finance costs	(1,642)
Profit before tax	6,894
Tax	(1,758)
Profit for the period from continuing operations	5,136

Bridport Ltd – Statement of financial position as at 30 June 20X1

	£'000
ASSETS	
Non-current assets	
Property, plant and equipment	42,792
Current assets	
Inventories	6,724
Trade receivables	5,278
Cash and cash equivalents	1,190
	13,192
Total assets	55,984
EQUITY AND LIABILITIES	
Equity	
Ordinary share capital (£1 shares)	16,000
Retained earnings	12,326
Total equity	28,326
Non-current liabilities	
Bank loans	20,400
	20,400
Current liabilities	
Trade payables	5,332
Tax liabilities	1,926
	7,258
Total liabilities	27,658
Total equity and liabilities	55,984

(a) **Identify the formulas that are used to calculate each of the following ratios:**

Return on shareholders' funds

Drop-down list:

Profit from operations/Total equity × 100
Profit after tax/Total equity × 100
Profit from operations/Total equity and liabilities × 100
Profit after tax/Total equity and liabilities × 100

Acid test ratio

Drop-down list:

Total assets/Total liabilities
Current assets/Current liabilities
Non-current liabilities/(Total equity + Non-current liabilities)
(Current Assets – Inventories)/Current liabilities

Inventory holding period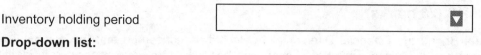

Drop-down list:

Cost of sales/Inventories
Revenue/Inventories
Inventories/Cost of sales × 365
Inventories/Revenue × 365

Asset turnover (net assets)

Drop-down list:

Revenue/Total assets
Profit from operations/Total assets
Revenue/(Total assets – Current liabilities)
Profit from operations/(Total assets – Current liabilities)

Gearing

Drop-down list:

Non-current liabilities/(Total equity + Non-current liabilities) × 100
Current assets/Current liabilities × 100
Revenue/(Total assets – Current liabilities) × 100
Profit from operations/(Total equity + Non-current liabilities) × 100

(b) **Calculate the above ratios to ONE DECIMAL PLACE**

Return on shareholders' funds   %

Acid test ratio   : 1

Inventory holding period   days

Asset turnover (net assets)   times

Gearing   %

Task 8 (23 marks)

Carol Bright, the Financial Director of Poole Ltd, is concerned that the company is not managing its working capital efficiently. She has asked for your assistance in identifying any problem area(s) and for your suggestions as to how these can be remedied.

You have calculated the following ratios in respect of Poole Ltd's latest financial statements and have also obtained each of their industry averages for comparative purposes.

	Poole Ltd	Industry average
Current ratio	5.1:1	2.3:1
Inventory turnover	7.2 times	6.8 times
Trade receivables collection period	63 days	45 days
Trade payables payment period	44 days	51 days

Prepare a reply to Carol that includes:

(a) **Comments on whether Poole Ltd has performed better or worse in respect of the calculated ratios, giving possible reasons, as compared to the industry averages.**

(b) **The steps to be taken to improve Poole Ltd's working capital cycle and any possible problems you think may arise from implementing these actions.**

AAT AQ2013 SAMPLE ASSESSMENT 1 FINANCIAL STATEMENTS

ANSWERS

Task 1 (21 marks)

Bookham Ltd

Statement of profit or loss and other comprehensive income for the year ended 30 June 20X1

	£'000
Revenue	78,241
Cost of sales (W)	(34,983)
Gross profit	43,258
Distribution costs (W)	(7,119)
Administrative expenses (W)	(27,390)
Profit from operations	8,749
Finance costs	(1,520)
Profit before tax	7,229
Tax (W)	(1,426)
Profit for the period from continuing operations	5,803
Other comprehensive income for the year	5,000
Total comprehensive income for the year	10,803

Workings

Costs of sales	£'000
Opening inventories	6,328
Purchases	36,148
Closing inventories	(7,493)
	34,983

Distribution costs	£'000
Distribution costs	7,249
Prepayment (156 × 10/12)	(130)
	7,119

Administrative expenses	£'000
Administrative expenses	27,338
Doubtful debts adjustment	47
Service costs	5
	27,390

Tax	£'000
Current year	1,486
Previous year	(60)
	1,426

Bookham Ltd

Statement of changes in equity for the year ended 30 June 20X1

	Share capital £'000	Revaluation reserve £'000	Retained earnings £'000	Total equity £'000
Balance at 1 July 20X0	32,000		7,462	39,462
Changes in equity				
Total comprehensive income		5,000	5,803	10,803
Dividends			(600)	(600)
Balance at 30 June 20X1	32,000	5,000	12,665	49,665

Task 2 (19 marks)

	£'000
ASSETS	
Non-current assets	
Property, plant and equipment (W)	51,357
Current assets	
Inventories	7,493
Trade and other receivables (W)	12,294
Cash and cash equivalents	3,820
	23,607
Total assets	74,964
EQUITY AND LIABILITIES	
Equity	
Share capital	32,000
Retained earnings (W)	12,665
Revaluation reserve	5,000
Total equity	49,665
Non-current liabilities	
Bank loans	17,000
	17,000
Current liabilities	
Trade and other payables	6,813
Tax liability	1,486
	8,299
Total liabilities	25,299
Total equity and liabilities	74,964

Workings

Property, plant and equipment	£'000
Property, plant and equipment – cost	64,229
Revaluation (19,000 – 14,000)	5,000
Accumulated depreciation	(17,867)
Servicing costs	(5)
	51,357

Trade and other receivables	£'000
Trade receivables	12,447
Prepayment	130
Allowance for doubtful debts (236 + 47)	(283)
	12,294

Retained earnings	£'000
Retained earnings at 1 July 20X0	7,462
Profit for the year	5,803
Dividends paid	(600)
	12,665

Task 3 (8 marks)

Note. Based on the information available at the time this book was written, we anticipate that this task would be human marked in the real assessment.

(a) The two fundamental characteristics of useful information are relevance and faithful representation.

(b) Income is defined as:

'Increases in economic benefits during the accounting period in the form of inflows or enhancements of assets or decreases of liabilities that result in increases in equity, other than those relating to contributions from equity participants'.

Task 4 (14 marks)

Note. Based on the information available at the time this book was written, we anticipate that this task would be human marked in the real assessment.

(a) The lease must be classified as a finance lease because the present value of the minimum lease payment (£28,000) amounts to at least substantially all of the fair value (£30,000) of the asset and because the lease term of 4 years is for the major part of the 5 year economic life of the asset. These two situations both indicate that the lease transfers substantially the risks and rewards of ownership from the lessor to the lessee.

(b) At the commencement of the lease term the finance lease must be recognised as an asset together with a corresponding liability to the lessor in the statement of financial position, at an amount equal to the lower of:

- The fair value of the machine (£30,000), and

- The present value of the minimum lease payments (£28,000)

The lease would therefore be recognised at £28,000.

The asset should be depreciated in accordance with the depreciation policy used for depreciable assets that are owned, over the shorter of the machine's useful life (5 years) and the lease term (4 years). The annual depreciation would therefore be £28,000/4 = £7,000.

Lease payments must be apportioned between the finance charge element, which is shown as an expense in the statement of profit or loss, and the reduction of the outstanding liability.

The total finance charge is calculated by the difference between:

- The total of the minimum lease payments (£36,000)

- The liability to the lessor which was established at the start of the lease (£28,000).

The finance charge of £8,000 should be allocated to each period during the lease term 'so as to produce a constant periodic rate of interest on the remaining balance of the liability'. This is normally implemented through use of the actuarial method, although IAS 17 does allow some form of approximation to be used in order to simplify the calculation (for example the sum of digits method).

Task 5 (17 marks)

(a) True ☐

 False ☑

(b)

 £53 ☑

 £60 ☐

 £62 ☐

 £69 ☐

Note. Net realisable value is £70 – 10 – 7 = £53, which is lower than cost of £62.

(c)

 £6,700 ☐

 £7,500 ☑

 £7,700 ☐

 £7,900 ☐

Working

	£
Operating profit	7,300
Decrease in inventories	500
Increase in receivables	(200)
Decrease in payables	(100)
	7,500

(d)

Contingent asset	Contingent liability	
Recognise in the statement of financial position as an asset	Disclosure is required	☐
Recognise in the statement of financial position as an asset	No disclosure is required	☐
No asset is recognised Disclosure is required	Disclosure is required	☐
No asset is recognised Disclosure is required	No disclosure is required	☑

(e)

£NIL	☐
£1,100	☐
£1,200	☑
£1,400	☐

Note. Fair value less costs of disposal is £18,200, which is less than value in use, so value in use of £18,400 is the recoverable amount. The impairment loss is the difference between the carrying amount of £19,600 and the recoverable amount, ie, £1,200.

(f)

10% of the company's voting power	☐
20% of the company's voting power	☑
40% of the company's voting power	☐
50% of the company's voting power	☐

Task 6 (28 marks)

	£'000
ASSETS	
Non-current assets	
Goodwill (W)	427
Property, plant and equipment	3,864
	4,291
Current assets	
Inventories (W)	754
Trade receivables	414
Cash and cash equivalents	112
	1,280
Total assets	5,571

	£'000
EQUITY AND LIABILITIES	
Equity	
Share capital	4,100
Retained earnings (W)	408
Non-controlling interest (W)	435
Total equity	4,943
Non-current liabilities	350
Current liabilities	
Trade payables	232
Taxation	46
	278
Total liabilities	628
Total equity and liabilities	5,571

Workings

Goodwill	£'000
Price paid	1,400
Share capital – attributable to Beacon plc (1,000 × 70%)	(700)
Retained earnings – attributable to Beacon plc (190 × 70%)	(133)
Revaluation reserve – attributable to Beacon plc (200 × 70%)	(140)
Goodwill	427

Inventories	£'000
Consolidated inventories (excluding any inter-company adjustment)	758
Inter-company adjustment (20,000 × 1/5)	(4)
	754

Retained earnings	£'000
Retained earnings – attributable to Beacon plc	370
Inter-company adjustment	(4)
Hill Ltd – attributable to Beacon plc (250 – 190 × 70%)	42
	408

Non-controlling interest (NCI)	£'000
Share capital – attributable to NCI (1,000 × 30%)	300
Retained earnings – attributable to NCI (250 × 30%)	75
Revaluation reserve – attributable to NCI (200 × 30%)	60
	435

Task 7 (20 marks)

(a) **Identify the formulas that are used to calculate each of the following ratios:**

Return on shareholders' funds | Profit after tax / Total equity × 100

Acid test ratio | (Current assets – Inventories) / Current liabilities

Inventory holding period | Inventories / Cost of sales × 365

Asset turnover (net assets) | Revenue / (Total assets – Current liabilities)

Gearing | Non-current liabilities / (Total equity + Non-current liabilities) × 100

(b) **Calculate the above ratios to ONE DECIMAL PLACE**

Return on shareholders' funds | 18.1 | % | (5,136/28,326)

Acid test ratio | 0.9 | : 1 | ((13,192 – 6,724)/7,258)

Inventory holding period | 58.3 | days | (6,724/42,126 × 365)

Asset turnover (net assets) | 1.2 | times | (58,914/(55,984 – 7,258))

Gearing | 41.9 | % | (20,400/(28,326 + 20,400))

Task 8 (23 marks)

Note. Based on the information available at the time this book was written, we anticipate that this task would be human marked in the real assessment.

Carol,

As requested I have analysed the working capital of Poole Limited by means of computing four accounting ratios for the company and comparing these to industry averages. My analysis is as follows:

(a) (i) Current ratio is better than the industry average.

- Poole Ltd has more current assets available to meet its current liabilities/ is more solvent.

- However, the ratio looks to be too high and indicates less efficient management of working capital.

- It may have higher levels of receivables, inventories or cash & cash equivalents/lower payables.

(ii) Inventory turnover is better than the industry average.

- Poole Ltd is selling its inventories slightly more quickly as compared to the industry average.

- Could be due to more effective inventory management systems or the company might have reduced its selling prices or employed better marketing techniques.

- Leads to lower storage costs and there is less risk of stock obsolescence.

(iii) Trade receivables collection period is worse than the industry average.

- Poole Ltd is taking longer to collect debts.
- This is bad for cash flow.
- Could be due to poor credit control procedures.
- May just be offering longer credit terms to boost sales.
- Could indicate the presence of irrecoverable debts.

(iv) Trade payables payment period may be considered to be better than the industry average (if linked to supplier goodwill) or worse (if linked to cash flow).

- Poole Ltd is paying its trade suppliers sooner.
- This is bad for cash flow
- This is good for supplier goodwill
- It may have negotiated additional settlement discounts with suppliers
- Suppliers may have dictated shorter payment terms.

(b) Suggestions to improve the working capital cycle and possible problems associated with these:

- Collect debts more quickly/reduce trade receivable days, eg improve debt collection procedures, reduce credit periods.

- Problem: possible loss of custom.

- Increase the length of time taken to pay suppliers/increase trade payable days, eg negotiate extended credit terms, improve payment procedures

- Problem: may lose supplier goodwill/settlement discounts.

AAT AQ2013 SAMPLE ASSESSMENT 2
FINANCIAL STATEMENTS

Time allowed: 2½ hours

Task 1 (33 marks)

You have been asked to prepare the statement of cash flows and statement of changes in equity for Fontwell Ltd for the year ended 30 June 20X1.

The most recent statement of profit or loss and statement of financial position (with comparatives for the previous year) of Fontwell Ltd can be viewed by clicking on the buttons below:

Fontwell Ltd – Statement of profit or loss for the year ended 30 June 20X1

	£'000
Continuing operations	
Revenue	89,463
Cost of sales	(51,279)
Gross profit	38,184
Loss on disposal of PPE	(39)
Dividends received	157
	38,302
Distribution costs	(11,389)
Administrative expenses	(15,126)
Profit from operations	11,787
Finance costs	(168)
Profit before tax	11,619
Tax	(2,712)
Profit for the period from continuing operations	8,907

Further information:

- The total depreciation charge for the year was £5,427,000.

- Property, plant and equipment with a carrying amount of £576,000 was sold in the year.

- All sales and purchases were on credit. Other expenses were paid for in cash.

- A dividend of £3,200,000 was paid during the year, and a further dividend of £1,300,000 was declared on 21 July 20X1 before the financial statements were authorised for issue.

Fontwell Ltd

Statement of financial position as at 30 June 20X1

	20X1 £'000	20X0 £'000
ASSETS		
Non-current assets		
Property, plant, equipment	47,835	32,691
Investments at cost	7,000	7,000
	54,835	39,691
Current assets		
Inventories	2,578	3,264
Trade receivables	7,964	9,325
Cash and cash equivalents	118	–
	10,660	12,589
Total assets	65,495	52,280
EQUITY AND LIABILITIES		
Equity		
Share capital	22,500	18,000
Share premium	8,900	6,300
Retained earnings	23,307	17,600
Total equity	54,707	41,900
Non-current liabilities		
Bank loans	2,800	2,400
	2,800	2,400
Current liabilities		
Trade payables	5,198	4,726
Tax liabilities	2,790	3,180
Bank overdraft	–	74
	7,988	7,980
Total liabilities	10,788	10,380
Total equity and liabilities	65,495	52,280

(a) **Prepare a reconciliation of profit from operations to net cash from operating activities for Fontwell Ltd for the year ended 30 June 20X1.**

(b) **Prepare the statement of cash flows for Fontwell Ltd for the year ended 30 June 20X1.**

Note. You don't have to use the workings boxes to achieve full marks on the task, however data in the workings will be taken into consideration if you make errors in the proforma.

[You will be asked to draft a statement of changes in equity in Task 2 using same data.]

Fontwell Ltd
Reconciliation of profit from operations to net cash from operating activities

		£'000
	▼	
Adjustments for:		
	▼	
	▼	
	▼	
	▼	
	▼	
	▼	
Cash generated by operations		
	▼	
	▼	
Net cash from operating activities		

Drop-down list:

Adjustment in respect of inventories
Adjustment in respect of trade payables
Adjustment in respect of trade receivables
Bank loans
Depreciation
Dividends received
Interest paid
Loss on disposal of PPE
Proceeds on disposal of PPE
Profit after tax
Profit before tax
Profit from operations
Purchase of investments
Purchases of PPE
Tax paid

Fontwell Ltd
Statement of cash flows for the year ended 30 June 20X1

	£'000
Net cash from operating activities	
Investing activities	
▼	
▼	
▼	
Net cash used in investing activities	
Financing activities	
▼	
▼	
▼	
Net cash from financing activities	
Net increase/(decrease) in cash and cash equivalents	
Cash and cash equivalents at beginning of year	
Cash and cash equivalents at end of year	

Drop-down list:

Adjustment in respect of inventories
Adjustment in respect of trade payables
Adjustment in respect of trade receivables
Bank loans
Dividends paid
Dividends received
Proceeds of share issue
Proceeds on disposal of PPE
Purchases of PPE

Workings

Proceeds on disposal of PPE		£'000
	▼	
	▼	

Drop-down list:

Carrying amount of PPE sold
Depreciation charge
Loss on disposal of PPE
PPE at end of year
PPE at start of year

Purchases of PPE		£'000
PPE at start of year		
	▼	
	▼	
	▼	
Total PPE additions		

Drop-down list:

Carrying amount of PPE sold
Depreciation charge
Loss on disposal of PPE
PPE at end of year

Tax paid		£'000
	▼	
	▼	
	▼	
Tax paid		

Drop-down list:

Tax charge to profit/loss
Tax liability at end of year
Tax liability at start of year

Task 2 (7 marks)

This task is a continuation of the scenario in Task 1 and uses the same data. You have been asked to prepare the statement of cash flows and statement of changes in equity for Fontwell Ltd for the year ended 30 June 20X1.

Draft the statement of changes in equity for Fontwell Ltd for the year ended 30 June 20X1.

Note. Additional notes and disclosures are not required. You don't need to use the workings tables to achieve full marks on the task, but data entered into the workings tables will be taken into consideration if you make errors in the proforma.

Fontwell Ltd – Statement of changes in equity for the year ended 30 June 20X1.

	Share capital £'000	Share premium £'000	Retained earnings £'000	Total equity £'000
Balance at 1 July 20X0				
Changes in equity				
Total profit				
Dividends				
Issue of share capital				
Balance at 30 June 20X1				

Task 3 (10 marks)

(a) The *Conceptual Framework for Financial Reporting* identifies 'Going concern' as an underlying assumption.

Explain the 'Going concern' assumption.

(b) The *Conceptual Framework for Financial Reporting* permits four alternative measurement bases to be used in the valuation of assets and liabilities. These are:

- Historical cost
- Current cost
- Realisable (settlement) value
- Present value

Briefly explain any TWO of these measurements.

Task 4 (12 marks)

Blair Ltd is a manufacturer of luxury outdoor spa baths which they sell to wealthy householders in the UK and Northern Europe.

The directors of Blair Ltd are now preparing the company's annual financial statements and are considering the requirements of IAS 36 *Impairment of Assets*. They understand that they will need to determine the recoverable amount of an asset and calculate whether the asset has suffered an impairment loss, when there is some indication that the asset might be impaired.

The following information relates to an item of plant and machinery owned by Blair Ltd at its accounting year end:

Original cost	£875,000
Accumulated depreciation	£481,000
Fair value	£341,000
Costs to sell	£15,000
Value in use	£367,000

Answer the following:

(a) **Explain how the directors of Blair Ltd should determine the recoverable amount of an asset, illustrating your answer with reference to the item of plant and machinery owned at the company's year end.**

(b) **Explain how the directors of Blair Ltd should calculate whether an asset has suffered an impairment loss, again illustrating your answer with reference to the item of plant and machinery owned at the year end.**

Task 5 (17 marks)

Fakenham Ltd is about to enter into a finance lease for a cutting machine.

Statement: The lease must be recognised as an asset and liability in the statement of financial position.

(a) **Is this statement true or false?**

True ☐

False ☐

Carlisle Ltd is preparing its financial statements for the year ending 30 June 20X1.

The trial balance shows the following in respect of corporation tax:

	£
Tax payable at 1 July 20X0	16,700
Tax paid during the year ended 30 June 20X1	14,900

The final agreed corporation tax liability in respect of the profits for the year ending 30 June 20X0 has been settled in full.

The estimated corporation tax liability based upon the profits for the year ending 30 June 20X1 is £17,300.

(b) **What is the tax charge that will be shown in the company's statement of profit or loss?**

£14,900 ☐

£15,500 ☐

£17,300 ☐

£19,100 ☐

Hereford Ltd values inventories using the weighted average cost method (AVCO).

At 1 July 20X0, there were 50 units in inventory valued at £8 each. On 9 March 20X1, 30 units were purchased for £12 each and on 12 May 20X1 a further 20 units were purchased for £15 each. On 27 June 20X1, 40 units were sold for £18 each.

(c) **What is the value of closing inventory at 30 June 20X1?**

£340 ☐

£424 ☐

£636 ☐

£740 ☐

Lingfield Ltd purchases a machine for £20,000 on 1 July 20X0. The machine is estimated to have a useful economic life of 4 years, after which it can be sold for £4,000. The company depreciates the machine using the straight line method, charging a full year's depreciation in both the year of purchase and sale. Lingfield Ltd prepares its financial statements to 30 June each year.

(d) **What will be the carrying amount of the machine at 30 June 20X3?**

£4,000 ☐

£5,000 ☐

£8,000 ☐

£12,000 ☐

Ayr Plc acquired 100% of the issued share capital and voting rights of Bath Ltd on 1 July 20X0.

The consolidated cost of sales of Ayr Plc and its subsidiary undertaking for the year ended 30 June 20X1, before taking into account any adjustments required in respect of the information below, is £70,000.

Additional data

During the year Ayr Plc sold goods which had cost £10,000 to Bath Ltd for £18,000.

One-quarter of these goods still remain in inventories at the end of the year.

(e) **What is the consolidated cost of sales for the year ending 30 June 20X1?**

£52,000 ☐

£54,000 ☐

£60,000 ☐

£62,000 ☐

(f) **Which of the following statements are correct with regard to property, plant and equipment (PPE)?**

(1) A revaluation reserve arises when an item of PPE is sold at a profit.
(2) All non-current assets must be depreciated.

(1) only ☐

(2) only ☐

Both ☐

Neither of them ☐

Task 6 (28 marks)

Purley Plc acquired 80% of the issued share capital and voting rights of Briar Ltd on 1 July 20X0 for £410,000. At that date Briar Ltd had issued share capital of £360,000 and retained earnings of £80,000.

An extract of the statement of financial position of Briar Ltd one year later at 30 June 20X1 and additional information can be accessed by clicking on the button below.

Briar Ltd Statement of financial position as at 30 June 20X1	£'000
Total assets	580
EQUITY AND LIABILITIES	
Equity	
Share capital	360
Retained earnings	140
Total equity	500
Total liabilities	80
Total equity and liabilities	580

Additional information

Purley Plc has decided that non-controlling interest will be valued at its proportionate share of the subsidiary's net assets.

(a) **Calculate the figures for goodwill and non-controlling interest that would be included in the consolidated statement of financial position of Purley Plc and its subsidiary undertaking as at 30 June 20X1.**

   Note. You don't have to use the workings tables to achieve full marks on the task, however data entered into the workings tables will be considered if you make errors in the proforma.

	£'000
Goodwill	
Non-controlling interest	

Workings

Goodwill		£'000
	▼	
	▼	
	▼	
Goodwill =		

Drop-down list:

Price paid
Retained earnings – attributable to Purley Plc
Share capital – attributable to Purley Plc
Total assets – attributable to Purley Plc

Non-controlling interest (NCI)		£'000
	▼	
	▼	
Non-controlling interest =		

Drop-down list:

Price paid
Retained earnings – attributable to NCI
Share capital – attributable to NCI
Total assets – attributable to NCI

Data

Danes Plc acquired 80% of the issued share capital and voting rights of Winter Ltd on 1 July 20X0. Extracts from both companies' statements of profit or loss for the year ended 30 June 20X1 and additional information can be accessed by clicking on the buttons shown below.

	Danes Plc £'000	Winter Ltd £'000
Continuing operations		
Revenue	18,560	9,350
Cost of sales	(12,346)	(5,256)
Gross profit	6,214	4,094
Other income	3,258	1,158
Distribution costs	(2,132)	(894)
Administrative expenses	(1,684)	(715)
Profit from operations	5,656	3,643
Finance costs	(360)	(193)
Profit before tax	5,296	3,450
Tax	(1,260)	(680)
Profit for the period from continuing operations	4,036	2,770

Additional information

During the year Danes Plc sold goods to Winter Ltd for £350,000. These goods had been purchased by Danes Plc at a cost of £210,000. Winter Ltd had sold half of these goods by the end of the year.

The other income of Danes Plc includes a dividend received of £320,000 from Winter Ltd.

(b) **Draft the consolidated statement of profit or loss for Danes Plc and its subsidiary undertaking for the year ended 30 June 20X1.**

Note. You don't need to use the workings to achieve full marks on the task, but data in the workings will be considered if you make errors in the proforma.

Danes plc
Consolidated statement of profit or loss for the year ended 30 June 20X1.

Continuing operations	£'000
Revenue	
Cost of sales	
Gross profit	
Other income	
Distribution costs	
Administrative expenses	
Profit from operations	
Finance costs	
Profit before tax	
Tax	
Profit for the period from continuing operations	

Attributable to	£'000
Equity holders of the parent	
Non-controlling interest	

Workings

Revenue	£'000
Danes Plc	
Winter Ltd	
Total inter-company adjustment	

Cost of sales	£'000
Danes Plc	
Winter Ltd	
Total inter-company adjustment	

Other income	£'000
Danes Plc	
Winter Ltd	
Total inter-company adjustment	

Task 7 (20 marks)

You have been given the financial statements of Femmy Ltd for the year ending 30 June 20X0. You are now required to prepare financial ratios to assist your manager in her analysis of the company.

Femmy Ltd's statement of profit or loss and statement of financial position can be viewed by clicking on the buttons below.

Femmy Ltd – Statement of profit or loss for the year ended 30 June 20X0

	£'000
Continuing operations	
Revenue	44,626
Cost of sales	(27,457)
Gross profit	17,169
Distribution costs	(3,754)
Administrative expenses	(2,963)
Profit from operations	10,452
Finance costs	(678)
Profit before tax	9,774
Tax	(1,947)
Profit for the period from continuing operations	7,827

Femmy Ltd – Statement of financial position as at 30 June 20X0

	£'000
ASSETS	
Non-current assets	
Property, plant, equipment	28,965
Current assets	
Inventories	8,419
Trade receivables	6,321
Cash and cash equivalents	785
	15,525
Total assets	44,490
EQUITY AND LIABILITIES	
Equity	
Ordinary share capital (£1 shares)	14,000
Retained earnings	11,125
Total equity	25,125
Non-current liabilities	
Bank loans	13,200
	13,200
Current liabilities	
Trade payables	4,218
Tax liabilities	1,947
	6,165
Total liabilities	19,365
Total equity and liabilities	44,490

(a) **Identify the formulas that are used to calculate each of the following ratios:**

Return on shareholders' funds   [　　　　　　　　　▼]

Interest cover   [　　　　　　　　　▼]

Current ratio   [　　　　　　　　　▼]

Operating profit percentage   [　　　　　　　　　▼]

Inventory turnover   [　　　　　　　　　▼]

BPP
LEARNING MEDIA

Drop-down list:

Profit from operations / Total equity × 100
Profit after tax / Total equity × 100
Profit from operations / (Total equity + Non-current liabilities) × 100
Profit after tax / (Total equity + Non-current liabilities) × 100

Revenue / Finance costs
Profit after tax / Finance costs
Profit from operations / Finance costs
Profit before tax / Finance costs

(Current assets – Inventories) / Current liabilities
(Current assets – Trade receivables) / Current liabilities
Total assets / Total liabilities
Current assets / Current liabilities

Gross profit / Revenue × 100
Profit from operations / Revenue × 100
Profit before tax / Revenue × 100
Profit after tax / Revenue × 100

Inventories / Revenue
Inventories / Cost of sales
Revenue / Inventories
Cost of sales / Inventories

(b) Calculate the above ratios to ONE decimal place.

Return on shareholders' funds   [   ] %

Interest cover   [   ] times

Current ratio   [   ] :1

Operating profit percentage   [   ] %

Inventory turnover   [   ] times

Task 8 (23 marks)

You are employed by Singh Ltd as a financial analyst. You have been asked to look at the profitability and interest cover of the company over the last two years.

You have calculated three key ratios for Singh Ltd in respect of its financial statements for the years 20X1 and 20X0, and an extract of the company's annual budget for 20X1 is also provided below.

Three key ratios:

	20X1	20X0
Gross profit %	31.6%	38.9%
Operating Profit %	11.3%	9.2%
Interest cover	5.2 times	3.9 times

Singh Ltd – Extract of annual budget for 20X1

	£'000
Revenue	940
Cost of sales	(630)
Gross profit	310
Operating expenses	(204)
Profit from operations	106
Finance costs	(23)
Profit before taxation	83

Prepare notes which include:

(a) **Comments on the relative performance of Singh Ltd in respect of the two years, giving possible reasons for any differences based upon the ratios calculated. (The extract of the annual budget may also assist you in some aspects of this.)**

(b) **THREE limitations of ratio analysis.**

AAT AQ2013 SAMPLE ASSESSMENT 2 FINANCIAL STATEMENTS

ANSWERS

Task 1 (33 marks)

(a) **Fontwell Ltd**
Reconciliation of profit from operations to net cash from operating activities

	£'000
Profit from operations	11,787
Adjustments for:	
Depreciation	5,427
Loss on disposal of PPE	39
Dividends received	(157)
Adjustment in respect of inventories (2,578 – 3,264)	686
Adjustment in respect of trade receivables (7,964 – 9,325)	1,361
Adjustment in respect of trade payables (5,198 – 4,726)	472
Cash generated by operations	19,615
Tax paid (W)	(3,102)
Interest paid	(168)
Net cash from operating activities	16,345

(b) **Fontwell Ltd**

Statement of cash flows for the year ended 30 June 20X1

	£'000
Net cash from operating activities	16,345
Investing activities	
Dividends received	157
Proceeds on disposal of PPE (W)	537
Purchase of PPE (W)	(21,147)
Net cash used in investing activities	(20,453)
Financing activities	
Bank loans	400
Proceeds of share issue	7,100
Dividends paid	(3,200)
Net cash from financing activities	4,300
Net increase/(decrease) in cash and cash equivalents	192
Cash and cash equivalents at beginning of year	(74)
Cash and cash equivalents at end of year	118

Workings

Proceeds on disposal of PPE	£'000
Carrying amount of PPE sold	576
Loss on disposal of PPE	(39)
Proceeds on disposal of PPE	537

Purchases of PPE	£'000
PPE at start of year	32,691
Depreciation charge	(5,427)
Carrying amount of PPE sold	(576)
PPE and end of year	(47,835)
Total PPE additions	(21,147)

Tax paid	£'000
Tax liability at start of year	3,180
Tax charge to profit/loss	2,712
Tax liability at end of year	(2,790)
Tax paid	3,102

Task 2 (7 marks)

Fontwell Ltd – Statement of changes in equity for the year ended 30 June 20X1.

	Share capital £'000	Share premium £'000	Retained earnings £'000	Total equity £'000
Balance at 1 July 20X0	18,000	6,300	17,600	41,900
Changes in equity				
Total profit			8,907	8,907
Dividends			(3,200)	(3,200)
Issue of share capital	4,500	2,600		7,100
Balance at 30 June 20X1	22,500	8,900	23,307	54,707

Task 3 (10 marks)

(a) **Going concern**

The assumption of going concern is that a company will continue in operational existence for the foreseeable future. Hence, it is assumed that the entity has neither the intention, nor the need to liquidate or curtail materially the scale of its operations; if such an intention or need exists, the financial statements may have to be prepared on a different basis and, if so, the basis used is disclosed.

(b) **Historical cost**

Assets are recorded at the amount of cash or cash equivalents (price) paid or the fair value of the consideration given to acquire them at the time of their acquisition. Liabilities are recorded at the amount of proceeds received in exchange for the obligation, or in some circumstances at the amount of cash or cash equivalents expected to be paid to satisfy the liability in the normal course of business.

Current cost

Assets are carried at the amount of cash or cash equivalents that would have to be paid if the same or an equivalent asset was acquired currently. Liabilities are carried at their settlement values; that is, the amount of cash that would be required to settle the obligation currently.

Realisable (settlement) value

Assets are carried at the amount of cash or cash equivalents that could currently be obtained by selling the asset in an orderly disposal. Liabilities are carried at their settlement values, that is, the undiscounted amounts of cash or cash equivalents expected to be paid to satisfy the liabilities in the normal course of business.

Present value

Assets are carried at the present discounted value of the future net cash inflows that the item is expected to generate in the normal course of business. Liabilities are carried at the present discounted value of the future net cash outflows that are expected to be required to settle the liabilities in the normal course of business.

....

Task 4 (12 marks)

(a) The recoverable amount is the greater of the fair value (market value) less costs to sell and the value in use.

Fair value is the price that would be received to sell an asset in an orderly transaction between market participants at the measurement date.

Value in use is the present value of the future cash flows expected to be derived from an asset.

Recoverable amount is the greater of:

Fair value less costs to sell	£341,000 – £15,000 = £326,000
Value in use	£367,000 = Recoverable amount

(b) An **impairment loss** is the amount by which the carrying amount of an asset exceeds its recoverable amount.

Carrying amount £875,000 – £481,000	= £394,000
Recoverable amount	= £367,000
Impairment loss	= £27,000

....

Task 5 (17 marks)

Statement: The lease must be recognised as an asset and liability in the statement of financial position.

(a) **Is this statement true or false?**

True ☑

False ☐

(b) **What is the tax charge that will be shown in the company's statement of profit or loss?**

£14,900 ☐

£15,500 ☑

£17,300 ☐

£19,100 ☐

Working

	£
Liability at 30 June 20X1	17,300
Overprovision in y/e 30 June 20X0:	
16,700 – 14,900	(1,800)
Tax charge	15,500

(c) **What is the value of closing inventory at 30 June 20X1?**

£340 ☐

£424 ☐

£636 ☑

£740 ☐

Working

- Total cost of units at 1 July 20X0 is £400 (50 × £8)

- Total cost of items purchased in the y/e 30 June 20X1 is £660 (30 × £12) + 20 × £15).

- Cost per item is £10.60 [(£400 + £660) ÷ (50 + 30 + 20)].

- Value of inventories: £636 (100 – 40) × £10.60).

(d) **What will be the carrying amount of the machine at 30 June 20X3?**

£4,000 ☐

£5,000 ☐

£8,000 ☑

£12,000 ☐

Working

	£
Cost at 1 July 20X0	20,000
Depreciation (3 years × [(20 – 4)/4]	(12,000)
Carrying amount at 30 June 20X3	8,000

(e) **What is the consolidated cost of sales for the year ending 30 June 20X1?**

£52,000 ☐

£54,000 ☑

£60,000 ☐

£62,000 ☐

Working

	£
Per question	70,000
Less intercompany	(18,000)
Unrealised profit (£18,000 – £10,000) × 25%	2,000
Tax charge	54,000

(f) **Which of the following statements are correct with regard to property, plant and equipment (PPE)?**

(1) A revaluation reserve arises when an item of PPE is sold at a profit.
(2) All non-current assets must be depreciated.

(1) only ☐

(2) only ☐

Both ☐

Neither of them ☑

Task 6 (28 marks)

(a) **Calculate the figures for goodwill and non-controlling interest that would be included in the consolidated statement of financial position of Purley Plc and its subsidiary undertaking as at 30 June 20X1.**

	£'000
Goodwill	58
Non-controlling interest	100

Workings

Goodwill	£'000
Price paid	410
Share capital – attributable to Purley plc (360 × 80%)	(288)
Retained earnings – attributable to Purley plc (80 × 80%)	(64)
Goodwill	58

Non-controlling interest (NCI)	£'000
Share capital – attributable to NCI (360 × 20%)	72
Retained earnings – attributable to NCI (140 × 20%)	28
	100

(b) **Draft the consolidated statement of profit or loss for Danes Plc and its subsidiary undertaking for the year ended 30 June 20X1.**

Note. You don't need to use the workings to achieve full marks on the task, but data in the workings will be considered if you make errors in the proforma.

Danes Plc
Consolidated statement of profit or loss for the year ended 30 June 20X1.

Continuing operations	£'000
Revenue (W)	27,560
Cost of sales (W)	(17,322)
Gross profit	10,238
Other income (W)	4,096
Distribution costs: 2,132 + 894	(3,026)
Administrative expenses: 1,684 + 715	(2,399)
Profit from operations	8,909
Finance costs: 360 + 193	(553)
Profit before tax	8,356
Tax: 1,260 + 680	(1,940)
Profit for the period from continuing operations	6,416

Attributable to	£'000
Equity holders of the parent	5,862
Non-controlling interest	554
	6,416

Workings

Revenue	£'000
Danes Plc	18,560
Winter Ltd	9,350
Total inter-company adjustment	(350)
	27,560

Cost of sales	£'000
Danes Plc	12,346
Winter Ltd	5,256
Total inter-company adjustment: 350 – [(350 – 210) × 50%]	(280)
	17,322

Other income	£'000
Danes Plc	3,258
Winter Ltd	1,158
Total inter-company adjustment	(320)
	4,096

....

Task 7 (20 marks)

(a) **Identify the formulas that are used to calculate each of the following ratios:**

Return on shareholders' funds | Profit after tax / Total equity × 100

Interest cover | Profit from operations / Finance costs

Current ratio | Current assets / Current liabilities

Operating profit percentage | Profit from operations / Revenue × 100

Inventory turnover | Cost of sales / Inventories

(b) **Calculate the above ratios to ONE decimal place.**

Return on shareholders' funds | 31.2 | % | (7,827/25,125)

Interest cover | 15.4 | times | (10,452/678)

Current ratio | 2.5 | :1 | (15,525/6,165)

Operating profit percentage | 23.4 | % | (10,452/44,626)

Inventory turnover | 3.2 | times | (27,457/8,419)

....

Task 8 (23 marks)

(a) **(i)** **20X1 Gross profit % is worse.**

- Less gross profit is being generated by sales/lower gross profit margins on sales.

- Selling prices may have decreased.

- Cost of sales/purchase costs may have increased.

- The mix of products sold may have changed in 20X1.

- The annual budget anticipated a reduction of gross profit (to 33%) but the drop is greater than expected.

(ii) **20X1 Operating profit % is better.**

- As the gross profit ratio has declined the improvement is due to lower overhead costs.

- More operating profit is being generated from sales.

- The operating profit achieved is in line with the budget.

- As gross profit is lower than the budget, this indicates that costs are lower than planned.

(iii) **20X1 Interest cover is better**.

- More profit is available to meet interest payments (less risky).

- May be caused by higher operating profits.

- May be caused by lower interest payments.

- May have paid off debt during the year.

- Interest rates may have declined.

- The improvement in interest cover was anticipated by the budget, but is better than expected.

(b) **Limitations of ratio analysis.**

Note. Only THREE required.

- *Different accounting policies*

  The choices of accounting policies may distort inter-company comparisons.

- *Creative accounting*

  Companies may try to show a better financial performance or position.

- *Outdated information in financial statements*

  Financial statements are likely to be out of date and will not reflect the current position.

- *Changes in accounting policy*

  Changes may affect the comparison of results between different accounting years.

- *Ratios are not definitive measures*

  Ratios only provide clues to the company's performance or financial situation.

- *Historical costs not suitable for decision making*

  Ratios based on historical costs may not be very useful for decision making.

- *Interpretation of the ratio*

  It is difficult to generalise about whether a particular ratio is 'good' or 'bad'.

- *Price changes*

  Inflation renders comparisons of results over time misleading.

- *Changes in accounting standard*

  Change will affect the comparison of results over a number of years.

- *Impact of seasons on trading*

  Some businesses are affected by seasons and can choose the best time to produce financial statements so as to show better results.

- *Different financial and business risk profile*

  Businesses may operate within the same industry but have different financial and business risk.

- *Different capital structures and size*

  Companies may have different capital structures which makes comparison difficult.

....

BPP PRACTICE ASSESSMENT 1
FINANCIAL STATEMENTS

Time allowed: 2½ hours

The following information is relevant to Task 1 and Task 2

You have been asked to help prepare the financial statements of Ricschtein Ltd for the year ended 31 March 20X7. The company's trial balance as at 31 March 20X7 is shown below.

Ricschtein Ltd

Trial balance as at 31 March 20X7

	Debit £'000	Credit £'000
Share capital		7,000
Trade payables		2,236
Property, plant and equipment – cost	39,371	
Property, plant and equipment – accumulated depreciation at 31 March 20X7		13,892
Trade receivables	4,590	
Accruals		207
7% bank loan repayable 20Y2		14,000
Cash at bank	423	
Retained earnings at 1 April 20X6		9,552
Interest	490	
Sales		36,724
Purchases	21,749	
Distribution costs	5,517	
Administrative expenses	4,251	
Inventories as at 1 April 20X6	6,120	
Dividends paid	1,100	
	83,611	83,611

Further information:

- The share capital of the company consists of ordinary shares with a nominal value of £1.

- At the beginning of the year the issued share capital was 7,000,000 ordinary shares. At the end of the year another 3,000,000 ordinary shares were issued at a price of £3.00 per share. Due to a misunderstanding about the date of the share issue, this has not been accounted for in the ledger accounts in the trial balance.

- The inventories at the close of business on 31 March 20X7 cost £7,304,000.

- Administrative expenses of £87,000 relating to February 20X7 have not been included in the trial balance.

- The company paid £36,000 insurance costs in June 20X6, which covered the period from 1 July 20X6 to 30 June 20X7. This was included in the administrative expenses in the trial balance.

- Interest on the bank loan for the last six months of the year has not been included in the accounts in the trial balance.

- The corporation tax charge for the year has been calculated as £1,170,000.

- All of the operations are continuing operations.

Task 1

(a) **Draft the statement of profit or loss and other comprehensive income for Ricschtein Ltd for the year ended 31 March 20X7.**

Ricschtein Ltd

Statement of profit or loss and other comprehensive income for the year ended 31 March 20X7

	£'000
Revenue	
Cost of sales	
Gross profit	
Distribution costs	
Administrative expenses	
Profit from operations	
Finance costs	
Profit before tax	
Tax	
Profit for the period from continuing operations	

Workings

(Complete the left hand column by writing in the correct narrative from the list provided.)

Cost of sales		£'000
	▼	
	▼	
	▼	

Picklist for narratives:

Accruals
Closing inventories
Opening inventories
Prepayments
Purchases

Administrative expenses	£'000
▼	
▼	
▼	

Picklist for narratives:

Accruals
Administrative expenses
Prepayments

(b) **Draft the statement of changes in equity for Ricschtein Ltd for the year ended 31 March 20X7.**

Ricschtein Ltd

Statement of changes in equity for the year ended 31 March 20X7

	Share capital £'000	Share premium £'000	Retained earnings £'000	Total equity £'000
Balance at 1 April 20X6				
Changes in equity				
Total comprehensive income				
Dividends				
Issue of share capital				
Balance at 31 March 20X7				

Task 2

Draft the statement of financial position for Ricschtein Ltd as at 31 March 20X7.

(Complete the left hand column by writing in the correct line item from the list)

Ricschtein Ltd
Statement of financial position as at 31 March 20X7

		£'000
Assets		
Non-current assets		
	▼	
Current assets		
	▼	
	▼	
	▼	
Total assets		
Equity and liabilities		
Equity		
	▼	
	▼	
	▼	
Total equity		
Non-current liabilities		
	▼	
Current liabilities		
	▼	
	▼	
Total liabilities		
Total equity and liabilities		

Picklist for line items

Bank loan
Cash and cash equivalents
Inventories
Property, plant and equipment
Retained earnings
Share capital
Share premium
Tax liability
Trade and other payables
Trade and other receivables

Workings

(Complete the left hand column by writing in the correct narrative from the list provided.)

Trade and other receivables	£'000
▼	
▼	

Picklist for narratives:

Accruals: trial balance
Additional administrative expenses accrual
Additional administrative expenses prepaid
Additional finance costs accrual
Additional finance costs prepaid
Trade and other payables
Trade and other receivables

Retained earnings	£'000
▼	
▼	
▼	

Picklist for narratives:

Dividends paid
Premium paid on share issue
Profit/(loss) for the period from continuing operations
Retained earnings at 1 April 20X6
Total profit for the year

Trade and other payables	£'000
▼	
▼	
▼	
▼	

Picklist for narratives:

Accruals: trial balance
Additional administrative expenses accrual
Additional administrative expenses prepaid
Additional finance costs accrual
Additional finance costs prepaid
Dividends
Tax liability
Trade and other payables
Trade and other receivables

Task 3

The IASB's *Conceptual Framework for Financial Reporting* states that there is one important assumption that underlies the preparation of general purpose financial statements. The *Conceptual Framework* also identifies and describes four qualitative characteristics that enhance the usefulness of financial information that is relevant and faithfully represented.

(a) **Identify and briefly explain the 'underlying assumption'.**

(b) **List the FOUR ENHANCING qualitative characteristics of useful financial information.**

(c) **Briefly explain ONE of these qualitative characteristics.**

Task 4

Oaktree Ltd publishes specialist magazines and technical manuals. The company prepares its financial statements to 31 March each year.

During the year ended 31 March 20X7, a customer took out a 12 month subscription for one of the company's monthly specialist magazines, starting on 1 July 20X6. Under the terms of the subscription, Oaktree Ltd supplied 20 copies of the magazine at the beginning of each month over the 12 month period. The price of the subscription was £1,500.

Oaktree Ltd also sold an old printing press for £5,000 during the year.

Prepare brief notes for a meeting with the directors of Oaktree Ltd to cover the following, in accordance with IAS 18 *Revenue*:

(a) **What is the definition of revenue?**

(b) **State the conditions which must be satisfied in order for revenue associated with the sale of goods to be recognised in the financial statements.**

(c) **Calculate the amount of revenue, if any, that should be recognised in the financial statements of Oaktree Ltd for the year ending 31 March 20X7 in respect of the subscription and the sale of the printing press.**

Task 5

(a) According to IAS 38 *Intangible Assets*, an internally generated brand name can be recognised as an intangible asset.

Is this statement True or False?

True	
False	

(b) At the beginning of the year, Broad Ltd had the following balance:

Accrued interest payable   £12,000 credit

During the year, Broad Ltd charged interest payable of £41,000 to profit or loss. The closing balance on accrued interest payable account at the end of the year was £15,000 credit.

How much interest paid should Broad Ltd show in its statement of cash flows for the year?

£38,000	
£41,000	
£44,000	
£53,000	

(c) **Which of the following statements are correct, according to IAS 36 *Impairment of Assets*?**

1   All non-current assets must be reviewed for impairment annually.

2   An impairment loss must be recognised immediately in profit or loss, except that all or part of a loss on a revalued asset should be charged against any related revaluation surplus.

1 only	
2 only	
Both 1 and 2	
Neither 1 nor 2	

(d) A company leases some plant on 1 January 20X4. The fair value of the plant is £9,000, and the company leases it for four years, paying four annual instalments of £3,000 beginning on 31 December 20X4.

The company uses the sum of the digits method to allocate interest.

What is the interest charge for the year ended 31 December 20X5?

£600	
£750	
£900	
£1,000	

(e) **Which of the following events after the reporting period would normally be classified as a *non-adjusting event*, according to IAS 10 *Events After the Reporting Period*?**

1 The company announced a plan to discontinue an operation.
2 A customer was discovered to be insolvent.

1 only	
2 only	
Both 1 and 2	
Neither 1 nor 2	

(f) Narrow Ltd is being sued by a customer and will have to pay an estimated £100,000 sum in compensation if it loses the case. At its accounting year end lawyers advise the company that it is possible (i.e. less than a 50% likelihood of occurrence) that it may lose the case.

In accordance with IAS 37 *Provisions, Contingent Liabilities and Contingent Assets* the possible future outflow should be:

Recognised in the statement of financial position as a provision	
Recognised in the statement of financial position as a contingent liability	
Only disclosed as a note to the financial statements	
Neither recognised in the statement of financial position nor included in the notes	

Task 6

The Managing Director of Harris plc has asked you to prepare the statement of financial position for the group. Harris plc has one subsidiary, Skye Ltd. The statements of financial position of the two companies as at 31 March 20X8 are set out below.

Statements of financial position as at 31 March 20X8

	Harris plc £'000	Skye Ltd £'000
Non-current assets		
Property, plant and equipment	47,875	31,913
Investment in Skye Ltd	32,000	
	79,875	31,913
Current assets		
Inventories	25,954	4,555
Trade and other receivables	14,343	3,656
Cash and cash equivalents	1,956	47
	42,253	8,258
Total assets	122,128	40,171
Equity and liabilities		
Equity		
Share capital	57,000	15,000
Retained earnings	26,160	14,340
Total equity	83,160	29,340
Non-current liabilities		
Long-term loans	20,000	7,000
Current liabilities		
Trade and other payables	14,454	3,685
Tax liabilities	4,514	146
	18,968	3,831
Total liabilities	38,968	10,831
Total equity and liabilities	122,128	40,171

Further information:

- The share capital of Skye Ltd consists of ordinary shares of £1 each. Ownership of these shares carries voting rights in Skye Ltd.
- Harris plc acquired 9,000,000 shares in Skye Ltd on 1 April 20X7.
- At 1 April 20X7 the balance of retained earnings of Skye Ltd was £11,260,000.
- The directors of Harris plc have concluded that goodwill has been impaired by £4,000,000 during the year.
- Non-controlling interest is measured as the proportionate share of the fair value of Skye Ltd's net assets.

Draft a consolidated statement of financial position for Harris plc and its subsidiary as at 31 March 20X8.

Harris plc

Consolidated statement of financial position as at 31 March 20X8

	£'000
Assets	
Non-current assets	
Intangible assets: goodwill	
Property, plant and equipment	
Current assets	
Inventories	
Trade and other receivables	
Cash and cash equivalents	
Total assets	
Equity and liabilities	
Equity	
Share capital	
Retained earnings	
Non-controlling interest	
Total equity	
Non-current liabilities	
Long-term loans	
Current liabilities	
Trade and other payables	
Tax liabilities	
Total liabilities	
Total equity and liabilities	

Workings

(Complete the left hand column by writing in the correct narrative from the list provided.)

Goodwill	£'000
▼	
▼	
▼	
▼	

Picklist for narratives:

Impairment
Price paid
Retained earnings – attributable to Harris plc
Share capital – attributable to Harris plc

Retained earnings	£'000
▼	
▼	
▼	

Picklist for narratives:

Harris plc
Impairment
Skye Ltd – attributable to Harris plc

Non-controlling interest (NCI)	£'000
▼	
▼	

Picklist for narratives:

Current assets – attributable to NCI
Impairment
Non-current assets – attributable to NCI
Price paid
Retained earnings – attributable to NCI
Share capital – attributable to NCI

Task 7

David Alexander is a shareholder in Cairngorm Ltd. He has asked you to assist him by calculating ratios in respect of the financial statements for the year ended 31 March 20X9. The financial statements of Cairngorm Ltd are set out below:

Cairngorm Ltd

Statement of profit or loss for the year ended 31 March 20X9

	£'000
Continuing operations	
Revenue	14,800
Cost of sales	(7,770)
Gross profit	7,030
Distribution costs	(3,700)
Administrative expenses	(2,072)
Profit from operations	1,258
Finance costs	(630)
Profit before tax	628
Tax	(294)
Profit for the period from continuing operations	334

Cairngorm Ltd

Statement of financial position as at 31 March 20X9

	£'000
Assets	
Non-current assets	
Property, plant and equipment	18,916
Current assets	
Inventories	1,632
Trade and other receivables	1,776
Cash and cash equivalents	0
	3,408
Total assets	22,324
Equity and liabilities	
Equity	
Share capital	6,500
Retained earnings	5,138
Total equity	11,638
Non-current liabilities	
Bank loans	9,000
Current liabilities	
Trade payables	855
Tax liabilities	294
Bank overdraft	537
	1,686
Total liabilities	10,686
Total equity and liabilities	22,324

(a) **State the formulae that are used to calculate the following ratios:**

(Write in the correct formula from the list provided)

(i) Inventory holding period	▼

Formulae:

Inventories/Cost of sales × 365

Inventories/Revenue × 365

Cost of sales/Inventories × 365

Revenue/Inventories × 365

(ii) Trade receivables collection period	▼

Formulae:

Trade payables/Cost of sales × 365

Trade receivables/Cost of sales × 365

Revenue/Trade receivables × 365

Trade receivables/Revenue × 365

(iii) Trade payables payment period	▼

Formulae:

Trade payables/Revenue × 365

Trade payables/Cost of sales × 365

Revenue/Trade payables × 365

Cost of sales/Trade payables × 365

(iv) Working capital cycle	▼

Formulae:

Current assets/Current liabilities

Current assets – Inventories/Current liabilities

Inventory days + Receivables days – Payables days

Inventory days + Receivables days + Payables days

(v) Gearing		
Formulae:		
Current assets/Current liabilities		
Revenue/Total assets – Current liabilities		
Non-current liabilities/Total equity + Non-current liabilities		
Profit after tax/Number of issued ordinary shares		

(b) **Calculate the following ratios to the nearest ONE DECIMAL PLACE.**

(i)	Inventory holding period (days)		days
(ii)	Trade receivables collection period		days
(iii)	Trade payables payment period		days
(iv)	Working capital cycle		days
(v)	Gearing ratio		%

Task 8

John Brams is a shareholder of Ma Leer Ltd. He has obtained some ratios that are based on the financial statements of the company for the last two years (to December 20X4 and 20X5). He is interested in how the directors have managed the business in the past year and in the company's financial performance. You have been asked to analyse the financial performance of the company using the ratios computed. The ratios John has obtained are set out below. Sales revenue has remained relatively stable throughout 20X4 and 20X5.

Ratio	20X5	20X4
Return on capital employed	15%	19%
Gross profit percentage	46%	42%
Operating profit percentage	20%	22%
Expense/revenue percentage	26%	24%
Asset turnover (based on net assets)	0.75	0.86

Prepare a report for John Brams that includes the following.

(a) **Your comments on the financial performance of Ma Leer Ltd for the two years based on your analysis of the ratios and what this tells you about the company.**

(b) **Your opinion, with reasons based on your analysis of the ratios above, as to how well the company has been managed during the year.**

BPP PRACTICE ASSESSMENT 1
FINANCIAL STATEMENTS

ANSWERS

Task 1

(a) **Ricschtein Ltd**

Statement of profit or loss and other comprehensive income for the year ended 31 March 20X7

	£'000
Revenue	36,724
Cost of sales (W)	(20,565)
Gross profit	16,159
Distribution costs	(5,517)
Administrative expenses (W)	(4,329)
Profit from operations	6,313
Finance costs (490 + 490)	(980)
Profit before tax	5,333
Tax	(1,170)
Profit for the period from continuing operations	4,163

Workings

Cost of sales	£'000
Opening inventories	6,120
Purchases	21,749
Closing inventories	(7,304)
	20,565

Administrative expenses	£'000
Administrative expenses	4,251
Accruals	87
Prepayments (36 × 3/12)	(9)
	4,329

(b) **Ricschtein Ltd**

Statement of changes in equity for the year ended 31 March 20X7

	Share capital £'000	Share premium £'000	Retained earnings £'000	Total equity £'000
Balance at 1 April 20X6	7,000		9,552	16,552
Changes in equity				
Total comprehensive income			4,163	4,163
Dividends			(1,100)	(1,100)
Issue of share capital	3,000	6,000	0	9,000
Balance at 31 March 20X7	10,000	6,000	12,615	28,615

Task 2

Ricschtein Ltd

Statement of financial position as at 31 March 20X7

	£'000
Assets	
Non-current assets	
Property, plant and equipment (39,371 – 13,892)	25,479
Current assets	
Inventories	7,304
Trade and other receivables (W)	4,599
Cash and cash equivalents (423 + 9,000)	9,423
	21,326
Total assets	46,805
Equity and liabilities	
Equity	
Share capital (7,000 + 3,000)	10,000
Share premium	6,000
Retained earnings (W)	12,615
Total equity	28,615
Non-current liabilities	
Bank loan	14,000
Current liabilities	
Trade and other payables (W)	3,020
Tax liability	1,170
	4,190
Total liabilities	18,190
Total equity and liabilities	46,805

Workings

Trade and other receivables	£'000
Trade and other receivables	4,590
Additional administrative expenses prepaid	9
	4,599

Retained earnings	£'000
Retained earnings at 1 April 20X6	9,552
Total profit for the year	4,163
Dividends paid	(1,100)
	12,615

Trade and other payables	£'000
Trade and other payables	2,236
Accruals: trial balance	207
Additional administrative expenses accrual	87
Additional finance costs accrual	490
	3,020

Task 3

Note. Based on the information available at the time this book was written, we anticipate that this task would be human marked in the real assessment.

(a) The underlying assumption is going concern.

Financial statements are normally prepared on the assumption that the entity will continue to operate for the foreseeable future. This means that its management does not intend or need to liquidate or curtail the scale of its operations materially. For example, if an entity is a going concern there should be no need to sell off any significant part of the business or restrict any of its normal trading activities.

(b) The four enhancing qualitative characteristics of useful financial information are:

- Comparability
- Verifiability
- Timeliness
- Understandability

(c) **Comparability**

Users need to be able to compare information about a reporting entity with similar information about other entities and with information about the same entity for a different period or another date.

Consistency helps to achieve comparability. Consistency is the use of the same methods for the same items from one period to the next and in a single period, the use of the same methods across entities.

Comparability does not mean uniformity. For information to be comparable, like things must look alike and different things must look different.

Verifiability

If information is verifiable, it means that different knowledgeable and independent observers could reach a consensus (broad agreement but not necessarily complete agreement) that a particular way of presenting an item is a faithful representation.

Verification can be direct (for example, through an observation, such as counting cash). It can also be indirect (for example, through checking the quantities and costs used in calculating the value of closing inventories and checking the calculation itself).

Timeliness

To be useful, information must be available to decision makers in time to be capable of influencing their decisions.

Generally, the older the information is, the less useful it is. For example, the latest set of financial statements is normally the most relevant for decision-making. However, older financial information may still be useful for identifying and assessing trends (for example, growth in profits over a number of years).

Understandability

Classifying, characterising and presenting information clearly and concisely makes it understandable.

However, some information is complex and cannot be made easier to understand. Excluding this information from the financial statements would make them more understandable, but they would also be incomplete and potentially misleading.

Financial reports are prepared for users who have a reasonable knowledge of business and economic activities and who review and analyse the information diligently. Users may sometimes need help from an adviser in order to understand complex financial information.

Note. Candidates only needed to explain ONE of the enhancing qualitative characteristics.

Task 4

Note. Based on the information available at the time this book was written, we anticipate that this task would be human marked in the real assessment.

(a) IAS 18 *Revenue* defines revenue as the 'gross inflow of economic benefits during the period arising in the course of the ordinary activities of the entity when those inflows result in increases in equity, other than increases relating to contributions from equity participants'.

(b) Revenue from the sale of goods should be recognised when the following conditions have been satisfied:

(i)   The entity has transferred to the buyer the significant risks and rewards of ownership of the goods

(ii) The entity retains neither continuing managerial involvement nor effective control over the goods sold

(iii) The amount of revenue can be measured reliably

(iv) It is probable that the economic benefits associated with the transaction will flow to the entity and

(v)   The costs incurred or to be incurred in respect of the transaction can be measured reliably.

(c) The subscription is effectively twelve separate purchases paid for in advance. At the year-end, the company has transferred nine of the twelve monthly issues to the customer, so it should recognise £1,125 (1,500 × 9/12).

The sale of the printing press does not arise in the course of the ordinary activities of the company, so the sale proceeds cannot be recognised as revenue.

Task 5

(a)

True	
False	✓

IAS 38 states that internally generated brands, mastheads, publishing titles, customer lists and items similar in substance should not be recognised as intangible assets.

(b)

£38,000	✓
£41,000	
£44,000	
£53,000	

	£
Opening balance	12,000
Profit or loss	41,000
Closing balance	(15,000)
	38,000

(c)

1 only	
2 only	✓
Both 1 and 2	
Neither 1 nor 2	

Statement 1 is incorrect. In most cases, an impairment review need only be carried out if there is some indication that impairment has incurred. Only goodwill and intangible assets with an indefinite useful life must be reviewed annually.

(d)

£600	
£750	
£900	✓
£1,000	

The interest charge is 3/10 × £3,000

(e)

1 only	✓
2 only	
Both 1 and 2	
Neither 1 nor 2	

(f)

Recognised in the statement of financial position as a provision	
Recognised in the statement of financial position as a contingent liability	
Only disclosed as a note to the financial statements	✓
Neither recognised in the statement of financial position nor included in the notes	

This is a contingent liability because the outflow of economic benefit is only possible, rather than probable. Contingent liabilities are only disclosed and are not recognised in the statement of financial position.

Task 6

Harris plc

Consolidated statement of financial position as at 31 March 20X8

	£'000
Assets	
Non-current assets	
Intangible assets: goodwill (W)	12,244
Property, plant and equipment	79,788
	92,032
Current assets	
Inventories	30,509
Trade and other receivables	17,999
Cash and cash equivalents	2,003
	50,511
Total assets	142,543
Equity and liabilities	
Equity	
Share capital	57,000
Retained earnings (W)	24,008
	81,008
Non-controlling interest (W)	11,736
Total equity	92,744
Non-current liabilities	
Long-term loans	27,000
Current liabilities	
Trade and other payables	18,139
Tax liabilities	4,660
	22,799
Total liabilities	49,799
Total equity and liabilities	142,543

Workings

Note: **Group structure**

Harris plc owns 60% of Skye Ltd (9,000,000/15,000,000)

Goodwill	£'000
Price paid	32,000
Share capital – attributable to Harris plc (60% × 15,000)	(9,000)
Retained earnings – attributable to Harris plc (60% × 11,260)	(6,756)
Impairment	(4,000)
	12,244

Retained earnings	£'000
Harris plc	26,160
Skye Ltd – attributable to Harris plc (60% × (14,340 – 11,260))	1,848
Impairment	(4,000)
	24,008

Non-controlling interest (NCI)	£'000
Share capital – attributable to NCI (40% × 15,000)	6,000
Retained earnings – attributable to NCI (40% × 14,340)	5,736
	11,736

Task 7

(a) **Formulae used to calculate the ratios**

(i)	Inventory holding period	$\dfrac{\text{Inventories}}{\text{Cost of sales}} \times 365$
(ii)	Trade receivables collection period	$\dfrac{\text{Trade receivables}}{\text{Revenue}} \times 365$
(iii)	Trade payables payment period	$\dfrac{\text{Trade payables}}{\text{Cost of sales}} \times 365$
(iv)	Working capital cycle	Inventory days + Receivables days – Payables days
(v)	Gearing ratio	$\dfrac{\text{Non-current liabilities}}{\text{Total equity + Non-current liabilities}} \times 100\%$

(b) **Calculation of the ratios**

(i)	**Inventory holding period (days)** $\dfrac{1,632}{7,770} \times 365$		76.7	days
(ii)	**Trade receivables collection period** $\dfrac{1,776}{14,800} \times 365$		43.8	days
(iii)	**Trade payables payment period** $\dfrac{855}{7,770} \times 365$		40.2	days
(iv)	**Working capital cycle** 76.7 + 43.8 – 40.2		80.3	days
(v)	**Gearing ratio** $\dfrac{9,000}{11,638 + 9,000} \times 100$		43.6	%

Task 8

Note. Based on the information available at the time this book was written, we anticipate that this task would be human marked in the real assessment.

REPORT

To: John Brams

From: Accounting Technician

Subject: Financial performance of Ma Leer Ltd

Date: 10 January 20X6

As requested, I have analysed the financial performance of Ma Leer Ltd, based on the ratios provided.

(a) **The financial performance of the company**

Return on capital employed

Return on capital employed has deteriorated significantly during the year. This suggests that investors are not obtaining as a good a return on the capital that they have invested as in previous years. There are two reasons for this. The company is slightly less profitable in 20X5 than it was in 20X4. In addition the company is not generating as much profit (or return) from its capital (assets) as in the previous year.

Gross profit percentage

This has improved significantly during the year. There could be several reasons for this. One reason is costs of sales may have fallen. Alternatively the company may have changed its 'sales mix', so that, although the overall sales revenue has remained stable, it has sold a greater proportion of products with a higher gross margin.

Operating profit percentage and expense/revenue percentage

There has been a slight fall in the company's operating profit percentage. This has occurred despite the improvement in the gross profit percentage during the year. There must have been a significant rise in operating expenses (such as administrative expenses). This is confirmed by the expenses/revenue percentage, which has risen slightly. This suggests that 'non-trading' expenses have risen fairly sharply compared with sales. Alternatively there may have been a large unusual expense of some kind during the year.

Asset turnover

Asset turnover has fallen during the year. The company appears to be operating less efficiently than in the previous year and is therefore generating less sales revenue relative to the capital invested in the business (represented by its net assets). There are a number of possible reasons for this, including investment in new assets towards the end of the year. However, the other ratios suggest that the most likely reason for the fall is either that sales have been disappointing following increased investment (an expected rise in sales has not materialised) or that the company now has a higher proportion of assets that are not being used to generate sales.

(b) **How well the company has been managed**

The overall picture is of a company which is probably not being managed as well as in previous years. Operating expenses seem to be disproportionately high compared with sales, suggesting poor control, and the company appears to be operating less efficiently than before, failing to turn increased investment in assets into additional profit. The fact that the company's gross profit percentage has increased despite this indicates that there is nothing fundamentally wrong with the business and that with better management there could be considerable scope for improvement in return on capital employed and overall performance.

BPP PRACTICE ASSESSMENT 2
FINANCIAL STATEMENTS

Time allowed: 2½ hours

PRACTICE ASSESSMENT 2

The following information is relevant to Task 1 and Task 2

You have been asked to prepare a statement of cash flows and a statement of changes in equity for Kenadie Ltd for the year ended 30 September 20X6. The statement of profit or loss and statement of financial position (with comparatives for the previous year) of Kenadie Ltd are set out below.

Kenadie Ltd

Statement of profit or loss for the year ended 30 September 20X6

	£'000
Continuing operations	
Revenue	31,461
Cost of sales	(16,304)
Gross profit	15,157
Loss on disposal of property, plant and equipment	(183)
Distribution costs	(5,663)
Administrative expenses	(3,681)
Profit from operations	5,630
Finance costs – interest on loan	(800)
Profit before tax	4,830
Tax	(919)
Profit for the period from continuing operations	3,911

Kenadie Ltd

Statement of financial position as at 30 September 20X6

	20X6 £'000	20X5 £'000
Assets		
Non-current assets		
Property, plant and equipment	29,882	19,100
Current assets		
Inventories	4,837	4,502
Trade receivables	5,244	4,978
Cash and cash equivalents	64	587
	10,145	10,067

Kenadie Ltd

Statement of financial position as at 30 September 20X6

	£'000	£'000
Total assets	40,027	29,167
Equity and liabilities		
Equity		
Share capital	8,000	5,000
Share premium account	2,500	1,000
Retained earnings	15,570	12,359
Total equity	26,070	18,359
Non-current liabilities		
Bank loan	10,000	7,000
Current liabilities		
Trade payables	3,038	2,954
Tax liabilities	919	854
	3,957	3,808
Total liabilities	13,957	10,808
Total equity plus liabilities	40,027	29,167

Further information:

- The total depreciation charge for the year was £2,172,000.

- Property, plant and equipment costing £1,103,000, with accumulated depreciation of £411,000, was sold in the year.

- All sales and purchases were on credit. Other expenses were paid for in cash.

- A dividend of £700,000 was paid during the year.

Task 1

(a) **Prepare a reconciliation of profit from operations to net cash from operating activities for Kenadie Ltd for the year ended 30 September 20X6.**

(Complete the left hand column by writing in the correct line item from the list provided.)

Reconciliation of profit from operations to net cash from operating activities

	£'000
▼	
Adjustments for:	
▼	
▼	
▼	
▼	
▼	
Cash generated by operations	
▼	
▼	
Net cash from operating activities	

Picklist for line items:

Adjustment in respect of inventories
Adjustment in respect of trade payables
Adjustment in respect of trade receivables
Depreciation
Loss on disposal of property, plant and equipment
Interest paid
New bank loans
Proceeds on disposal of property, plant and equipment
Profit after tax
Profit before tax
Profit from operations
Purchases of property, plant and equipment
Tax paid

(b) **Prepare the statement of cash flows for Kenadie Ltd for the year ended 30 September 20X6.**

(Complete the left hand column by writing in the correct line item from the list provided.)

Kenadie Ltd

Statement of cash flows for the year ended 30 September 20X6

	£'000
Net cash from operating activities	
Investing activities	
▼	
▼	
Net cash used in investing activities	
Financing activities	
▼	
▼	
▼	
Net cash from financing activities	
Net increase/(decrease) in cash and cash equivalents	
Cash and cash equivalents at the beginning of the year	
Cash and cash equivalents at the end of the year	

Picklist for line items:

Adjustment in respect of inventories
Adjustment in respect of trade payables
Adjustment in respect of trade receivables
Dividends paid
New bank loans
Proceeds of share issue
Proceeds on disposal of property, plant and equipment
Purchases of property, plant and equipment

Workings

(Complete the left hand column by writing in the correct narrative from the list provided.)

Proceeds on disposal of property, plant and equipment (PPE)		£'000
	▼	
	▼	

Picklist for narratives:

Carrying amount of PPE sold
Depreciation charge
Loss on disposal
PPE at end of year
PPE at start of year

Purchases of property, plant and equipment (PPE)		£'000
PPE at start of year		
	▼	
	▼	
	▼	
Total PPE additions		

Picklist for narratives:

Carrying amount of PPE sold
Depreciation charge
Loss on disposal of PPE
PPE at end of year

Task 2

Draft the statement of changes in equity for Kenadie Ltd for the year ended 30 September 20X6.

(Complete the left hand column by writing in the correct line item from the list provided.)

Kenadie Ltd

Statement of changes in equity for the year ended 30 September 20X6

	Share capital £'000	Share premium £'000	Retained earnings £'000	Total equity £'000
Balance at 1 October 20X5				
Changes in equity				
Profit for the year				
Dividends				
Issue of share capital				
Balance at 30 September 20X6				

Task 3

(a) **What is the objective of general purpose financial reporting according to the IASB *Conceptual Framework for Financial Reporting*?**

(b) **Give ONE example of a PRIMARY user of general purpose financial reports (financial statements) and explain their need for the information in financial statements.**

(c) **Briefly explain ONE limitation of general purpose financial reports.**

Task 4

Otto Line is the managing director of Morel Ltd. He would like you to advise him on the accounting treatment of some matters that have arisen during the financial year as follows.

- During the year an incident at one of the company's factories resulted in poisonous waste material being discharged into a river, causing serious damage to the environment. In an interview with the local newspaper, the managing director accepted responsibility for the damage and promised that the company would clean up the discharge and restore the river to its previous condition, even though it is not legally obliged to do so. The board of directors has a reliable estimate that the cost of cleaning up the damage would be £850,000.

- During the year three people were seriously injured as a result of food poisoning. It was claimed that the food poisoning came from products sold by Morel Ltd. Legal proceedings have started seeking damages from the company of £2,000,000. Lawyers working for Morel Ltd have advised that it is probable that the company will not be found liable.

Prepare notes for a meeting with the directors to answer the following questions.

(a) **What is meant by a 'provision', according to IAS 37 *Provisions, Contingent Liabilities and Contingent Assets.*?**

(b) **When should a provision be recognised?**

(c) **How should Morel Ltd should treat the two matters set out in the data above in its financial statements?**

....

Task 5

(a) The following measures relate to a non-current asset:

   (i)   Carrying amount £20,000
   (ii) Fair value less costs of disposal £18,000
   (iii) Value in use £22,000
   (iv) Replacement cost £50,000

   What is the recoverable amount of the asset, according to IAS 36 *Impairment of Assets*?

£18,000	
£20,000	
£22,000	
£50,000	

(b) A company purchased a machine at a cost of £24,000. Delivery costs totalled £1,000, the cost of installing the machine was £2,000 and there were also general administrative expenses of £3,500 in connection with the purchase.

   What amount should be recognised as the cost of the machine, according to IAS 16 *Property, Plant and Equipment*?

£24,000	
£25,000	
£27,000	
£30,500	

(c) At the year-end, Chabrol Ltd has the following liabilities:

   (i)   Loan notes issued five years ago, due for repayment within one year.

   (ii) Trade payables due for settlement more than twelve months after the year-end, within the normal course of the operating cycle.

   (iii) Trade payables due for settlement within twelve months after the year end, within the normal course of the operating cycle.

   (iv) Bank overdrafts.

   According to IAS 1 *Presentation of Financial Statements,* which of these liabilities is a current liability?

All four items	
(i), (iii) and (iv) only	
(i) and (ii) only	
(ii), (iii) and (iv) only	

(d) Goodwill arising on a business combination is never amortised.

   Is this statement True or False?

True	
False	

(e) A business sells three products and at the year-end details of the inventories of these products are:

	Cost £	Selling price £	Selling costs £
Basic	14,300	15,700	2,400
Standard	21,600	21,300	1,000
Premium	17,500	28,600	1,800

   At what value should closing inventories be recognised in the statement of financial position?

£51,100	
£53,100	
£53,400	
£65,600	

(f) The corporation tax charge of Roamer Ltd based upon its profits for the current year is £48,000. The company had under-estimated its corporation tax liability for the previous year by £9,000.

What will be the corporation tax charge and corporation tax liability recognised in the financial statements of Roamer Ltd at the end of the current accounting period?

Corporation tax charge	Corporation tax liability	
£39,000	£39,000	
£39,000	£48,000	
£57,000	£48,000	
£57,000	£57,000	

Task 6

The Managing Director of Wraymand plc has asked you to prepare the statement of profit or loss. The company has one subsidiary, Blonk Ltd. The statements of profit or loss of the two companies for the year ended 31 March 20X7 are set out below.

Statements of profit or loss for the year ended 31 March 20X7

	Wraymand plc £'000	Blonk Ltd £'000
Continuing operations		
Revenue	38,462	12,544
Cost of sales	(22,693)	(5,268)
Gross profit	15,769	7,276
Other income – dividend from Blonk Ltd	580	–
Distribution costs	(6,403)	(2,851)
Administrative expenses	(3,987)	(2,466)
Profit from operations	5,959	1,959
Finance costs	(562)	(180)
Profit before tax	5,397	1,779
Tax	(1,511)	(623)
Profit for the period from continuing operations	3,886	1,156

Further information:

- Wraymand plc acquired 75% of the ordinary share capital of Blonk Ltd on 1 April 20X6.

- During the year Wraymand plc sold goods which had cost £1,100,000 to Blonk Ltd for £1,600,000. Three quarters of the goods had been sold by Blonk Ltd by the end of the year.

Draft a consolidated statement of profit or loss for Wraymand plc and its subsidiary for the year ended 31 March 20X7.

Wraymand plc

Consolidated statement of profit or loss for the year ended 31 March 20X7

	£'000
Continuing operations	
Revenue	
Cost of sales	
Gross profit	
Other income	
Distribution costs	
Administrative expenses	
Profit from operations	
Finance costs	
Profit before tax	
Tax	
Profit for the period from continuing operations	
Attributable to:	
Equity holders of the parent	
Non-controlling interest	

Workings

Revenue	£'000
Wraymand plc	
Blonk Ltd	
Total inter-company adjustment	

Cost of sales	£'000
Wraymand plc	
Blonk Ltd	
Total inter-company adjustment	

Task 7

You have been asked to assist a shareholder in Forth Ltd. She has asked you to calculate ratios in respect of the financial statements of the company for the year ending 31 October 20X7. The financial statements of Forth Ltd are set out below:

Forth Ltd

Statement of profit or loss for the year ended 31 October 20X7

	£'000
Continuing operations	
Revenue	2,400
Cost of sales	(1,392)
Gross profit	1,008
Distribution costs	(540)
Administrative expenses	(240)
Profit from operations	228
Finance costs	(91)
Profit before tax	137
Tax	(44)
Profit for the period from continuing operations	93

Forth Ltd

Statement of financial position as at 31 October 20X7

Assets	£'000
Non-current assets	
Property, plant and equipment	4,750
Current assets	
Inventories	320
Trade receivables	360
Cash and cash equivalents	0
	680
Total assets	5,430
Equity and liabilities	
Equity	
Share capital	2,500
Retained earnings	1,239
Total equity	3,739
Non-current liabilities	
Bank loans	1,300
Current liabilities	
Trade payables	195
Tax liabilities	44
Bank overdraft	152
	391
Total liabilities	1,691
Total equity and liabilities	5,430

(a) **State the formulae that are used to calculate each of the following ratios:**

(Write in the correct formula from the list provided)

(i) Gross profit percentage	▼

Formulae:
Gross profit/Total equity × 100
Gross profit/Revenue × 100
Gross profit/Total assets × 100
Gross profit/Total assets – Current liabilities

(ii) Operating profit percentage	▼

Formulae:
Profit from operations/Revenue × 100
Profit from operations/Total assets × 100
Profit from operations/Total equity + Non-current liabilities × 100
Profit from operations/Finance costs × 100

(iii) Administrative expenses/revenue percentage	▼

Formulae:
Administrative expenses/Revenue × 100
Distribution costs + Administrative expenses/Revenue × 100
Administrative expenses/Cost of sales × 100
Revenue/Administrative expenses × 100

(iv) Current ratio	▼

Formulae:
Total assets/Total liabilities
Current assets – Inventories/Current liabilities
Current assets/Current liabilities
Total assets – Inventories/Total liabilities

(v) Inventory holding period	▼
Formulae:	
Inventories/cost of sales × 365	
Inventories/revenue × 365	
Cost of sales/inventories × 365	
Revenue/inventories × 365	

(b) **Calculate the ratios to the nearest ONE DECIMAL PLACE.**

(i) Gross profit percentage		%
(ii) Operating profit percentage		%
(iii) Administrative expenses/revenue percentage		%
(iv) Current ratio		:1
(v) Inventory holding period		days

Task 8

You have been asked by the Managing Director of Gariroads Ltd to advise the company on the feasibility of raising a loan to finance the expansion of its activities.

A meeting has already been held with the bank and they have been sent a copy of the financial statements of the company for the past two years. The Managing Director wants you to comment on the likelihood of the bank lending the company money on the basis of the financial position revealed in the financial statements alone.

You have calculated the following ratios in respect of Gariroads Ltd's financial statements for the last two years to assist you in your analysis.

		20X7	20X6
(i)	Current ratio	2.2	2.1
(ii)	Quick ratio	0.8	1.3
(iii)	Gearing ratio	51.1%	31.2%
(iv)	Interest cover	1.8 times	4.5 times

Prepare a letter for the Managing Director of Gariroads that includes the following:

(a) **Comments on how the liquidity and financial position of Gariroads Ltd has changed over the two years based solely on the ratios calculated, suggesting possible reasons for the changes.**

(b) **A conclusion, with reasons, as to whether it is likely that the bank will lend the company money based solely on the ratios calculated and their analysis.**

....

BPP PRACTICE ASSESSMENT 2
FINANCIAL STATEMENTS

ANSWERS

Task 1

(a) **Reconciliation of profit from operations to net cash from operating activities**

	£'000
Profit from operations	5,630
Adjustments for:	
Depreciation	2,172
Loss on disposal of property, plant and equipment	183
Adjustment in respect of inventories (4,837 – 4,502)	(335)
Adjustment in respect of trade receivables (5,244 – 4,978)	(266)
Adjustment in respect of trade payables (3,038 – 2,954)	84
Cash generated by operations	7,468
Tax paid	(854)
Interest paid	(800)
Net cash from operating activities	5,814

(b) **Kenadie Ltd**

Statement of cash flows for the year ended 30 September 20X6

	£'000
Net cash from operating activities	5,814
Investing activities	
Purchases of property, plant and equipment (W)	(13,646)
Proceeds on disposal of property, plant and equipment (W)	509
Net cash used in investing activities	(13,137)
Financing activities	
Proceeds of share issue (10,500 – 6,000)	4,500
New bank loans (10,000 – 7,000)	3,000
Dividends paid	(700)
Net cash from financing activities	6,800
Net increase/(decrease) in cash and cash equivalents	(523)
Cash and cash equivalents at the beginning of the year	587
Cash and cash equivalents at the end of the year	64

Workings

Proceeds on disposal of property, plant and equipment (PPE)	£'000
Carrying amount of PPE sold	692
Loss on disposal	(183)
	509

Purchases of property, plant and equipment (PPE)	£'000
PPE at start of year	19,100
Depreciation charge	(2,172)
Carrying amount of PPE sold	(692)
PPE at end of year	(29,882)
Total PPE additions	(13,646)

Task 2

Kenadie Ltd

Statement of changes in equity for the year ended 30 September 20X6

	Share capital £'000	Share premium £'000	Retained earnings £'000	Total equity £'000
Balance at 1 October 20X5	5,000	1,000	12,359	18,359
Changes in equity				
Profit for the year			3,911	3,911
Dividends			(700)	(700)
Issue of share capital	3,000	1,500		4,500
Balance at 30 September 20X6	8,000	2,500	15,570	26,070

Task 3

Note. Based on the information available at the time this book was written, we anticipate that this task would be human marked in the real assessment.

(a) The IASB *Conceptual Framework for Financial Reporting* states that the objective of general purpose financial reporting is to provide financial information about the reporting entity that is useful to existing and potential investors, lenders and other creditors in making decisions about providing resources to the entity.

(b) Examples of primary users of financial information and their information needs:

Existing and potential investors

Investors and potential investors need information to help them determine whether they should buy, hold or sell their investment. They need information which helps them to assess the ability of the entity to pay dividends and to assess the potential changes in the market price of their investment.

Existing and potential lenders and other creditors

Lenders need information that helps them to make decisions about providing or settling loans. They need information which helps them to assess whether their loans and the interest attaching to them will be paid when due.

Tutorial note: Candidates only needed to write about ONE example of a PRIMARY user. According to the IASB *Conceptual Framework*, the primary users are the providers of capital (ie, those given in the answer to part (a) above). Although there may be other users of financial statements, eg, employees, the government, the public, general purpose financial statements are not primarily prepared for them.

(c) Limitations of general purpose financial reports (according to the IASB *Conceptual Framework*):

- **They are not designed to show the value of a reporting entity** (the market value of the company's shares). However, they provide information that may help users to estimate its value.

- **They may not meet the needs of every individual user**. Individual investors, lenders and other creditors (primary users) may have different information needs, which may conflict.

- **They are prepared primarily for existing and potential investors, lenders and other creditors**. Other groups of people, such as regulators and members of the public, may be interested in financial information about an entity. These groups may find general purpose financial reports useful, but they are **not primarily directed towards these other groups**.

- **They are based on estimates, judgements and models rather than exact depictions.** The *Conceptual Framework* establishes the concepts that underlie those estimates, judgements and models.

Tutorial note: Candidates only needed to write about ONE example.

Task 4

Note. Based on the information available at the time this book was written, we anticipate that this task would be human marked in the real assessment.

(a) IAS 37 *Provisions, Contingent Liabilities and Contingent Assets* defines a provision as a liability of uncertain timing or amount. A liability is a present obligation of the entity arising from past events, the settlement of which is expected to result in an outflow of economic benefits.

(b) A provision should be recognised when:

- An entity has a present obligation as a result of a past event. The obligation can be either legal or constructive; and

- It is probable that an outflow of resources embodying economic benefits will be required to settle the obligation; and

- A reliable estimate can be made of the amount of the obligation.

(c) **Accounting treatment of matters arising during the financial year**

(i) **Clean up costs**

Morel Ltd has a constructive obligation because it has publicly accepted responsibility for the damage to the environment and has created a valid expectation that it will restore the river to its previous condition. As the incident and the interview appear to have taken place before the year end the company has a present obligation as the result of a past event. It is probable that there will be an outflow of resources embodying economic benefits: the company will incur costs as a result of cleaning up the discharge. A reliable estimate has been made of the costs. Therefore the company should recognise a provision of £850,000 at its year end.

(ii) **Legal proceedings**

Because the company will probably not be liable it is unlikely that there is a present obligation or that there will be an outflow of resources embodying economic benefits. Therefore no provision should be made. However, the company does have a contingent liability (unless the chances of its being found liable for damages are remote). Details of the claim should be disclosed in the notes to the financial statements.

Task 5

(a)

£18,000	
£20,000	
£22,000	✓
£50,000	

Recoverable amount is the higher of value in use and fair value less costs of disposal.

(b)

£24,000	
£25,000	
£27,000	✓
£30,500	

The cost of property, plant and equipment is the cost of bringing it into working condition for its intended use. Therefore the cost includes delivery and installation costs but does not include the administrative expenses.

	£
Cost	
Purchase price	24,000
Delivery costs	1,000
Installation costs	2,000
	27,000

(c)

All four items	✓
(i), (iii) and (iv) only	
(i) and (ii) only	
(ii), (iii) and (iv) only	

IAS 1 states that a liability is current if an entity expects to settle it within its normal operating cycle. Even though item (ii) is due more than twelve months after the year end it is a current liability.

Note. This situation is extremely rare.

(d)

True	✓
False	

Goodwill arising on a business combination is recognised at cost in the statement of financial position and reviewed for impairment each year.

(e)

£51,100	✓
£53,100	
£53,400	
£65,600	

	Inventory value £
Basic – NRV (15,700 – 2,400)	13,300
Standard – NRV (21,300 – 1,000)	20,300
Premium – cost	17,500
	51,100

(f)

Corporation tax charge	Corporation tax liability	
£39,000	£39,000	
£39,000	£48,000	
£57,000	£48,000	✓
£57,000	£57,000	

Tax charge:

	£
Tax on profits for the year	48,000
Adjustments relating to previous years	9,000
	57,000

Task 6

Wraymand plc

Consolidated statement of profit or loss for the year ended 31 March 20X7

	£'000
Continuing operations	
Revenue (W)	49,406
Cost of sales (W)	(26,486)
Gross profit	22,920
Other income	–
Distribution costs (6,403 + 2,851)	(9,254)
Administrative expenses (3,987 + 2,466)	(6,453)
Profit from operations	7,213
Finance costs (562 + 180)	(742)
Profit before tax	6,471
Tax (1,511 + 623)	(2,134)
Profit for the period from continuing operations	4,337
Attributable to:	
Equity holders of the parent	4,048
Non-controlling interest (25% × 1,156)	289
	4,337

Workings

Revenue	£'000
Wraymand plc	38,462
Blonk Ltd	12,544
Total inter-company adjustment	(1,600)
	49,406

Cost of sales	£'000
Wraymand plc	22,693
Blonk Ltd	5,268
Total inter-company adjustment (1,600 – (1/4 × 500))	(1,475)
	26,486

Task 7

(a) Formulae used to calculate the ratios

(i)	Gross profit percentage	$\dfrac{\text{Gross profit}}{\text{Revenue}} \times 100\%$
(ii)	Operating profit percentage	$\dfrac{\text{Profit from operations}}{\text{Revenue}} \times 100\%$
(iii)	Administrative expenses/revenue percentage	$\dfrac{\text{Administrative expenses}}{\text{Revenue}} \times 100\%$
(iv)	Current ratio	$\dfrac{\text{Current assets}}{\text{Current liabilities}}$
(v)	Inventory holding period	$\dfrac{\text{Inventories}}{\text{Cost of sales}} \times 365$

(b) Calculation of ratios

(i)	Gross profit percentage $\dfrac{1,008}{2,400} \times 100$	42.0	%
(ii)	Operating profit percentage $\dfrac{228}{2,400} \times 100$	9.5	%
(iii)	Administrative expenses/revenue percentage $\dfrac{240}{2,400} \times 100$	10.0	%
(iv)	Current ratio $\dfrac{680}{391}$	1.7	:1
(v)	Inventory holding period $\dfrac{320}{1,392} \times 365$	83.9	days

Task 8

Note. Based on the information available at the time this book was written, we anticipate that this task would be human marked in the real assessment.

Accounting Technician

20 High Street

Anytown

20 June 20X7

Dear Sir,

As requested, I have reviewed the key ratios calculated from the financial statements of Gariroads Ltd to establish whether further finance could be obtained for expansion.

(a) **Commentary on liquidity and financial position**

There has been a slight increase in the current ratio in the year which is positive and the overall ratio is at a comfortable level above 2. The company's current assets have increased relative to its current liabilities.

However, the quick ratio shows a worsening position as it has fallen from 1.3 to 0.8 showing that Gariroads may struggle to meet its obligations from assets that are quickly convertible into cash. The fact that the current ratio has risen while the quick ratio has fallen suggests that it is the level of inventories that has risen, rather than trade receivables or cash. It is quite likely that the level of cash has fallen during the year, possibly even that a positive cash balance has become an overdraft.

The gearing ratio has increased in the year from a relatively safe 31% to a high 51%. New loans have been taken out during the year and the company is likely to be seen as risky by future lenders. The sharp increase in the gearing ratio suggests that total borrowings may have more than doubled compared with the previous year.

Interest cover has decreased from 4.5 times to 1.8 times which again would be seen as a risk factor by lenders. The most obvious reason for the worrying fall in interest cover is the sharp increase in the amount that the company has borrowed. Other reasons for this could include a fall in profit from operations and/or higher interest rates on the additional loan. Because there are less profits available to cover the interest payments, future lenders would be very cautious about lending money to Gariroads Ltd.

(b) **Conclusion**

Overall, Gariroads has a worsening liquidity position and increased gearing in 20X7 compared to 20X6. While the company is still able to meet its interest payments, the ability to do so has decreased. If the fall in interest cover is partly the result of falling profits, this is a very worrying sign.

Gariroads is already very highly geared. A potential lender would view the company as a risky and unattractive prospect. On the basis of these four ratios, it is unlikely that the bank would lend further cash to the business at the moment, unless there is a very strong possibility of increased profits and much better interest cover in the near future.

Yours faithfully

Accounting Technician

BPP PRACTICE ASSESSMENT 3
FINANCIAL STATEMENTS

Time allowed: 2½ hours

The following information is relevant to Task 1 and Task 2

You have been asked to help prepare the financial statements of Nevis Ltd for the year ended 31 March 20X9. The company's trial balance as at 31 March 20X9 is shown below.

Nevis Ltd

Trial balance as at 31 March 20X9

	Debit	Credit
	£'000	£'000
Share capital		12,000
Share premium		2,000
Trade and other payables		2,642
Motor vehicles – cost	21,840	
Motor vehicles – acc depreciation at 1 April 20X8		4,675
Plant and equipment – cost	32,800	
Plant and equipment – acc depreciation at 1 April 20X8		16,000
Trade and other receivables	4,567	
Accruals		239
6% bank loan repayable 20Y6		12,000
Cash at bank	3,519	
Retained earnings at 1 April 20X8		6,590
Interest	360	
Sales		65,113
Purchases	44,000	
Distribution costs	2,905	
Administrative expenses	4,098	
Inventories as at 1 April 20X8	5,640	
Dividends paid	1,530	
	121,259	121,259

Further information:

- The inventories at the close of business on 31 March 20X9 were valued at £6,806,000.

- The company hired some temporary office space for the period 1 March to 31 May 20X9. The contract price for the three months was £144,000 and this was paid in full on 8 March. Office rental is included in administrative expenses.

- Depreciation is to be provided for the year to 31 March 20X9 as follows:

Motor vehicles	25% per annum	Straight line basis
Plant and equipment	20% per annum	Diminishing balance basis

  Depreciation is apportioned as follows:

	%
Cost of sales	50
Distribution costs	20
Administrative expenses	30

- Interest on the bank loan for the last six months of the year has not been included in the accounts in the trial balance.

- The corporation tax charge for the year has been calculated as £2,540,000.

- The company issued 2,000,000 new ordinary shares during the year. They had a nominal value of £1 but were sold for £1.50 per share. This transaction is included in the trial balance above.

- All of the operations are continuing operations.

Task 1

(a) **Draft the statement of profit or loss and other comprehensive income for Nevis Ltd for the year ended 31 March 20X9.**

Nevis Ltd

Statement of profit or loss and other comprehensive income for the year ended 31 March 20X9

	£'000
Revenue	
Cost of sales	_____
Gross profit	
Distribution costs	
Administrative expenses	_____
Profit from operations	
Finance costs	_____
Profit before tax	
Tax	_____
Profit for the period from continuing operations	_____

Workings

(Complete the left hand column by writing in the correct narrative from the list provided.)

Cost of sales		£'000
	▼	
	▼	
	▼	
	▼	

Picklist for narratives:

Accruals
Closing inventories
Depreciation
Opening inventories
Prepayments
Purchases

Distribution costs		£'000
	▼	
	▼	

Picklist for narratives:

Accruals
Depreciation
Distribution costs
Prepayments

Administrative expenses		£'000
	▼	
	▼	
	▼	

Picklist for narratives:

Accruals
Administrative expenses
Depreciation
Prepayment

(b) **Draft the statement of changes in equity for Nevis Ltd for the year ended 31 March 20X9.**

Nevis Ltd

Statement of changes in equity for the year ended 31 March 20X9

	Share capital £'000	Share premium £'000	Retained earnings £'000	Total equity £'000
Balance at 1 April 20X8				
Changes in equity				
Total comprehensive income				
Dividends				
Issue of share capital				
Balance at 31 March 20X9				

Task 2

(a) **Draft the statement of financial position for Nevis Ltd as at 31 March 20X9.**

Nevis Ltd

(Complete the left hand column by writing in the correct line item from the list provided)

Statement of financial position as at 31 March 20X9

	£'000
Assets	
Non-current assets	
▽	_____
Current assets	
▽	
▽	
▽	_____
	_____
Total assets	=====
Equity and liabilities	
Equity	
▽	
▽	
▽	_____
Total equity	_____
Non-current liabilities	
▽	_____
Current liabilities	
▽	
▽	_____
	_____
Total liabilities	_____
Total equity and liabilities	=====

Picklist for line items:

Bank loan
Cash and cash equivalents
Inventories
Property, plant and equipment
Retained earnings
Share capital
Share premium
Tax liabilities
Trade and other payables
Trade and other receivables

Workings

(Complete the left hand column by writing in the correct narrative from the list provided.)

Property, plant and equipment		£'000
	▼	
	▼	
	▼	
	▼	

Picklist for narratives:

Accumulated depreciation – motor vehicles
Accumulated depreciation – plant and equipment
Motor vehicles – Cost
Plant and equipment – Cost

Trade and other receivables		£'000
	▼	
	▼	

Picklist for narratives:

Accruals: trial balance
Additional administrative expenses accrual
Additional administrative expenses prepaid
Additional finance costs accrued
Additional finance costs prepaid
Prepayments
Trade and other payables
Trade and other receivables

Retained earnings		£'000
	▼	
	▼	
	▼	

Picklist for narratives:

Dividends paid
Other comprehensive income for the year
Retained earnings at 1 April 20X8
Total comprehensive income for the year
Total profit for the year

Trade and other payables		£'000
	▼	
	▼	
	▼	

Picklist for narratives:

Accruals: trial balance
Additional administrative expenses accrual
Additional administrative expenses prepaid
Additional finance costs accrual
Additional finance costs prepaid
Dividends
Prepayments
Tax liabilities
Trade and other payables
Trade and other receivables

....

Task 3

In accordance with the IASB *Conceptual Framework for Financial Reporting*

(a) **Explain what is meant by 'measurement'.**

(b) **Identify the FOUR possible measurement bases.**

(c) **Explain how assets are measured under ONE measurement base.**

....

Task 4

The directors of Munro Ltd believe that one of the company's machines may have become impaired. The machine has a carrying amount of £45,000 and the directors estimate that it will generate cash flows with a net present value of £38,000 over the remainder of its useful life. It could be sold for £42,000 and disposal costs would be £1,000.

Prepare brief notes to answer the following points for the directors:

(a) **State how, according to IAS 36 *Impairment of Assets*, an impairment loss is calculated and which two figures are needed.**

(b) **Explain what is meant by each of these figures.**

(c) **Calculate the impairment loss relating to the machine and state how this should be treated in the financial statements.**

Task 5

(a) Webb Ltd has a possible obligation as a result of a claim against it by a customer. The company's solicitors have advised the directors that there is a 30% chance that the claim will be successful.

In the financial statements for the period, Webb Ltd should recognise a contingent liability.

Is this statement True or False?

True	
False	

(b) According to IAS 28 *Investments in Associates and Joint Ventures*, an investor will normally have significant influence over a company in which it holds an investment if it holds a certain minimum percentage or more of that company's voting power.

This percentage is:

10%	
20%	
25%	
50%	

(c) A company sold some plant which had cost £100,000 for £20,000. At the time of sale the carrying amount of the plant was £18,000.

Which of the following correctly states the treatment of the transaction in the company's statement of cash flows for the period?

Proceeds of sale	Profit on sale	
Cash inflow under financing activities	Deducted from profit in calculating net cash from operating activities	
Cash inflow under investing activities	Added to profit in calculating net cash from operating activities.	
Cash inflow under financing activities	Added to profit in calculating net cash from operating activities	
Cash inflow under investing activities	Deducted from profit in calculating net cash from operating activities	

(d) A company has three different products in its inventories. The following information applies:

Product	Costs incurred to date £	Estimated selling costs £	Selling price £
(i)	738	208	915
(ii)	800	294	1,120
(iii)	640	220	900

At what value should the inventories be stated in the company's financial statements in accordance with IAS 2 *Inventories*?

£2,147	
£2,178	
£2,900	
£2,935	

(e) **According to IAS 38 *Intangible Assets*, which of the following statements are true?**

(i) Internally generated brands should never be capitalised

(ii) Intangible assets can be revalued upwards

(i) only	
(ii) only	
Both (i) and (ii)	
Neither (i) nor (ii)	

(f) On 1 January 20X1 Stockbridge Ltd purchased a machine for £560,000. The residual value was estimated as £80,000 and the useful life was expected to be 10 years Stockbridge Ltd depreciates plant on a straight line basis.

At 1 January 20X6 the machine's remaining useful life was reassessed to be 4 years and the residual value was still considered to be £80,000.

What is the depreciation charge for the item of plant for the current year to 31 December 20X6?

£32,000	
£56,000	
£60,000	
£80,000	

Task 6

Data

Teal plc acquired 80% of the issued share capital of Amber Ltd on 1 January 20X9 for £4,600,000. At that date Amber Ltd had issued share capital of £3,000,000 and retained earnings of £840,000.

The summarised statements of financial position for the two companies one year later at 31 December 20X9 are as follows:

	Teal plc £'000	Amber Ltd £'000
Assets		
Investment in Amber Ltd	4,600	
Non-current assets	7,500	4,590
Current assets	3,800	1,570
Total assets	15,900	6,160
Equity and liabilities		
Equity		
Share capital	5,000	3,000
Retained earnings	7,800	1,510
Total equity	12,800	4,510
Non-current liabilities	1,000	750
Current liabilities	2,100	900
Total liabilities	3,100	1,650
Total equity and liabilities	15,900	6,160

Additional data

- The fair value of the non-current assets of Amber Ltd at 1 January 20X9 was £4,200,000. The book value of the non-current assets at 1 January 20X9 was £3,900,000. The revaluation has not been recorded in the books of Amber Ltd (ignore any effect on the depreciation for the year).

- The directors of Teal plc have decided that non-controlling interest will be valued at the proportionate share of Amber Ltd's net assets.

(a) **Draft the consolidated statement of financial position for Teal plc and its subsidiary as at 31 December 20X9.**

Teal plc

Consolidated statement of financial position as at 31 December 20X9

	£'000
Assets	
Non-current assets:	
Intangible assets: goodwill	
Property, plant and equipment	
Current assets	
Total assets	
Equity and liabilities	
Equity	
Share capital	
Retained earnings	
Non-controlling interest	
Total equity	
Non-current liabilities	
Current liabilities	
Total liabilities	
Total equity and liabilities	

Workings

(Complete the left hand column by writing in the correct narrative from the list provided.)

Goodwill		£'000
	▼	
	▼	
	▼	
	▼	

Picklist for narratives:

Price paid
Retained earnings – attributable to Teal plc
Revaluation reserve – attributable to Teal plc
Share capital – attributable to Teal plc

Retained earnings		£'000
	▼	
	▼	

Picklist for narratives:

Amber Ltd – attributable to Teal plc
Revaluation
Teal plc

Non-controlling interest (NCI)		£'000
	▼	
	▼	
	▼	

Picklist for narratives:

Current assets – attributable to NCI
Non-current assets – attributable to NCI
Price paid
Retained earnings – attributable to NCI
Revaluation reserve – attributable to NCI
Share capital – attributable to NCI

Data

Blue plc acquired 75% of the issued share capital of Brown Ltd on 1 January 20X9.

Summarised statements of profit or loss for the year ended 31 December 20X9 are shown below:

	Blue plc £'000	Brown Ltd £'000
Continuing operations		
Revenue	61,200	22,300
Cost of sales	(29,100)	(8,600)
Gross profit	32,100	13,700
Other income – dividend from Brown Ltd	2,500	–
Operating expenses	(3,750)	(1,900)
Profit from operations	30,850	11,800

Additional data

- During the year Blue plc sold goods which had cost £600,000 to Brown Ltd for £1,000,000. None of these goods remain in inventory at the end of the year.

- Goodwill of £900,000 arose on the acquisition. The directors of Blue plc have concluded that goodwill has been impaired by 10% during the year.

(b) **Draft the consolidated statement of profit or loss for Blue plc and its subsidiary up to and including the profit from operations line for the year ended 31 December 20X9.**

Blue plc

Consolidated statement of profit or loss for the year ended 31 December 20X9

	£'000
Continuing operations	
Revenue	
Cost of sales	
Gross profit	
Other income	
Operating expenses	
Profit from operations	

Workings

Revenue	£'000
Blue plc	
Brown Ltd	
Total inter-company adjustment	

Cost of sales	£'000
Blue plc	
Brown Ltd	
Total inter-company adjustment	

Task 7

Lucy Carmichael is considering buying shares in Tweed Ltd. She wishes to assess the level of profitability and risk of the company. She has asked you to assist her by calculating ratios in respect of the financial statements of the company for the year ended 31 March 20X8. The financial statements of Tweed Ltd are set out below.

Tweed Ltd

Statement of profit or loss for the year ended 31 March 20X8

	£'000
Continuing operations	
Revenue	16,000
Cost of sales	(8,640)
Gross profit	7,360
Distribution costs	(3,600)
Administrative expenses	(2,880)
Profit from operations	880
Finance costs	(308)
Profit before tax	572
Tax	(117)
Profit for the period from continuing operations	455

Tweed Ltd

Statement of financial position as at 31 March 20X8

Assets	£'000
Non-current assets	
Property, plant and equipment	9,800
Current assets	
Inventories	1,728
Trade receivables	1,600
Cash and cash equivalents	0
	3,328
Total assets	13,128
Equity and liabilities	
Share capital	3,000
Retained earnings	4,372
Total equity	7,372
Non-current liabilities	£'000
Bank loans	4,400
Current liabilities	
Trade payables	1,210
Tax liabilities	117
Bank overdraft	29
	1,356
Total liabilities	5,756
Total equity and liabilities	13,128

(a) **State the formulae that are used to calculate each of the following ratios:**

(Write in the correct formula from the list provided)

(i) Return on capital employed	▼

Formulae:

Profit after tax/Total equity × 100

Profit from operations/Total equity × 100

Profit after tax/Total equity + Non-current liabilities × 100

Profit from operations/Total equity + Non-current liabilities × 100

(ii) Return on shareholders' funds	▼

Formulae:

Profit after tax/Total equity × 100

Profit before tax/Total equity × 100

Profit from operations/Total equity × 100

Profit from operations/Total equity + Non-current liabilities × 100

(iii) Gross profit percentage	▼

Formulae:

Gross profit/Total equity × 100

Gross profit/Revenue × 100

Gross profit/Total assets × 100

Gross profit/Total assets – Current liabilities

(iv) Quick (acid test) ratio	▼

Formulae:

Current assets/Current liabilities

Total assets – Inventories/Total liabilities

Total assets/Total liabilities

Current assets – Inventories/Current liabilities

(v) Interest cover	▼

Formulae:

Finance costs/Profit from operations

Finance costs/Revenue

Profit from operations/Finance costs

Revenue/Finance costs

(b) **Calculate the following ratios to the nearest ONE DECIMAL PLACE.**

(i) Return on capital employed	%
(ii) Return on shareholders' funds	%
(iii) Gross profit percentage	%
(iv) Quick (acid test) ratio	:1
(v) Interest cover	times

Task 8

Clare Miller, a shareholder in Selston plc, is debating whether to keep or sell her shares in the company. Her main concern is the level of return she is receiving from Selston plc, but she also wishes to ensure that her shareholding is safe.

She has asked you to analyse the company's most recent financial statements with a view to assisting her in her decision.

You have calculated the following three accounting ratios for Selston plc, for years 20X8 and 20X7, and an extract from the company's statement of cash flows is also provided below.

	20X8	20X7
Return on shareholders' funds	7.2%	12.8%
Asset turnover (non-current assets)	2.5 times	3.6 times
Interest cover	1.7 times	4.1 times

Selston plc: Statement of cash flows (extract) for year 20X8

	£'000
Operating activities	140
Investing activities	(220)
Financing activities	200
Increase in cash and cash equivalents	120

Prepare notes for Clare that include:

(a) **Comments on the relative performance of Selston plc in respect of the two years, giving possible reasons for any differences (the extract of the statement of cash flows may assist you in some aspects of this) based upon the ratios calculated;**

(b) **Advice to Clare, with ONE principal reason only to support this, as to whether or not she should keep or sell her shares in the company.**

BPP PRACTICE ASSESSMENT 3
FINANCIAL STATEMENTS

ANSWERS

Task 1

(a) **Nevis Ltd**

Statement of profit or loss and other comprehensive income for the year ended 31 March 20X9

	£'000
Revenue	65,113
Cost of sales (W)	(47,244)
Gross profit	17,869
Distribution costs (W)	(4,669)
Administrative expenses (W)	(6,648)
Profit from operations	6,552
Finance costs (6% × 12,000)	(720)
Profit before tax	5,832
Tax	(2,540)
Profit for the period from continuing operations	3,292

Workings

Cost of sales	£'000
Opening inventories	5,640
Purchases	44,000
Depreciation (50% × 8,820)	4,410
Closing inventories	(6,806)
	47,244

Distribution costs	£'000
Distribution costs	2,905
Depreciation (20% × 8,820)	1,764
	4,669

Administrative expenses	£'000
Administrative expenses	4,098
Depreciation (30% × 8,820)	2,646
Prepayment (144 × 2/3)	(96)
	6,648

Depreciation

	£'000
Motor vehicles (25% × 21,840)	5,460
Plant and equipment (20% × 32,800 – 16,000)	3,360
	8,820

(b) **Nevis Ltd**

Statement of changes in equity for the year ended 31 March 20X9

	Share capital £'000	Share premium £'000	Retained earnings £'000	Total equity £'000
Balance at 1 April 20X8	10,000	1,000	6,590	17,590
Changes in equity				
Total comprehensive income			3,292	3,292
Dividends			(1,530)	(1,530)
Issue of share capital	2,000	1,000		3,000
Balance at 31 March 20X9	12,000	2,000	8,352	22,352

Share premium

	£'000
As at 31 March 20X9	2,000
On shares issued during the year (50p × 2,000)	(1,000)
As at 1 April 20X8	1,000

Task 2

(a) **Nevis Ltd**

Statement of financial position as at 31 March 20X9

	£'000
Assets	
Non-current assets	
Property, plant and equipment (W)	25,145
Current assets	
Inventories	6,806
Trade and other receivables (W)	4,663
Cash and cash equivalents	3,519
	14,988
Total assets	40,133
Equity and liabilities	
Equity	
Share capital	12,000
Share premium	2,000
Retained earnings (W)	8,352
Total equity	22,352
Non-current liabilities	
Bank loan	12,000
Current liabilities	
Trade and other payables (W)	3,241
Tax liabilities	2,540
	5,781
Total liabilities	17,781
Total equity and liabilities	40,133

Workings

Property, plant and equipment	£'000
Motor vehicles – Cost	21,840
Plant and equipment – Cost	32,800
Accumulated depreciation – motor vehicles (4,675 + 5,460)	(10,135)
Accumulated depreciation – plant and equipment (16,000 + 3,360)	(19,360)
	25,145

Trade and other receivables	£'000
Trade and other receivables	4,567
Additional administrative expenses prepaid	96
	4,663

Retained earnings	£'000
Retained earnings at 1 April 20X8	6,590
Total profit for the year	3,292
Dividends paid	(1,530)
	8,352

Trade and other payables	£'000
Trade and other payables	2,642
Accruals: trial balance	239
Additional finance costs accrual	360
	3,241

Task 3

Note. Based on the information available at the time this book was written, we anticipate that this task would be human marked in the real assessment.

(a) Measurement is the process of determining the monetary amounts at which items are recognised and carried in the financial statements.

(b) The four measurement bases are:
- Historic cost
- Current cost
- Realisable value
- Present value

(c) **Historical cost**: Assets are recorded at the amount of cash paid or the fair value of the consideration given to acquire them at the time of the acquisition.

Current cost: Assets are carried at the amount of cash that would have to be paid if the same or a similar asset was acquired currently.

Realisable value: Assets are carried at the amount of cash that could currently be obtained by selling the asset.

Present value: Assets are carried at the present discounted value of the future net cash inflows that the item is expected to generate in the normal course of business.

Note. Candidates only needed to give ONE of the above.

Task 4

Note. Based on the information available at the time this book was written, we anticipate that this task would be human marked in the real assessment.

(a) IAS 36 *Impairment of Assets* states that if an asset's carrying amount is greater than its recoverable amount, the asset is impaired. The impairment loss is the difference between an asset's carrying amount and its recoverable amount.

(b) The carrying amount of an asset is the amount at which it is recognised in the statement of financial position after deducting accumulated depreciation or amortisation and accumulated impairment losses.

An asset's recoverable amount is the higher of its fair value less costs of disposal and its value in use. IAS 36 defines value in use as the present value of the future cash flows expected to be derived from an asset, including any cash flows arising on its disposal.

(c) The recoverable amount of the machine is £41,000. This is its fair value less costs of disposal (42,000 – 1,000), which is higher than its value in use of £38,000.

The impairment loss is £4,000: the difference between the carrying amount and the recoverable amount (45,000 – 41,000).

The impairment loss should be recognised immediately in profit or loss.

Task 5

(a)

True	
False	✓

The company should disclose a contingent liability in the notes to the financial statements. No liability is recognised because an outflow of economic benefits is not probable.

(b)

10%	
20%	✓
25%	
50%	

(c)

Proceeds of sale	Profit on sale	
Cash inflow under financing activities	Deducted from profit in calculating net cash from operating activities	
Cash inflow under investing activities	Added to profit in calculating net cash from operating activities	
Cash inflow under financing activities	Added to profit in calculating net cash from operating activities	
Cash inflow under investing activities	Deducted from profit in calculating net cash from operating activities	✓

The company has made a profit on disposal, so this amount is deducted in calculating net cash from operating activities.

(d)

£2,147	✓
£2,178	
£2,900	
£2,935	

£'000

Inventories

Product I (915 – 208)	707
Product II (Cost)	800
Product III (Cost)	640
	2,147

(e)

(i) only	
(ii) only	
Both (i) and (ii)	✓
Neither (i) nor (ii)	

Although it is rare for an intangible asset to be revalued, IAS 38 allows a choice between the cost model and the revaluation model.

(f)

£32,000	
£56,000	
£60,000	✓
£80,000	

Net carrying amount at 1 January 20X6:

	£
Cost	560,000
Depreciation ((560,000 – 80,000) ÷ 10 × 5)	(240,000)
	320,000
Charge for 20X6 (320,000 – 80,000 ÷ 4)	60,000

Task 6

(a) **Teal plc**

   Consolidated statement of financial position as at 31 December 20X9

	£'000
Assets	
Non-current assets:	
Intangible assets: goodwill (W)	1,288
Property, plant and equipment (7,500 + 4,590 + 300)	12,390
Current assets	5,370
Total assets	19,048
Equity and liabilities	
Equity	
Share capital	5,000
Retained earnings (W)	8,336
Non-controlling interest (W)	962
Total equity	14,298
Non-current liabilities	1,750
Current liabilities	3,000
Total liabilities	4,750
Total equity and liabilities	19,048

Workings

Goodwill	£'000
Price paid	4,600
Share capital – attributable to Teal plc (80% × 3,000)	(2,400)
Retained earnings – attributable to Teal plc (80% × 840)	(672)
Revaluation reserve – attributable to Teal plc (80% × 300)	(240)
	1,288

Retained earnings	£'000
Teal plc	7,800
Amber Ltd – attributable to Teal plc (80% × (1,510 – 840))	536
	8,336

Non-controlling interest (NCI)	£'000
Share capital – attributable to NCI (20% × 3,000)	600
Retained earnings – attributable to NCI (20% × 1,510)	302
Revaluation reserve – attributable to NCI (20% × 300)	60
	962

(b) **Blue plc**

Consolidated statement of profit or loss for the year ended 31 December 20X9

	£'000
Continuing operations	
Revenue (W)	82,500
Cost of sales (W)	(36,700)
Gross profit	45,800
Other income	0
Operating expenses (3,750 + 1,900 + 90)	(5,740)
Profit from operations	40,060

Workings

Revenue	£'000
Blue plc	61,200
Brown Ltd	22,300
Total inter-company adjustment	(1,000)
	82,500

Cost of sales	£'000
Blue plc	29,100
Brown Ltd	8,600
Total inter-company adjustment	(1,000)
	36,700

Task 7

(a) Formulae used to calculate the ratios

(i)	Return on capital employed	$\dfrac{\text{Profit from operations}}{\text{Total equity + non-current liabilities}} \times 100\%$
(ii)	Return on shareholders' funds	$\dfrac{\text{Profit after tax}}{\text{Total equity}} \times 100\%$
(iii)	Gross profit percentage	$\dfrac{\text{Gross profit}}{\text{Revenue}} \times 100\%$
(iv)	Quick (acid test) ratio	$\dfrac{\text{Current assets – inventories}}{\text{Current liabilities}}$
(v)	Interest cover	$\dfrac{\text{Profit from operations}}{\text{Finance costs}}$

(b) Calculation of the ratios

(i)	Return on capital employed	$\dfrac{880}{7,372 + 4,400} \times 100$	7.5	%
(ii)	Return on shareholders' funds	$\dfrac{455}{7,372} \times 100$	6.2	%
(iii)	Gross profit percentage	$\dfrac{7,360}{16,000} \times 100$	46.0	%
(iv)	Quick (acid test) ratio	$\dfrac{1,600}{1,356}$	1.2	:1
(v)	Interest cover	$\dfrac{880}{308}$	2.9	times

Task 8

Note. Based on the information available at the time this book was written, we anticipate that this task would be human marked in the real assessment.

Notes for Clare Miller on the performance of Selston plc

(a) **Return on shareholders' funds**

Return on shareholders' funds has deteriorated significantly. This means that the company has made less profit than in the previous year, relative to the total shareholders' funds invested in the company.

The most obvious reason for this is that profit after tax is lower in 20X8 than it was in 20X7.

It is also possible that shareholders' funds have increased during the year, either because there has been an issue of shares, or because the company's net assets have increased, possibly as a result of purchasing non-current assets. The cash flow information suggests that either or both these things may have happened: there has been a cash outflow from investing activities and a cash inflow from financing activities.

Asset turnover

Asset turnover (based on non-current assets) has also become significantly worse. The company is generating less sales revenue from its assets than in the previous year.

Sales revenue may be lower in 20X8 than in 20X7.

Another possible reason for the fall is that the company's non-current assets have increased during the year. The assets may have been revalued upwards. Because there has been a large cash outflow in investing activities a more likely explanation is that the company has made major asset purchases during the year.

Unless the asset purchases were made early in the year they will not have generated a full year's revenue in 20X8. Therefore asset turnover (and financial performance generally) should improve in future.

Interest cover

Interest cover has fallen significantly. There is less profit available to meet interest payments and therefore less profit available for distribution to shareholders.

Operating profit may have fallen in the year.

Alternatively, interest payments may be higher than in previous years, probably because the company has taken out additional loans (possibly to purchase the new non-current assets). The cash inflow from financing activities suggests that this is the main reason for the fall.

If the company has increased its borrowings, gearing will be higher. This means that the company is now a riskier investment. Profits for ordinary shareholders may become more volatile, because a greater proportion of operating profit will be used to pay loan interest. The company may find it harder to raise additional finance if this is needed in the future.

(b) On the basis of the information provided, you are advised to sell your shares in Selston plc. The ratios suggest that you will receive a lower rate of return on your investment in future. The company has also become a riskier investment.

Note. Candidates were asked for ONE reason why Clare should keep or sell her shares in the company. Another possible answer would be that Clare should keep the shares, because the company's investment in non-current assets suggests that profits may improve in future periods.

BPP PRACTICE ASSESSMENT 4
FINANCIAL STATEMENTS

Time allowed: 2½ hours

The following information is relevant to Task 1 and Task 2

You have been asked to help prepare the financial statements of Martin Ltd for the year ended 31 October 20X9. The company's trial balance as at 31 October 20X9 is shown below.

Martin Ltd

Trial balance as at 31 October 20X9

	Debit	Credit
	£'000	£'000
Share capital		9,000
Trade and other payables		1,347
Property, plant and equipment – cost	39,880	
Property, plant and equipment – accumulated depreciation at 31 October 20X9		21,780
Trade and other receivables	2,234	
Accruals		146
8% bank loan repayable 20Y6		14,000
Cash at bank	9,654	
Retained earnings at 1 November 20X9		3,465
Interest	560	
Sales		46,433
Purchases	32,553	
Distribution costs	2,450	
Administrative expenses	3,444	
Inventories as at 1 November 20X8	4,466	
Dividends paid	930	
	96,171	96,171

Additional data:

- The inventories at the close of business on 31 October 20X9 were valued at £4,987,000. On 4 November 20X9, goods included in this total at a value of £550,000 were found to be damaged and were sold for £300,000.

- Land, which is non-depreciable, is included in the trial balance at a value of £8,000,000. It is to be revalued at £12,000,000 and this revaluation is to be included in the financial statements for the year ended 31 October 20X9.

- The company paid £512,000 for one year's insurance on 1 February 20X9, this is due to expire on 31 January 20Y0. Insurance is included in administrative expenses.

- Distribution costs of £66,000 owing at 31 October 20X9 are to be accrued.

- Interest on the bank loan for the last six months of the year has not been included in the accounts in the trial balance.

- The corporation tax charge for the year has been calculated as £980,000.
- All of the operations are continuing operations.

Task 1

(a) **Draft the statement of profit or loss and other comprehensive income for Martin Ltd for the year ended 31 October 20X9.**

Martin Ltd

Statement of profit or loss and other comprehensive Income for the year ended 31 October 20X9

	£'000
Revenue	
Cost of sales	_____
Gross profit	
Distribution costs	
Administrative expenses	_____
Profit from operations	
Finance costs	
Profit before tax	
Tax	_____
Profit for the period from continuing operations	
Other comprehensive income	
Gain on revaluation	_____
Total comprehensive income for the year	_____

Workings

(Complete the left hand column by writing in the correct narrative from the list provided.)

Cost of sales		£'000
	▼	
	▼	
	▼	

Picklist for narratives:

Accruals
Closing inventories
Opening inventories
Prepayments
Purchases

Distribution costs		£'000
	▼	
	▼	

Picklist for narratives:

Accruals
Distribution costs
Prepayments

Administrative expenses		£'000
	▼	
	▼	

Picklist for narratives:

Accruals
Administrative expenses
Prepayment

(b) **Draft the statement of changes in equity for Martin Ltd for the year ended 31 October 20X9.**

Martin Ltd

Statement of changes in equity for the year ended 31 October 20X9

	Share capital £'000	Revaluation reserve £'000	Retained earnings £'000	Total equity £'000
Balance at 1 November 20X8				
Changes in equity				
Total comprehensive income				
Dividends				
Balance at 31 October 20X9				

Task 2

Draft the statement of financial position for Martin Ltd as at 31 October 20X9.

Martin Ltd

(Complete the left hand column by writing in the correct line item from the list provided)

Statement of financial position as at 31 October 20X9

	£'000
Assets	
Non-current assets	
▼	
Current assets	
▼	
▼	
▼	
Total assets	

	£'000
Equity and liabilities	
Equity	
▼	
▼	
▼	_____
Total equity	_____
Non-current liabilities	
▼	_____
Current liabilities	
▼	
▼	_____
	_____
Total liabilities	_____
Total equity and liabilities	_____

Picklist for line items:

Bank loan
Cash and cash equivalents
Inventories
Property, plant and equipment
Retained earnings
Revaluation reserve
Share capital
Tax liabilities
Trade and other payables
Trade and other receivables

Workings

(Complete the left hand column by writing in the correct narrative from the list provided.)

Property, plant and equipment	£'000
▼	
▼	
▼	

Picklist for narratives:

Property, plant and equipment – Cost
Property, plant and equipment -Accumulated depreciation
Revaluation

Trade and other receivables		£'000
	▼	
	▼	

Picklist for narratives:

Accruals: trial balance
Additional distribution costs accrual
Additional distribution costs prepaid
Additional finance costs accrual
Additional finance costs prepaid
Administrative expenses accrual
Administrative expenses prepaid
Trade and other payables
Trade and other receivables

Retained earnings		£'000
	▼	
	▼	
	▼	

Picklist for narratives:

Dividends paid
Other comprehensive income for the year
Retained earnings at 1 November 20X8
Revaluation reserve
Total comprehensive income for the year
Total profit for the year

Trade and other payables		£'000
	▼	
	▼	
	▼	
	▼	

Picklist for narratives:

Accruals: trial balance
Additional distribution costs accrual
Additional distribution costs prepaid
Additional finance costs accrual
Additional finance costs prepaid
Administrative expenses accrual
Administrative expenses prepaid
Dividends
Tax payable
Trade and other payables
Trade and other receivables

···

Task 3

(a) **List the elements that appear in financial statements according to the *Conceptual Framework for Financial Reporting*.**

(b) **Define the elements that appear in the statement of financial position of a company in accordance with the definitions in the *Conceptual Framework for Financial Reporting*.**

···

Task 4

The directors of Sydenham Ltd have recently purchased a new item of manufacturing equipment. The invoiced price of the equipment was £37,000, delivery costs were £1,600, and installation and testing costs were £4,500. As part of the process of testing the equipment, the company produced some samples, which were slightly imperfect and were sold for £1,800. After the equipment had been successfully installed and tested the company incurred costs of £3,000 in training staff to use it.

Prepare brief notes for the directors of Sydenham Ltd to cover the following:

(a) **When should items of property, plant and equipment be recognised as assets?**

(b) **Which costs should be included on initial recognition of property, plant and equipment?**

(c) **Calculate the amount that should be recognised in property, plant and equipment as the cost of the new item of manufacturing equipment.**

···

Task 5

(a) **Which, if any, of the following two statements are correct, according to IAS 1** *Presentation of Financial Statements*?

(i) Financial statements should be prepared at least annually.

(ii) A complete set of financial statements must include notes.

(i) only	
(ii) only	
Both (i) and (ii)	
Neither (i) nor (ii)	

(b) Which of the following items would **not appear as a line item** in a company's statement of changes in equity, according to IAS 1 *Presentation of Financial Statements?*

Dividends paid	
Gain on revaluation of properties	
Issue of share capital	
Total comprehensive income for the year	

(c) Which one of the following would normally be classified as a cash flow arising from operating activities, according to IAS 7 *Statement of Cash Flows?*

Cash paid to a supplier	
Cash received from a share issue	
Cash paid to purchase property	
Cash received from the sale of an investment	

(d) The directors of Worcester Ltd consider that a machine with a carrying amount of £15,000 may have become impaired. At present it could be sold for £12,000 and disposal costs would be £400. The directors estimate that the machine will generate cash flows with a net present value of £11,500 over the remainder of its useful life.

What is the amount of the impairment loss that will be recognised in the statement of profit or loss, in accordance with IAS 36 *Impairment of Assets?*

£Nil	
£3,000	
£3,400	
£3,500	

(e) On 15 March 20X7, Yare Ltd received an order for goods with a sales value of £900,000. The customer paid a deposit of £90,000.

At 31 March 20X7 the goods had not yet been despatched.

According to IAS 18 *Revenue*, how should Yare Ltd report this transaction in its financial statements for the year ended 31 March 20X7?

Revenue £900,000; trade receivable £810,000	
Revenue £90,000; trade receivable £nil	
Revenue £nil; trade payable £90,000	
Revenue £90,000; trade payable £90,000; trade receivable £90,000	

(f) Ouse plc owns 45% of the voting rights of Avon Ltd, is exposed to variable returns from its involvement with Avon Ltd and has the ability to affect those returns through its power over Avon Ltd.

In relation to Ouse plc, Avon Ltd is an associate.

Is this statement True or False?

True	
False	

Task 6

The Managing Director of Wells plc has asked you to prepare the statement of financial position for the group.

Wells plc has one subsidiary, Wilkie Ltd.

The statements of financial position of the two companies as at 31 October 20X9 are set out below.

Statements of financial position as at 31 October 20X9

	Wells plc £'000	Wilkie Ltd £'000
Non-current assets		
Property, plant and equipment	44,352	19,884
Investment in Wilkie Ltd	19,000	
	63,352	19,884
Current assets		
Inventories	14,670	3,432
Trade and other receivables	6,756	2,249
Cash and cash equivalents	1,245	342
	22,671	6,023
Total assets	86,023	25,907
Equity and liabilities		
Equity		
Share capital	35,000	12,000
Retained earnings	26,036	8,332
Total equity	61,036	20,332
Non-current liabilities		
Long-term loans	14,000	4,000
Current liabilities		
Trade and other payables	8,877	1,445
Tax liabilities	2,110	130
	10,987	1,575
Total liabilities	24,987	5,575
Total equity and liabilities	86,023	25,907

Additional data

- The share capital of Wilkie Ltd consists of ordinary shares of £1 each. Ownership of these shares carries voting rights in Wilkie Ltd.

- Wells plc acquired 9,000,000 shares in Wilkie Ltd on 1 November 20X8.

- At 1 November 20X8 the balance of retained earnings of Wilkie Ltd was £5,344,000.

- Included in trade and other receivables for Wells plc and in trade and other payables for Wilkie Ltd is an inter-company transaction for £1,250,000 that took place in early October 20X9.

- The directors of Wells plc have concluded that goodwill has been impaired by £1,500,000 during the year.

- Wells plc has decided non-controlling interests will be valued at their proportionate share of net assets.

Draft a consolidated statement of financial position for Wells plc and its subsidiary as at 31 October 20X9.

Wells plc

Consolidated statement of financial position as at 31 October 20X9

	£'000
Assets	
Non-current assets	
Intangible assets: goodwill	
Property, plant and equipment	
Current assets	
Inventories	
Trade and other receivables	
Cash and cash equivalents	
Total assets	
Equity and liabilities	
Equity	
Share capital	
Retained earnings	
Non-controlling interest	
Total equity	

	£'000
Non-current liabilities	
Long-term loans	
Current liabilities	
Trade and other payables	
Tax liabilities	
Total liabilities	
Total equity and liabilities	

Workings

(Complete the left hand column by writing in the correct narrative from the list provided.)

Goodwill	£'000
▼	
▼	
▼	
▼	

Picklist for narratives:

Impairment
Price paid
Retained earnings – attributable to Wells plc
Share capital – attributable to Wells plc

Retained earnings	£'000
▼	
▼	
▼	

Picklist for narratives:

Impairment
Wells plc
Wilkie Ltd – attributable to Wells plc

Non-controlling interest (NCI)	£'000
▽	
▽	

Picklist for narratives:

Current assets – attributable to NCI
Impairment
Non-current assets – attributable to NCI
Price paid
Retained earnings – attributable to NCI
Share capital – attributable to NCI

....

Task 7

You have been asked to calculate ratios for Sienna Ltd in respect of its financial statements for the year ending 31 October 20X9 to assist your manager in his analysis of the company.

Sienna Ltd's statement of profit or loss and statement of financial position are set out below.

Sienna Ltd

Statement of profit or loss for the year ended 31 October 20X9

	£'000
Continuing operations	
Revenue	37,384
Cost of sales	(21,458)
Gross profit	15,926
Distribution costs	(6,142)
Administrative expenses	(6,158)
Profit from operations	3,626
Finance costs	(639)
Profit before tax	2,987
Tax	(687)
Profit for the period from continuing operations	2,300

Sienna Ltd

Statement of financial position as at 31 October 20X9

Assets	£'000
Non-current assets	
Property, plant and equipment	23,366
Current assets	
Inventories	4,461
Trade receivables	3,115
Cash and cash equivalents	213
	7,789
Total assets	31,155
Equity and liabilities	
Equity	
Share capital	3,000
Retained earnings	16,679
Total equity	19,679
Non-current liabilities	
Bank loans	8,000
Current liabilities	
Trade and other payables	2,789
Tax liabilities	687
	3,476
Total liabilities	11,476
Total equity plus liabilities	31,155

(a) **State the formulae that are used to calculate each of the following ratios:**

(Write in the correct formula from the list provided)

(i) Operating profit percentage	▼

Formulae:

Profit from operations/Revenue × 100

Profit from operations/Total assets × 100

Profit from operations/Total equity + Non-current liabilities × 100

Profit from operations/Finance costs × 100

(ii) Return on shareholders' funds	▼

Formulae:

Profit after tax/Total equity × 100

Profit before tax/Total equity × 100

Profit from operations/Total equity × 100

Profit from operations/Total equity + Non-current liabilities × 100

(iii) Quick (acid test) ratio	▼

Formulae:

Current assets/Current liabilities

Total assets – Inventories/Total liabilities

Total assets/Total liabilities

Current assets – Inventories/Current liabilities

(iv) Inventory turnover	▼

Formulae:

Cost of sales/Inventories

Inventories/Cost of sales

Inventories/Revenue

Revenue/Inventories

(v)	Interest cover		
Formulae:			
Finance costs/Profit from operations			
Finance costs/Revenue			
Profit from operations/Finance costs			
Revenue/Finance costs			

(b) **Calculate the ratios to the nearest ONE DECIMAL PLACE.**

(i)	Operating profit percentage		%
(ii)	Return on shareholders' funds		%
(iii)	Quick (acid test) ratio		:1
(iv)	Inventory turnover		times
(v)	Interest cover		times

Task 8

Louise Michaels is a shareholder in Hoy Ltd. She wishes to assess the effectiveness of the management in using its resources. She has asked you to assist her by analysing the financial statements of the company, which are set out below.

Louise has obtained a report from the internet that gives the industry ratio averages for the sector in which Hoy Ltd operates.

She has emailed you and asked you to explain some of the points she is unsure about. A copy of the email is shown below

From: lm1000@warmmail.com

To: aatstudent@dfsexam

Date: 27 November 20X9

Subject: Accounting ratios

Hi

I found these sector ratios on the internet. This is the same sector as the company I have invested in. The profit figures are straightforward but I'm a bit lost about the rest. Can you help?

Many thanks

Louise

	Industry averages	Hoy Ltd
Gearing	65.00%	88.65%
Current ratio	1.6:1	1.9:1
Acid test ratio	0.9:1	0.7:1
Trade receivables collection period	33 days	25.6 days
Trade payables payment period	36 days	32.9 days

Prepare an email reply for Louise that includes:

(a) **Comments on whether the company has performed better or worse, based on the ratios calculated compared to the industry averages and what this tells you about the company.**

(b) **Advice, with reasons, to Louise as to whether or not to continue with her investment.**

••

BPP PRACTICE ASSESSMENT 4
FINANCIAL STATEMENTS

ANSWERS

Task 1

(a) **Martin Ltd**

Statement of profit or loss for the year ended 31 October 20X9

	£'000
Revenue	46,433
Cost of sales (W)	(32,282)
Gross profit	14,151
Distribution costs (W)	(2,516)
Administrative expenses (W)	(3,316)
Profit from operations	8,319
Finance costs (8% × 14,000)	(1,120)
Profit before tax	7,199
Tax	(980)
Profit for the period from continuing operations	6,219
Other comprehensive income	
Gain on revaluation (12,000 – 8,000)	4,000
Total comprehensive income for the year	10,219

Workings

Cost of sales	£'000
Opening inventories	4,466
Purchases	32,553
Closing inventories (4,987 – 250)	(4,737)
	32,282

Distribution costs	£'000
Distribution costs	2,450
Accruals	66
	2,516

Administrative expenses	£'000
Administrative expenses	3,444
Prepayment (512 × 3/12)	(128)
	3,316

(b)   **Martin Ltd**

Statement of changes in equity for the year ended 31 October 20X9

	Share capital £'000	Revaluation reserve £'000	Retained earnings £'000	Total equity £'000
Balance at 1 November 20X8	9,000		3,465	12,465
Changes in equity				
Total comprehensive income		4,000	6,219	10,219
Dividends			(930)	(930)
Balance at 31 October 20X9	9,000	4,000	8,754	21,754

Task 2

Martin Ltd

Statement of financial position as at 31 October 20X9

	£'000
Assets	
Non-current assets	
Property, plant and equipment (W)	22,100
Current assets	
Inventories (4,987 – 250)	4,737
Trade and other receivables (W)	2,362
Cash and cash equivalents	9,654
	16,753
Total assets	38,853

	£'000
Equity and liabilities	
Equity	
Share capital	9,000
Revaluation reserve	4,000
Retained earnings (W)	8,754
Total equity	21,754
Non-current liabilities	
Bank loan	14,000
Current liabilities	
Trade and other payables (W)	2,119
Tax liabilities	980
	3,099
Total liabilities	17,099
Total equity and liabilities	38,853

Workings

Property, plant and equipment	£'000
Property, plant and equipment – Cost	39,880
Property, plant and equipment – Accumulated depreciation	(21,780)
Revaluation	4,000
	22,100

Trade and other receivables	£'000
Trade and other receivables	2,234
Administrative expenses prepaid	128
	2,362

Retained earnings	£'000
Retained earnings at 1 November 20X8	3,465
Total profit for the year	6,219
Dividends paid	(930)
	8,754

Trade and other payables	£'000
Trade and other payables	1,347
Accruals: trial balance	146
Additional distribution costs accrual	66
Additional finance costs accrual	560
	2,119

Task 3

Note. Based on the information available at the time this book was written, we anticipate that this task would be human marked in the real assessment.

(a) The elements that appear in financial statements are:

- Assets
- Liabilities
- Equity
- Income
- Expenses

(b) Assets, liabilities and equity appear in the statement of financial position of a company. The *Conceptual Framework for Financial Reporting* defines them as follows:

Assets are resources controlled by an entity as a result of past events and from which future economic benefits are expected to flow to the entity.

Liabilities are present obligations of an entity arising from past events, the settlement of which is expected to result in an outflow from the entity of resources embodying economic benefits.

Equity is the residual interest in the assets of an entity after deducting all its liabilities.

Task 4

Note. Based on the information available at the time this book was written, we anticipate that this task would be human marked in the real assessment.

(a) IAS 16 states that items of property, plant, and equipment should be recognised as assets when two conditions are met:

- It is probable that future economic benefits associated with the item will flow to the entity; and

- The cost of the asset can be measured reliably.

(b) The cost of an item of property, plant and equipment is:

- Its purchase price, including import duties and after deducting trade discounts and rebates; and

- Any costs directly attributable to bringing the item to the location and condition necessary for it to be capable of operating in the manner intended by management.

(c) Cost of new item of manufacturing equipment:

	£
Invoiced price of the equipment	37,000
Delivery costs	1,600
Installation and testing costs	4,500
Proceeds from the sale of samples produced when testing equipment	(1,800)
Net costs	41,300

Only costs that are directly attributable to bringing the asset to the location and condition necessary for it to be capable of operating in the manner intended by management may be included. Staff training costs are not included.

· ·

Task 5

(a)

(i) only	
(ii) only	
Both (i) and (ii)	✓
Neither (i) nor (ii)	

(b)

Dividends paid	
Gain on revaluation of properties	✓
Issue of share capital	
Total comprehensive income for the year	

A gain on revaluation of properties is reported as a line item in other comprehensive income, but in the statement of changes in equity it forms part of total comprehensive income for the year.

(c)

Cash paid to a supplier	✓
Cash received from a share issue	
Cash paid to purchase property	
Cash received from the sale of an investment	

Cash received from a share issue is a cash flow from financing activities. Cash paid to purchase property and cash received from the sale of an investment are cash flows from investing activities.

(d)

£Nil	
£3,000	
£3,400	✓
£3,500	

Recoverable amount is fair value less costs of disposal of £11,600 (12,000 – 400) as this is higher than value in use of £11,500. The recoverable amount is lower than carrying amount so the impairment loss is £3,400 (15,000 – 11,600).

(e)

Revenue £900,000; trade receivable £810,000	
Revenue £90,000; trade receivable £nil	
Revenue £nil; trade payable £90,000	✓
Revenue £90,000; trade payable £90,000; trade receivable £90,000	

No revenue should be recognised, because Yare Ltd has not yet transferred the significant risks and rewards of ownership to the buyer.

(f)

True	
False	✓

Although Ouse plc owns less than 50% of the voting rights, it controls Avon Ltd.

....

Task 6

Wells plc

Consolidated statement of financial position as at 31 October 20X9

	£'000
Assets	
Non-current assets	
Intangible assets: goodwill (W)	4,492
Property, plant and equipment	64,236
	68,728
Current assets	
Inventories	18,102
Trade and other receivables (6,756 + 2,249 − 1,250)	7,755
Cash and cash equivalents	1,587
	27,444
Total assets	96,172
Equity and liabilities	
Equity	
Share capital	35,000
Retained earnings (W)	26,777
	61,777
Non-controlling interest (W)	5,083
Total equity	66,860

	£'000
Non-current liabilities	
Long-term loans	18,000
Current liabilities	
Trade and other payables (8,877 + 1,445 – 1,250)	9,072
Tax liabilities	2,240
	11,312
Total liabilities	29,312
Total equity and liabilities	96,172

Workings

Note: **Group structure**

Wells plc owns 75% of Wilkie Ltd (9,000,000/12,000,000)

Goodwill	£'000
Price paid	19,000
Share capital – attributable to Wells plc (75% × 12,000)	(9,000)
Retained earnings – attributable to Wells plc (75% × 5,344)	(4,008)
Impairment	(1,500)
	4,492

Retained earnings	£'000
Wells plc	26,036
Wilkie Ltd – attributable to Wells plc (75% × (8,332 – 5,344))	2,241
Impairment	(1,500)
	26,777

Non-controlling interest (NCI)	£'000
Share capital – attributable to NCI (25% × 12,000)	3,000
Retained earnings – attributable to NCI (25% × 8,332)	2,083
	5,083

Task 7

(a) Formulae used to calculate the ratios

(i)	Operating profit percentage	$\dfrac{\text{Profit from operations}}{\text{Revenue}} \times 100\%$
(ii)	Return on shareholders' funds	$\dfrac{\text{Profit after tax}}{\text{Total equity}} \times 100\%$
(iii)	Quick (acid test) ratio	$\dfrac{\text{Current assets} - \text{inventories}}{\text{Current liabilities}}$
(iv)	Inventory turnover	$\dfrac{\text{Cost of sales}}{\text{Inventories}}$
(v)	Interest cover	$\dfrac{\text{Profit from operations}}{\text{Finance costs}}$

(b) Calculation of the ratios

(i)	Operating profit percentage $\dfrac{3,626}{37,384} \times 100$	9.7	%
(ii)	Return on shareholders' funds $\dfrac{2,300}{19,679} \times 100$	11.7	%
(iii)	Quick (acid test) ratio $\dfrac{7,789 - 4,461}{3,476}$	0.96	:1
(iv)	Inventory turnover $\dfrac{21,458}{4,461}$	4.8	times
(v)	Interest cover $\dfrac{3,626}{639}$	5.7	times

Task 8

Note. Based on the information available at the time this book was written, we anticipate that this task would be human marked in the real assessment.

From: aatstudent@dfsexam

To: lm1000@warmmail.com

Date: 2 December 20X9

Subject: Comparison of accounting ratios of Hoy Ltd with industry averages

As requested, I have compared the accounting ratios computed from the financial statements of Hoy Ltd with the industry averages. I set out my comments below.

(a) **Gearing**

At 88.5%, Hoy Ltd's gearing ratio is considerably higher than the industry average. This shows that Hoy Ltd has a relatively high level of long-term borrowings or debt, which means that it is a riskier investment than most other companies in the industry.

Current ratio

The current ratio is better than the industry average. Hoy Ltd's current liabilities are covered almost twice by its current assets.

Acid test (quick) ratio

This is lower than the industry average; Hoy Ltd's current liabilities are greater than its trade receivables plus its cash. This means that Hoy Ltd is less likely to be able to meet its liabilities in the short term than most other companies in the industry sector. Because the current ratio is relatively high, Hoy Ltd must have a high level of inventories.

Trade receivables collection period

At 25.6 days, this is considerably better than the industry average and suggests that Hoy Ltd is more efficient at collecting its debts than most other companies in the industry. This means that more cash will be available to pay suppliers and lenders.

Trade payables payment period

Again, this is slightly lower than the industry average. This suggests that Hoy Ltd pays its suppliers relatively quickly, possibly more quickly than is necessary. This may be one of the reasons that the company has relatively few 'quick' assets.

(b) **Conclusion**

On the basis of these ratios, you should not continue to invest in this company. The low acid test ratio, together with the low trade payables payment period, suggest that the company is not managing its liquid resources particularly well. The high gearing ratio is a worrying sign. The company appears to be a risky investment and probably suffers a high level of interest. This means that fewer profits will be available for shareholders.

BPP PRACTICE ASSESSMENT 5
FINANCIAL STATEMENTS

Time allowed: 2½ hours

The following information is relevant to Task 1 and Task 2

You have been asked to prepare the statement of cash flows and statement of changes in equity for Phantom Ltd for the year ended 31 October 20X1.

The most recent statement of profit or loss and statement of financial position (with comparatives for the previous year) of Phantom Ltd are set out below.

Phantom Ltd – Statement of profit or loss for the year ended 31 October 20X1.

Continuing operations	£'000
Revenue	85,000
Cost of sales	(50,400)
Gross profit	34,600
Dividends received	200
Gain on disposal of property, plant and equipment	756
Distribution costs	(18,480)
Administrative expenses	(15,120)
Profit from operations	1,956
Finance costs	(420)
Profit before tax	1,536
Tax	(705)
Profit for the period from continuing operations	831

Phantom Ltd – Statement of financial position as at 31 October 20X1

	20X1	20X0
	£'000	£'000
Assets		
Non-current assets		
Property, plant and equipment	35,783	26,890
Current assets		
Inventories	6,552	5,544
Trade receivables	6,720	5,880
Cash and cash equivalents	0	476
	13,272	11,900
Total assets	49,055	38,790
Equity and liabilities		
Equity		
Share capital	9,000	6,000
Share premium	3,000	2,000
Retained earnings	24,863	24,198
Total equity	36,863	32,198
Non-current liabilities		
Bank loans	6,000	800
	6,000	800
Current liabilities		
Trade payables	5,040	4,536
Tax liabilities	705	1,256
Bank overdraft	447	0
	6,192	5,792
Total liabilities	12,192	6,592
Total equity and liabilities	49,055	38,790

Further information:

- The total depreciation charge for the year was £2,898,000.

- Property, plant and equipment costing £998,000 with accumulated depreciation of £256,000 was sold in the year.

- All sales and purchases were on credit. Other expenses were paid for in cash.

- A dividend of £166,000 was paid during the year.

Task 1

(a) **Prepare a reconciliation of profit from operations to net cash from operating activities for Phantom Ltd for the year ended 31 October 20X1.**

(Complete the left hand column by writing in the correct line item from the list provided.)

Reconciliation of profit from operations to net cash from operating activities

		£'000
	▼	
Adjustments for:		
	▼	
	▼	
	▼	
	▼	
	▼	
	▼	
Cash generated by operations		
	▼	
	▼	
Net cash from operating activities		

Picklist for line items:
Adjustment in respect of inventories
Adjustment in respect of trade payables
Adjustment in respect of trade receivables
Depreciation
Dividends received
Gain on disposal of property, plant and equipment
Interest paid
New bank loans
Proceeds on disposal of property, plant and equipment
Profit after tax
Profit before tax
Profit from operations
Purchases of property, plant and equipment
Tax paid

(b) **Prepare the statement of cash flows for Phantom Ltd for the year ended 31 October 20X1.**

(Complete the left hand column by writing in the correct line item from the list provided.)

Phantom Ltd

Statement of cash flows for the year ended 31 October 20X1

	£'000
Net cash from operating activities	
Investing activities	
▼	
▼	
▼	
Net cash used in investing activities	
Financing activities	
▼	
▼	
▼	
Net cash from financing activities	
Net increase/(decrease) in cash and cash equivalents	
Cash and cash equivalents at the beginning of the year	
Cash and cash equivalents at the end of the year	

Picklist for line items:

Adjustment in respect of inventories
Adjustment in respect of trade payables
Adjustment in respect of trade receivables
Dividends paid
Dividends received
New bank loans
Proceeds of share issue
Proceeds on disposal of property, plant and equipment
Purchases of property, plant and equipment

Workings

(Complete the left hand column by writing in the correct narrative from the list provided.)

Proceeds on disposal of property, plant and equipment (PPE)	£'000
▼	
▼	

Picklist for narratives:

Carrying amount of PPE sold
Depreciation charge
Gain on disposal
PPE at end of year
PPE at start of year

Purchases of property, plant and equipment (PPE)	£'000
PPE at start of year	
▼	
▼	
▼	
Total PPE additions	

Picklist for narratives:

Carrying amount of PPE sold
Depreciation charge
Gain on disposal of PPE
PPE at end of year

Task 2

Draft the statement of changes in equity for Phantom Ltd for the year ended 31 October 20X1.

Phantom Ltd

Statement of changes in equity for the year ended 31 October 20X1

	Share capital £'000	Share premium £'000	Retained earnings £'000	Total equity £'000
Balance at 1 November 20X0				
Changes in equity				
Profit for the year				
Dividends				
Issue of share capital				
Balance at 31 October 20X1				

Task 3

(a) State the two conditions that must be met before an asset or a liability can be recognised in the financial statements according to the *Conceptual Framework for Financial Reporting*.

(b) Give ONE example of an asset that is recognised in the financial statements and briefly explain why it meets these conditions.

(c) Give ONE example of an asset that is not recognised in the financial statements and briefly explain why it does not meet these conditions.

Task 4

During the year ended 31 October 20X1, Birch Ltd carried out two separate research and development projects:

(i) The company spent £50,000 on researching new environmentally friendly building techniques. Work on this project is still at an early stage.

(ii) The company also spent £75,000 on developing a special type of new packaging material. This second project was completed shortly before the year-end. Since the year-end, Birch Ltd has begun to use the new material in its operations. The directors believe that the new material will reduce the company's distribution costs by approximately £35,000 a year for at least the next five years.

Prepare brief notes for the directors of Birch plc to answer the following questions:

(a) What is meant by an intangible asset according to IAS 38 *Intangible Assets*?

(b) What would Birch plc have to demonstrate about an intangible asset arising from development activities before it can be recognised as an intangible asset in the financial statements?

(c) How much of the research and development expenditure can be recognised as an intangible asset in the financial statements for the year ended 31 October 20X1?

....

Task 5

(a) According to IAS 36 *Impairment of Assets*, the recoverable amount of an asset is the lower of fair value less costs of disposal and value in use.

Is this statement True or False?

True	
False	

(b) Glasbury Ltd prepares its financial statements to 31 October each year. The following events took place between 31 October and the date on which the financial statements were authorised for issue.

(i) A customer claimed to have been injured by a faulty product and has started legal proceedings to claim damages from the company. The faulty product was purchased on 10 December.

(ii) The company made a 1 for 6 bonus issue of £1 ordinary shares.

Which of the above is likely to be classified as a non-adjusting event according to IAS 10 *Events After the Reporting Period*?

(i) only	
(ii) only	
Both	
Neither of them	

(c) Vowchurch Ltd purchased a building for £600,000 on 1 November 20X0. The building was depreciated over 20 years on a straight line basis.

On 1 November 20X4 the building was valued at £700,000 and its remaining useful life was estimated at 20 years.

Vowchurch Ltd has chosen to adopt the cost model in IAS 16 *Property, Plant and Equipment*.

What is the total net carrying amount of the building at 31 October 20X5?

£456,000	
£475,000	
£570,000	
£665,000	

(d) Knighton Ltd is preparing its first set of financial statements for the three months to . 31 December.

The cost of purchases was £120 per unit until 15 November, when the company's supplier increased it to £130 per unit. Purchases and sales took place evenly over the period.

The directors have arrived at three possible alternative ways of valuing inventories at 31 December.

(i) At £120 per unit (cost at the beginning of the period)

(ii) At £130 per unit (cost at the end of the period)

(iii) At £125 per unit (average cost)

Which methods of valuing inventories are allowed, according to IAS 2 *Inventories*?

(i) and (ii)	
(ii) and (iii)	
(i) and (iii)	
All of them	

(e) At 1 November 20X0, Brilley Ltd had an estimated current tax liability of £157,000.

In February 20X1 the company paid corporation tax of £165,000.

At 31 October 20X1, the current tax liability for the year has been estimated at £188,000.

What is the total tax expense in profit or loss for the year ended 31 October 20X1?

£165,000	
£180,000	
£188,000	
£196,000	

(f) At the end of an accounting period, a company has a contingent asset where an inflow of economic benefits is **possible** and a contingent liability where the likelihood of an outflow of resources is **possible**.

Which of the following would be the correct accounting treatment for each of these items?

Contingent asset	Contingent liability	
Disclosure is required	Disclosure is required	
Disclosure is required	No disclosure is required	
No disclosure is required	Disclosure is required	
No disclosure is required	No disclosure is required	

Task 6

Data

Bestwood plc acquired 75% of the issued share capital and voting rights of Torkard Ltd on 1 November 20X0 for £3,400,000. At that date Torkard Ltd had issued share capital of £2,000,000, share premium of £500,000 and retained earnings of £560,000.

An extract of the statement of financial position of Torkard Ltd one year later at 31 October 20X1 is shown below.

Torkard Ltd: Statement of financial position at 31 October 20X1

	£'000
Total assets	5,430
EQUITY AND LIABILITIES	
Equity	
Share capital	2,000
Share premium	500
Retained earnings	912
Total equity	3,412
Total liabilities	2,018
Total equity and liabilities	5,430

Additional data:

- Bestwood plc has decided non-controlling interest will be valued at their proportionate share of net assets.

(a) **Calculate the figures for goodwill and non-controlling interest that would be included in the consolidated statement of financial position of Bestwood plc and its subsidiary as at 31 October 20X1.**

Felley plc

Consolidated statement of financial position as at 31 October 20X1

	£'000
Goodwill	
Non-controlling interest	

Workings

(Complete the left hand column by writing in the correct narrative from the list provided.)

Goodwill	£'000
▼	
▼	
▼	
▼	

Picklist for narratives:

Price paid
Retained earnings – attributable to Bestwood plc
Share capital – attributable to Bestwood plc
Share premium – attributable to Bestwood plc
Total assets – attributable to Bestwood plc

Non-controlling interest (NCI)		£'000
	▼	
	▼	
	▼	

Picklist for narratives:

Price paid
Retained earnings – attributable to NCI
Share capital – attributable to NCI
Share premium – attributable to NCI
Total assets – attributable to NCI

Data

Strelley plc acquired 60% of the issued share capital and voting rights of **Barber Ltd** on 1 November 20X0.

Extracts of each company's statement of profit or loss for the year ended 31 October 20X1 are shown below:

	Strelley plc £'000	Barber Ltd £'000
Continuing operations		
Revenue	270,600	54,300
Cost of sales	(108,300)	(22,350)
Gross profit	162,300	31,950
Other income	9,000	
Distribution costs	(24,600)	(10,050)
Administrative expenses	(35,550)	(8,850)
Profit from operations	111,150	13,050
Finance costs	(7,350)	(1,050)
Profit before tax	103,800	12,000
Tax	(21,900)	(2,400)
Profit for the period from continuing operations	81,900	9,600

Additional data:

- During the year Strelley plc sold goods which had cost £900,000 to Barber Ltd for £1,080,000. Half of these goods still remain in inventories at the end of the year.

- Other income of Strelley plc consists of a dividend of £5,520 received from Barber Ltd and rental income received from another company.

(b) **Draft the consolidated statement of profit or loss for Strelley plc and its subsidiary for the year ended 31 October 20X1.**

Strelley plc

Consolidated statement of profit or loss for the year ended 31 October 20X1

	£'000
Continuing operations	
Revenue	
Cost of sales	
Gross profit	
Other income	
Distribution costs	
Administrative expenses	
Profit from operations	
Finance costs	
Profit before tax	
Tax	
Profit for the year	
Attributable to:	
Equity holders of the parent	
Non-controlling interests	

Workings

Revenue	£'000
Strelley plc	
Barber Ltd	
Total inter-company adjustment	

Cost of sales	£'000
Strelley plc	
Barber Ltd	
Total inter-company adjustment	

Task 7

You have been asked to calculate ratios for Hampden Ltd in respect of its financial statements for the year ending 31 October 20X1 to assist your manager in her analysis of the company.

Hampden Ltd's statement of profit or loss and statement of financial position are set out below.

Hampden Ltd – Statement of profit or loss for the year ended 31 October 20X1

	£'000
Continuing operations	
Revenue	22,600
Cost of sales	(10,735)
Gross profit	11,865
Distribution costs	(5,424)
Administrative expenses	(4,068)
Profit from operations	2,373
Finance costs	(770)
Profit before tax	1,603
Tax	(294)
Profit for the period from continuing operations	1,309

Hampden Ltd – Statement of financial position as at 31 October 20X1

	£'000
Assets	
Non-current assets	
Property, plant and equipment	22,916
Current assets	
Inventories	1,932
Trade receivables	1,808
Cash and cash equivalents	582
	4,322
Total assets	27,238
Equity and liabilities	
Equity	
Share capital (£1 ordinary shares)	8,000
Retained earnings	6,334
Total equity	14,334
Non-current liabilities	
Bank loans	11,000
	11,000
Current liabilities	
Trade payables	1,610
Tax liabilities	294
	1,904
Total liabilities	12,904
Total equity and liabilities	27,238

(a) **State the formulae that are used to calculate each of the following ratios**

(Write in the correct formula from the list provided)

(i) Return on capital employed	▼

Formulae:

Profit after tax/Total equity × 100

Profit from operations/Total equity × 100

Profit after tax/Total equity + Non-current liabilities × 100

Profit from operations/Total equity + Non-current liabilities × 100

(ii) Current ratio	▼

Formulae:

Total assets/Total liabilities

Current assets – inventories/Current liabilities

Current assets/Current liabilities

Total assets – inventories/Total liabilities

(iii) Trade receivables collection period	▼

Formulae:

Cost of sales/Trade receivables × 365

Revenue/Trade receivables × 365

Trade receivables/Cost of sales × 365

Trade receivables/Revenue × 365

(iv) Trade payables payment period	▼

Formulae:

Trade payables/Revenue × 365

Trade payables/Cost of sales × 365

Revenue/Trade payables × 365

Cost of sales/Trade payables × 365

(v)	Asset turnover (net assets)	▼
Formulae:		
Revenue/Total assets – Current liabilities		
Revenue/Total assets – Total liabilities		
Total assets – Current liabilities/Revenue		
Total assets – Total liabilities/Revenue		

(b) **Calculate the ratios to the nearest ONE DECIMAL PLACE.**

(i)	Return on capital employed	%
(ii)	Current ratio	:1
(iii)	Trade receivables collection period	days
(iv)	Trade payables payment period	days
(v)	Asset turnover (net assets)	times

Task 8

Lewis Baingle is interested in buying shares as a means of investment and has heard that some shares are riskier than others. He wishes to assess the merits of two local companies with a view to buying shares in one of them.

Lewis would like to invest in a profitable company but his main concern is that his investment is safe. He has managed to find the most recent financial statements of the companies and you have used these to calculate the following ratios to assist you in your analysis.

	Anica Ltd	Papaca Ltd
Gross profit percentage	45.0%	52.5%
Operating profit percentage	9.0%	11.5%
Gearing	13.3%	71.1%
Interest cover	11.6 times	3.1 times
Quick (acid test) ratio	1.2:1	0.6:1

Prepare a letter for Lewis that includes:

(a) **Comments on which company has performed better, based on the ratios calculated and what this tells you about the two companies.**

(b) **Advice, with reasons based on the ratios you have calculated, to Lewis as to which company to invest in.**

BPP PRACTICE ASSESSMENT 5
FINANCIAL STATEMENTS

ANSWERS

Task 1

(a) **Phantom Ltd**

Reconciliation of profit from operations to net cash from operating activities

	£'000
Profit from operations	1,956
Adjustments for:	
Depreciation	2,898
Dividends received	(200)
Gain on disposal of property, plant and equipment	(756)
Adjustment in respect of inventories (6,552 – 5,544)	(1,008)
Adjustment in respect of trade receivables (6,720 – 5,880)	(840)
Adjustment in respect of trade payables (5,040 – 4,536)	504
Cash generated by operations	2,554
Tax paid	(1,256)
Interest paid	(420)
Net cash from operating activities	878

(b) **Phantom Ltd**

Statement of cash flows for the year ended 31 October 20X1

	£'000
Net cash from operating activities	878
Investing activities	
Purchases of property, plant and equipment (W)	(12,533)
Proceeds on disposal of property, plant and equipment (W)	1,498
Dividends received	200
Net cash used in investing activities	(10,835)

	£'000
Financing activities	
Proceeds of share issue (12,000 – 8,000)	4,000
New bank loans (6,000 – 800)	5,200
Dividends paid	(166)
Net cash from financing activities	9,034
Net increase/(decrease) in cash and cash equivalents	(923)
Cash and cash equivalents at the beginning of the year	476
Cash and cash equivalents at the end of the year	(447)

Workings

Proceeds on disposal of property, plant and equipment (PPE)	£'000
Carrying amount of PPE sold	742
Gain on disposal	756
	1,498

Purchases of property, plant and equipment (PPE)	£'000
PPE at start of year	26,890
Depreciation charge	(2,898)
Carrying amount of PPE sold	(742)
PPE at end of year	(35,783)
Total PPE additions	(12,533)

Task 2

Phantom Ltd

Statement of changes in equity for the year ended 31 October 20X1

	Share capital £'000	Revaluation reserve £'000	Retained earnings £'000	Total equity £'000
Balance at 1 November 20X0	6,000	2,000	24,198	32,198
Changes in equity				
Profit for the year			831	831
Dividends			(166)	(166)
Issue of share capital	3,000	1,000		4,000
Balance at 31 October 20X1	9,000	3,000	24,863	36,863

Task 3

Note. Based on the information available at the time this book was written, we anticipate that this task would be human marked in the real assessment.

(a) An item that meets the definition of an element (eg, an asset or a liability) should be recognised if:

- It is **probable** that any future economic benefit associated with the item will flow to or from the entity.

- The item has a cost or value that can be measured with **reliability**.

(b) Plant and machinery is recognised in the financial statements. It meets both conditions:

- It will be used to produce goods that will be sold to generate cash and profits (an inflow of economic benefits).

- It has a cost that is a matter of fact and can be verified (reliable measurement).

Note. Other examples of assets that meet the criteria are land and buildings, vehicles, inventories, trade receivables, cash.

(c) Internally generated goodwill cannot be recognised in the financial statements. It meets the first condition, but not the second:

- It contributes to sales and therefore generates an inflow of economic benefits
- It cannot be valued reliably/objectively

Task 4

Note. Based on the information available at the time this book was written, we anticipate that this task would be human marked in the real assessment.

(a) IAS 38 *Intangible Assets* defines an intangible asset as 'an identifiable, non-monetary asset without physical substance'.

(b) IAS 38 states that an intangible asset arising from development can only be recognised if an entity can demonstrate all of the following:

- The technical feasibility of completing the intangible asset so that it will be available for use or sale.

- Its intention to complete the intangible asset and use or sell it.

- Its ability to use or sell the intangible asset.

- How the intangible asset will generate probable future economic benefits.

- The availability of adequate technical, financial and other resources to complete the development and to use or sell the intangible asset.

- Its ability to measure reliably the expenditure attributable to the intangible asset during its development.

(c) Project (i) is still in its 'research phase'. It is not clear that the project will generate any future economic benefit. The expenditure of £50,000 should be recognised in profit or loss for the year.

Project (ii) is now complete and the new material is being used successfully. Using the new material is expected to result in cost savings of £175,000 over the next five years. This is considerably more than the cost of carrying out the project. Project (ii) is already generating economic benefits (cost savings) and it meets all the recognition criteria above. Therefore Birch Ltd should recognise an intangible asset of £75,000 at 31 October 20X1.

Task 5

(a)

True	
False	✓

Recoverable amount is the higher of fair value less costs of disposal and value in use.

(b)

(i) only	
(ii) only	
Both	✓
Neither of them	

(c)

£456,000	✓
£475,000	
£570,000	
£665,000	

	£
Cost	600,000
Depreciation to 20X4 (600,000 ÷ 20 × 4)	(120,000)
Net carrying amount at 1 November 20X4	480,000
Depreciation for 20X5 (480,000 ÷ 20)	(24,000)
Net carrying amount at 31 October 20X5	456,000

(d)

(i) and (ii)	
(ii) and (iii)	✓
(i) and (iii)	
All of them	

Method 1 is Last-in-First-out (LIFO) and is prohibited by IAS 2. Method 2 is First-in-First-out (FIFO).

(e)

£165,000	
£180,000	
£188,000	
£196,000	✓

	£
Expense for current year	188,000
Adjustment in respect of prior period	8,000
Tax expense in profit or loss	196,000

(f)

Contingent asset	Contingent liability	
Disclosure is required	Disclosure is required	
Disclosure is required	No disclosure is required	
No disclosure is required	Disclosure is required	✓
No disclosure is required	No disclosure is required	

Task 6

(a)

	£'000
Goodwill	1,105
Non-controlling interest	853

Workings

Goodwill	£'000
Price paid	3,400
Share capital – attributable to Bestwood plc (75% × 2,000)	(1,500)
Share premium – attributable to Bestwood plc (75% × 500)	(375)
Retained earnings – attributable to Bestwood plc (75% × 560)	(420)
	1,105

Non-controlling interest (NCI)	£'000
Share capital – attributable to NCI (25% × 2,000)	500
Share premium – attributable to NCI (25% × 500)	125
Retained earnings – attributable to NCI (25% × 912)	228
	853

(b) **Strelley plc**

Consolidated statement of profit or loss for the year ended 31 October 20X1

	£'000
Continuing operations	
Revenue	323,820
Cost of sales	(129,660)
Gross profit	194,160
Other income (9,000 – 5,520)	3,480
Distribution costs	(34,650)
Administrative expenses	(44,400)
Profit from operations	118,590
Finance costs	(8,400)
Profit before tax	110,190
Tax	(24,300)
Profit for the year	85,890
Attributable to:	
Equity holders of the parent	82,050
Non-controlling interests (9,600 × 40%)	3,840
	85,890

Workings

Revenue	£'000
Strelley plc	270,600
Barber Ltd	54,300
Total inter-company adjustment	(1,080)
	323,820

Cost of sales	£'000
Strelley plc	108,300
Barber Ltd	22,350
Total inter-company adjustment (1,080 – (180/2)	(990)
	129,660

Task 7

(a) Formulae used to calculate the ratios

(i)	Return on capital employed	$\dfrac{\text{Profit from operations}}{\text{Total equity + non-current liabilities}} \times 100\%$
(ii)	Current ratio	$\dfrac{\text{Current assets}}{\text{Current liabilities}}$
(iii)	Trade receivables collection period	$\dfrac{\text{Trade receivables}}{\text{Revenue}} \times 365$
(iv)	Trade payables payment period	$\dfrac{\text{Trade payables}}{\text{Cost of sales}} \times 365$
(v)	Asset turnover (net assets)	$\dfrac{\text{Revenue}}{\text{Total assets} - \text{current liabilities}}$

(b) Calculation of the ratios

(i)	Return on capital employed $\dfrac{2,373}{14,334 + 11,000} \times 100$	9.4	%
(ii)	Current ratio $\dfrac{4,322}{1,904}$	2.3	:1
(iii)	Trade receivables collection period $\dfrac{1,808}{22,600} \times 365$	29.2	days
(iv)	Trade payables payment period $\dfrac{1,610}{10,735} \times 365$	54.7	days
(v)	Asset turnover (net assets) $\dfrac{22,600}{27,238 - 1,904}$	0.9	times

Task 8

Note. Based on the information available at the time this book was written, we anticipate that this task would be human marked in the real assessment.

Sender's address

Lewis Baingle

Address

Date

Dear Lewis,

Performance of Anica Ltd and Papaca Ltd

As you requested, I have compared the profitability of Anica Ltd and Papaca Ltd, based on ratios calculated from their most recent financial statements. I have also compared the two companies in terms of their riskiness for a potential investor.

(a) **Comparison of the two companies**

Gross profit percentage

Both companies have healthy gross profit percentages, but Papaca Ltd is clearly the more profitable of the two. It generates significantly more direct trading profit, relative to its sales, than Anica Ltd.

Operating profit percentage

Again, both companies are reasonably profitable, but Papaca Ltd has the better operating profit percentage of the two. However, the difference between the overall profitability of the two companies is fairly small.

Gearing

Anica Ltd has a much lower gearing ratio than Papaca Ltd. Papaca Ltd appears to have a worryingly high level of debt and would be a very risky investment. In comparison, Anica Ltd has some debt, but this forms only a small proportion of its total financing. On this basis, Anica Ltd would be a much safer investment.

Interest cover

Anica Ltd has a much higher level of interest cover than Papaca Ltd. The ratio suggests that it can comfortably meet its interest payments from its operating profit and that this will continue to be the case even if interest rates rise or profits fall significantly. Papaca Ltd's interest cover is acceptable at the moment, but on this basis again Anica Ltd is clearly a much safer investment than Papaca Ltd.

Quick (acid test) ratio

Anica Ltd has a much better quick ratio than Papaca Ltd. Its liquid assets exceed its current liabilities and this indicates that it should easily be able to meet its payments to suppliers and other short term obligations as they fall due. Papaca Ltd's quick ratio is low enough to suggest that the company has liquidity problems: yet another indication that it would be a very risky investment.

(b) Conclusion

Because your main concern is the riskiness of your investment I would advise you to invest in Anica Ltd. Anica Ltd is profitable, with no apparent gearing or liquidity problems.

In contrast, although Papaca Ltd is the more profitable of the two companies, it is very highly geared and may have liquidity problems. Taken together, the high level of debt and the low quick ratio are extremely worrying and suggest that the company is in danger of becoming insolvent. Papaca Ltd would clearly be a very risky investment.

I hope you have found this analysis helpful.

Yours sincerely,

Accounting Technician

Notes

Notes

Notes

Notes